WITHDRAWN

Arthur Schnitzler and Politics

Studies in Austrian Literature, Culture, and Thought

Major Figures of Modern Austrian Literature
Edited by Donald G. Daviau

Introducing Austria. A Short History
By Lonnie Johnson

The Verbal and Visual Art of Alfred Kubin
By Phillip H. Rhein

*Austrian Foreign Policy Yearbook:
Report of the Austrian Federal Ministry
for Foreign Affairs for the Year 1988*

From Wilson to Waldheim
Edited by Peter Pabisch

Arthur Schnitzler and Politics
By Adrian Clive Roberts

Translation Series:

February Shadows
By Elisabeth Reichart
Translated by Donna L. Hoffmeister

Arthur Schnitzler and Politics

Adrian Clive Roberts

Ariadne Press
270 Goins Court
Riverside, California 92507

Library of Congress Cataloging-in-Publication Data

Robert, Adrian Clive.

Arthur Schnitzler and politics/Adrian Clive Roberts.
p. cm. — (Studies in Austrian literature, culture, and thought)
Bibliography: p. 192-210
Includes indexes.
1. Schnitzler, Arthur, 1862-1931—Political and social views.
I. Title. II. Series.

PT2638.N5z8484 1989	89-6678
833'.8—dc20	CIP

ISBN: 0-929497-06-6
ISBN: 0-929497-14-7 (pbk.)

Cover picture by Georg Eisler, Vienna

Acknowledgments

I would first like to thank my editors, Professor Donald G. Daviau and Professor Richard H. Lawson for their criticism and help in revising this work.

I am indebted to the late Professor Heinrich Schnitzler for his interesting insights and kind words, as well as for permission to work with his father's diaries and posthumous documents in Marbach and at the University of California, Los Angeles.

Frau Gerda Niedieck of Niedieck Linder AG most graciously allowed me to cite Schnitzler's unpublished diaries, an unpublished letter to Josef Körner, his unpublished essay on Romain Rolland, and his school essay, "Kann uns zum Vaterland die Fremde werden?" Thanks go also to Mrs. Sonja Dobbins of the Williams Verlag AG for permission to publish two of Stefan Zweig's as yet unpublished letters to Arthur Schnitzler.

I am also extremely grateful to Professor Werner Welzig of the Austrian Academy of Sciences in Vienna (which is in the process of publishing Arthur Schnitzler's diaries) for his kind permission to cite extracts from the Diplomatic Copy in Vienna of the as yet unpublished portions of the diaries. Peter Michael Braunwarth was good enough to supply me with the official versions of the diary entries, which he painstakingly collated with the copies I had obtained in Marbach am Neckar at the German Literature Archive and in the Special Collections Section of the Research Library at the University of California, Los Angeles. All quotations from Schnitzler's diary shall be appropriately designated as being from the Diplomatic Copy.

My appreciation goes also to Professors Cynthia Walk and James K. Lyon for their guidance during the original project, and to Dr. Knut Beck and Frau Beatrix Wulf of the S. Fischer Verlag for permission to quote from several of Schnitzler's letters already published by that press.

I would like to thank Dr. Werner Volke and Herr Feifel of the Literature Archive in Marbach for their assistance in making Arthur Schnitzler's diaries accessible to me.

Last but not least, my eternal gratitude to Mr. Conrad Mouton of San Diego, California, who lent me his computer (to word process the manuscript) for "a couple of months"—which soon became a year—without once asking when it would be returned.

Adrian Clive Roberts,
Monterey, California
December 1988

Dedication

To my daughters, Gwendolyn Heather and Annemarie Catherine, and my parents, Alfred Oscar Hoexter and Valerie. Their love was my motivation.

**Pencil sketch of Arthur Schnitzler
by Georg Eisler, Vienna**

Table of Contents

1

Introduction

Over a span of fifty years Arthur Schnitzler dealt in his literary works and essays with numerous social and political issues, but virtually none appears with the frequency of the subjects war, militarism and the Austro-Hungarian army. These themes are so significant throughout his works, that he clearly deserves recognition as a pacifist writer.

Schnitzler's pacifism was unusual in an era noted for its enthusiastic support of war. Throughout the First World War, and especially during its early months, numerous Austrian and German authors were caught up in the patriotic fervor of the times. Such notable writers as Gerhart Hauptmann, Hugo von Hofmannsthal, Thomas Mann, Robert Musil, and initially even Stefan Zweig contributed to the prowar propaganda efforts of Germany and Austria-Hungary.

Hauptmann and Thomas Mann both published essays supporting the war, and Hofmannsthal and Zweig wrote for such government propaganda journals as *Das Kriegsarchiv*. In addition to his publishing activities Hofmannsthal undertook numerous semiofficial diplomatic propaganda missions outside Austria to promote the war effort. Zweig, after volunteering in 1914, was posted to the War Archives to assist in the dissemination of propaganda. As an officer in the Austro-Hungarian army, Robert Musil served two years in the infantry before being transferred to Vienna, where he was put in charge of a propaganda publication called *Heimat*.

By contrast, Schnitzler's opposition to the First World War is evident in his war essays. His is a fundamental, principled opposition to war per se—evident already in his early diary entries of 1880, when he was not yet eighteen years old. Many of the ideas he first expressed here reappear in his dramas and narrative works and above all in his essays on war, written during the First World War. Although he was always opposed to war in theory, Schnitzler's pacifism developed slowly over the years preceding the War, blossoming during its first months.

With each new decade Schnitzler explored a different aspect of the topic ".war" in his literature. During the first phase of his interest in the problem of war, beginning in 1880, he sketched the causes of what he considered to be the three types of war. The first is brought about by the perpetuation of traditional rivalries and hatreds between peoples of neighboring countries, aided by the human instinct of aggression. Here Schnitzler anticipates Freud's theory on the repression of the instinct of aggression, and its unfortunate outlet in the form of war. More importantly, however, Schnitzler sees as the underlying cause for this first type of war the misdirected sense of the ego, as in his critique of patriotism ("Über den Patriotismus"—an essay published in a Munich newspaper in 1880). The second type—war for imperialistic purposes—is caused by the despotism of the state, which seeks to expand its power through the extension of its boundaries. This form of rule is maintained at the expense of the common citizens who have little if anything to gain but everything to lose from expansion of state power. The third type of war—revolution—like the first has its roots in the personal ego, in this case combined with internal national corruption and social injustice.

Between 1890 and the turn of the century, as Schnitzler's professional interests turned from medicine to literature, he experimented with a variety of forms and subjects. Through the medium of the historical drama, Schnitzler dramatized the kinds of war outlined previously in the early phase: wars of rivalry and revolution.

From 1900 to the outbreak of the First World War, Schnitzler continued to write historical dramas on the subject of war, but these new works dealt more closely with the effects of war. Through the recollections of soldiers, vivid battle scenes are described, and the senselessness of war is made evident through the exposure of the falseness of such concepts as "Ehre" and "Vaterland." Here, Schnitzler for the first time condemns the compulsion governments place on their citizens to fight wars.

Between 1914 and 1919 Schnitzler produced several essays and numerous aphorisms condemning war in general, and the First World War specifically. Though not published until 1939, eight years after his death, these essays served as source material for dramatic and narrative works. Several fragments from this period deal with war; two, written between 1915 and 1918, are actually set during the War.

In 1917 Schnitzler returned to a theme used frequently in his early works: the duel. Now, however, given the similar nature of the two activities and the historical period during which Schnitzler is writing, the duel may be seen as an analogy to war. The analogy is all the more persuasive since the duel had virtually ceased to exist in Austria after 1911. Before 1900 Schnitzler stated that he intended to write works against the duel. Now war and conscription had superseded the duel as contemporary institutions of evil, yet he persisted in writing about the duel.

From 1920 until his death, Schnitzler fought the label "versunkene Welt," attached by critics to the subject matter of his post-War works in which he chose largely to write about pre-War Vienna. Actually Schnitzler returned to the historical drama not because he was unable to face the "new age," but because he saw in past ages similarities to his own period. He also disguised contemporary political figures in the cloak of history, perhaps to avoid retribution, but more importantly to illustrate the immutability of human nature.

Schnitzler also attacked what he considered to be the underlying causes of the First World War. Like Karl Kraus, he criticized journalists who sensationalize news and contribute to the dissemination of false information designed to inflame hatred between the peoples of the warring nations. Schnitzler illustrated the shortsightedness of the masses who live only for the moment and ignore the larger threatening problems around them. He revealed the greed of speculators who use the capitalist system for personal profit at the expense of others—even if it helps bring about a World War. He condemned the monarchs of Europe who stood passively by and allowed their politicians and diplomats to start a war they could not stop.

Before his death in 1931 Schnitzler worked on several new fragments relating to wars from different historical periods. He had first used the medium of the historical drama as a practical proving ground for his theories on the different types of war he had outlined earlier.

After the War he used the historical drama as an indirect way of revealing contemporary figures and events. Despite the differences in magnitude he was able to demonstrate the similarities between the causes of war in the eighteenth and twentieth centuries. His portrayal of war developed beyond a condemnation of war's effects on society, to a critical exposé of its psychological and political causes.

Schnitzler's critique of war is accompanied by a study of the underlying attitudes that produce conflicts within and between states. The primary factor is the ideology of militarism. The term "militarism," coined in France, came into vogue all over Europe in the late nineteenth century. Alfred Vagts writes of the derogatory sense in which the term was used at the turn of the century in Europe to connote the "domination of the military man over the civilian, an undue preponderance of military demands, an emphasis on military considerations, spirit, ideals, and scales of values, in the life of states."[1] Vagts's definition points to the broader character of militarism as a pervasive influence on the political, social, and cultural life of a nation.

Herbert Spencer, one of the fathers of modern sociology (and one of Bertha von Suttner's sources for pacifist theory) engaged in a systematic analysis of militarism in the mid 1880s. His theories on the centralization of the state and the close binding of the individuals of a society into a whole closely reflect the patterns of industrialization during the late nineteenth century. Volker R. Berghahn, author of *Militarism 1861-1979*, writes of Spencer's definition of militarism:

> In the mid-1880s he [Spencer] advanced what appeared to have been the first systematic analysis of militarism, although he preferred to call it an examination of a "militant type of society." Individualism will be unacceptable. The citizen's life "is not his own, the individual is owned by the state," which in turn requires strong controls and "a system of centralization." Seen in a different light, the "process of militant organization" is tantamount to a "process of regimentation which, primarily taking place in the army, secondarily affects the whole community." Ultimately, all aspects of public life would have to be supervised and enforced.[2]

Schnitzler examines the duel as both a military and a militaristic institution by placing military and civilian figures in opposition. He believed that a man enlisting in the army would be aware of the potential obligation to duel that such a career might place on him. The civilian, though, simply by virtue of his birth, became subject to the same code of honor that compelled the military man to engage in duels.

Schnitzler criticizes the duel first as a military institution that obliges its members to engage in a foolish and dangerous activity actually counterproductive to the interests of the army itself. Second, he attacks the duel as a militarist institution imposed on civilian society in order to perpetuate the rule of the aristocracy through the distinction of the social classes. The Austro-Hungarian army is represented in many of Schnitzler's works. Ill at ease in a society at peace, Schnitzler's military figures are often virtual caricatures of members of the strict, archaic Austrian army that was still obsessed with the code of honor and the duel in an age of technology and international politics.

Schnitzler was willing to take a public stand on the issue of the duel, but he was more cautious in his publications on war—perhaps as a result of the scandal over *Leutnant Gustl.* But he consistently opposed war and militarism privately in his diary, in his correspondence, and in his essays on war, published posthumously in 1939. These documents offer substantiation not only for the development of Schnitzler's pacifism—but also for the thesis that Schnitzler's oeuvre reflects the same attitudes as those presented in his private documents. Caution did not entirely prevent him from commenting on and criticizing both war and militarism in his dramatic and narrative works. An important aspect of the present study therefore involves an examination of the various literary techniques Schnitzler employs alternately to cover up and to reveal his criticism of war and militarism. These techniques include the historical mode, irony, ambiguity, and polemical debate.

Though fear of censorship, hostile criticism, or media misrepresentation certainly played a role in Schnitzler's reluctance to speak out openly on politics and militarism (Schnitzler gave up his medical practice in the 1890s and relied entirely on his literary publications and the staging of his plays for his income), the main reason for his stance seems to lie elsewhere. For Schnitzler opposed all dogmatism, even the dogma of absolute pacifism as represented by such contemporary figures as Alfred Fried, Romain Rolland, Bertha von Suttner, and later Fritz von Unruh and Stefan Zweig. Invariably, he felt, some prejudice (as in the case of Rolland) or weakness (as in the case of Fried) on the part of a leading figure of a group pursuing the lofty goal of world peace could serve only to detract from the ideal—a goal which Schnitzler did not believe could be attained in foreseeable human history. Schnitzler the individualist refused to be associated with any group, especially for a cause that concerned him as deeply as peace. Although war is never the main subject of a Schnitzler work, it plays a significant role in no less than eleven plays and short stories. Apart from the recollections of old soldiers, there is no major battle scene in any of Schnitzler's works. Nevertheless, the threat of war hangs over his characters, making the presence of certain personal conflicts all the more evident.

A contributing factor to the "backstage" character of war in Schnitzler's writings (with the notable exception of his essays on war) is that he stressed the psychology of human relationships and addressed social and political issues as a result of this interaction. This is not to say that Schnitzler did not write about issues or problems, as some critics have asserted. Those critics who do address problems in Schnitzler's works, however, focus almost exclusively on love and death, and on such social issues as the hypocritical condemnation by the upper-classes of decadent middle-class morality or the rising tide of anti-Semitism. The result is that such topics as war and militarism have been too lightly passed over by Schnitzler scholarship.

Peter Brock, author of one of the foremost histories on pacifism in Europe,[3] describes the relatively recent genesis of "absolute pacifism" (the total rejection of war, on moral grounds). According to Gordon N. Bergquist, the increase in the last century of the incidence of universal conscription worldwide has ushered in a hitherto unmatched age of absolute pacifism based on conscientious objection.[4] On moral grounds Schnitzler unequivocally condemns conscription (in his diaries and essays he refers to it more than once as "Sklaverei") and war in his essays and aphorisms on war. He objects to the infringement by the state on the right of the individual to self determination, and rejects propagandistic rhetoric that hypocritically decries on "humanitarian" grounds the killing of civilians in wartime while remaining silent on the large scale killing of soldiers in battle. For Schnitzler human life was without exception sacred. His dramatic and narrative works dealing with war and militarism complement the pacifist message of Schnitzler's essays and aphorisms on war, the content of which alone justifies his recognition as an absolute pacifist.

Although such contemporary writers as Andreas Latzko, Erich Maria Remarque, Bertha von Suttner, Fritz von Unruh, and Arnold Zweig won renown as pacifist authors, Schnitzler remains to this day largely unrecognized for his pacifism, despite the publication of his essays and aphorisms against war. His dramatic and narrative works contain many of the same antiwar statements propounded by Suttner, yet Schnitzler's subtlety of presentation makes his pacifist stance less obvious.

Suttner's antiwar novel *Die Waffen nieder* (1889) gained her international recognition as a pacifist, as well as the Nobel Prize. Unruh's antiwar Expressionist plays written during the last years of the First World War were followed by pacifist novels and decades of worldwide lectures on pacifism. Both Latzko and Remarque gained renown for their realistic depictions of battle-scene horrors—the former writing his first pacifist novel, *Menschen im Krieg*, in 1916. The latter found his fame more than a decade later for his novel *Im Westen nichts Neues* (1929). Arnold Zweig, like Schnitzler before him, illustrates the underlying causes and the destructive effects of militarism in *Der Streit um den Sergeanten Grischa* (1928). The innocent Russian Grischa falls victim to the struggle between the archaic, traditional militarism of the aristocracy and the even more brutal twentieth century militarism of the rising German middle class.

In contrast to the activist stance of the above writers, Schnitzler chose to remain publicly silent on the War, while privately writing his antiwar essays and aphorisms. It appears that he later used these as thematic material for his post-War literary works.

The duel motif has been dealt with as a social problem for decades, but Rena Schlein, in "Das Duellmotiv in Schnitzlers Dramen 'Ritterlichkeit', *Das weite Land* und *Das Wort*" (1975), was the first to point out Schnitzler's condemnation of the political implications. Her interpretation is limited, however, to the persecution of Jews who were excluded from dueling as "satisfaktionsunfähig." Klaus Laermann, in *Arthur Schnitzler: Zur Diagnose des Wiener Bürgertums im Fin de siècle* (1977), discusses the legal battle over the duel between the military and the government. At the turn of the last century, civilian opposition to the military code of honor was almost nonexistent. In fact the monarchy secretly approved of dueling because it helped maintain a state of military readiness for impending wars through the honing of combat skills in real-life situations.

Very little has been published on the subjects of Schnitzler's pacifism or politics. In 1968 Reinhard Urbach edited Schnitzler's anti-war poem "Ballade von den drei Brüdern" along with six letters from Schnitzler to various individuals, including the Nobel prize winning pacifist Alfred Hermann Fried, on the subject of politics. Urbach adds no commentary, nor was there any subsequent review of the poem or the majority of the letters. Only one letter, to Schnitzler's sister-in-law Elisabeth Steinrück dated 22 December 1914, received critical attention, in Friedrich Vollhardt's "Wer etwas zu sagen hat, trete vor und schweige!: Anmerkungen zu einer unbekannten Erklärung Dr. Arthur Schnitzlers (Zum Fall Ernst Toller) aus dem Jahr 1919"[5] as well as in Robert Kann's "Die historische Situation und die entscheidenden politischen Ereignisse zur Zeit und im Leben Arthur Schnitzlers" (1982).[6]

Vollhardt takes as a basis for his argument a statement made by Schnitzler in 1919 but discovered among his posthumous documents only in 1981. In a letter to the *Wiener Arbeiter-Zeitung* (19 June 1919), Schnitzler observes that the signature on a telegram published in the *Münchner Post* attributed to him was a forgery. Nevertheless, not only did Schnitzler concur with the sentiments of the telegram objecting to the intended execution of the German dramatist and then-communist, Ernst Toller, he went even further, condemning all political persecution by any country at any time. Vollhardt examines Schnitzler's silence during the First World War and concludes that although it might be construed as having been a political statement, it does little to contradict the prevalent notion that Schnitzler was an apolitical writer. Vollhardt further attempts to equate Schnitzler's attitude with that of one of his characters, Professor Bernhardi, who despite an apolitical nature became very active politically within the personal sphere, but he fails to address the theme of war and pacifism in Schnitzler's oeuvre. And it is here that the true political character of Schnitzler's writing is to be found.

Robert A. Kann addresses the subject of Schnitzler and politics in a more general manner but he makes a stronger case for the political interpretation of Schnitzler's writings than does Vollhardt. In order to address as many of Schnitzler's works as possible, as well as to evoke the political atmosphere of the period (in much the same way as he did in a 1959 article entitled "Das Österreich Arthur Schnitzlers"),[7] Kann foregoes any meaningful interpretation of a single play or narrative work. Nevertheless, he provides stimulation for a more in-depth study of Schnitzler's writings when he quotes from Schnitzler's letter of 22 December 1914 to Elisabeth Steinrück, to show Schnitzler claiming that his pre-War works anticipated and commented upon the political situation of Europe:

> Wenn ich auch in keinem Schützengraben liege—ja es sogar vermeide, mich da und dort "zum Welt-krieg" mich zu äußern, ich sehe mich mit beiden Beinen in unserem Zeitalter stehen wie irgend einer—und habe ich auch nicht eben leitartikel-oder feuilletongerechte Gedanken über Vaterland, Heldentum und Politik—es ist mir wahrscheinlich vernünftigeres durch den Kopf gegangen, als vielen, die sich lyrisch und essayistisch betätigen...Ich wage es zu behaupten, dab in manchen der Sachen, die ich schon vor dem Kriege geschrieben habe, und fast allen, die ich entworfen...eine Ahnung oder besser ein Vorverstehen dieser Epoche herauszuspüren ist...Wenn einer nicht mitschießt, ja nicht einmal mittrommelt, ist er noch kein "Abseitssteher."[8]

Kann makes the connection between Schnitzler's statement and his historical drama Der junge Medardus on the basis of the patriotic figure Eschenbacher. Kann fails, however, to grasp the possibility of an intended parallel between the two epochs and dismisses further study of Medardus. To him the play cannot be considered relevant to the twentieth century because it is set in Vienna over one hundred years before the First World War.

Schnitzler's posthumous papers, long available to scholars, contain a great many political writings relating to the War and to the post-War period.[9] A number of these essays and aphorisms were published by Robert O. Weiss in the volume Aphorismen und Betrachtungen (1967). Schnitzler's essays on war contained here, collectively entitled "Und einmal wird der Friede wiederkommen...," form the main reference for my work.

Despite the increased accessibility of Schnitzler's essays on war since 1967, no major study has investigated whether similar pacifist tendencies are to be found in Schnitzler's dramatic and narrative works. To be sure, Brigitte Schneider-Halvorson brings up the possibility of a connection between Schnitzler's aphoristic writings and his postwar plays in The Late Dramatic Works of Arthur Schnitzler.[10]

Although her study is limited to four post-War dramas, Schneider-Halvorson is the first to point out the significance of the war and peace theme in Schnitzler's late dramatic works. The present study might therefore be regarded as an extension and documentation of speculation and unanswered questions in her work.

To trace the development of Schnitzler's ideas on war, militarism, and pacifism over the course of the author's life, I follow a chronological approach. My historical method involves more, however, than simply tracing the history of an idea. Schnitzler's works are known for their thematic intricacy and complexity. Perhaps one of the reasons for Schnitzler's lack of recognition as a pacifist writer is the fact that he places a higher priority on creating realistic characters and producing literary works of high quality than on using the literary medium as a forum for his personal beliefs.

Although I shall focus on the political nature of his works on war and militarism, I shall also attempt to detect the thread which ties together the lives of individual characters and the political direction of societies and nations. This thread consists of Schnitzler's recognition, evident already in his essay from 1880, "Über den Patriotismus," that the strong sense of self awareness ("das Bewutsein des Ich") is largely responsible for conflicts between individuals and nations alike. Previous research has tended to focus on the psychology of individual characters at the expense of larger political themes. This study, while addressing primarily the latter, attempts to place the political aspect in perspective with the psychological aspect. I will trace the development of Schnitzler's anti- militarist and pacifist stance in his narrative, dramatic, and aphoristic works from 1880 to 1931 to demonstrate a progression, moving from a theoretical polemic on the evils of patriotism and an analysis of three types of war, to a condemnation of the specific causes of war.

It is clear that Schnitzler developed his own ideas on militarism and pacifism, but there is also evidence that he was influenced by the European pacifist movement before, during, and after the First World War. Schnitzler rejected dogmatism and refused to join any organized movement against war. Although his essays on war were not published until eight years after his death, Schnitzler's post-War works contain much of the pacifist dialogue contained in those essays. This refutes the generally accepted belief that Schnitzler remained silent on the War.

Through ambiguity and the use of the historical drama as a parallel to contemporary history, Schnitzler criticized his own period and anticipated future events without subjecting himself to censorship. I challenge the commonly held view that Schnitzler stagnated in his post-1918 works simply because the works continue for the most part to be set before the First World War. Such works as *Komödie der Verführung* and *Der Gang zum Weiher*, written after the First World War, are as relevant today as they would have been in 1914.

Schnitzler's technique of combining psychological studies with political themes makes the political realm accessible to the reader. He demonstrated that the average person is involved in the political process, even though that person may not have realized it. Schnitzler attacked politicians, diplomats, and journalists who conspire to seize power from the general populace. He believed they must be restrained through the modification of social and political institutions whose primary role will be to prevent future wars. Schnitzler sought to expose the false code of honor imposed on individuals (through the institution of the duel) and whole nations (through the institution of war) by the militarist ideology of governments and despotic rulers. The critique of war and militarism was the goal of many of his essays, and often of his dramatic and narrative works as well.

2

Austro-Hungarian Militarism Versus Pacifism: 1880-1889

2.1 Schnitzler's Early Ideas on Patriotism and the Causes of War

"Es fehlt mir die Ehrfurcht vor jeder militärischen Charge. Der Kampf gegen den Militarismus ist kein Kampf gegen eine Institution, sondern gegen eine Weltanschauung."

Theodor Reik[1]

Periodically Schnitzler read through his old diaries to refresh his memory and obtain ideas for his literary works. He mentions such an occasion in his diary entry of 4 April 1916, significantly, in the middle of the First World War: "Seltsam berührten mich die Bemerkungen über Militarismus, die ich als achtzehnjähriger [sic] schrieb, und über den Krieg,—wie ich sie heute nicht verständiger schreiben könnte."[2] Indeed, as seen, his diary entry of 28 April 1880 reveals surprisingly mature reflections on patriotism, militarism, and war.

While still a schoolboy, Schnitzler was assigned the task of writing an essay on the question of whether it was possible to become completely at home in a foreign country. The title of the essay, Schnitzler's "2. Schularbeit," was "Kann uns zum Vaterland die Fremde werden?" (included here in Appendix 2). This thought-provoking topic was possibly the catalyst for his diary entry of 28 April 1880 on the subjects patriotism and war, as well as his published essay, "Über den Patriotismus."[3]

In his diary Schnitzler approaches the topic of patriotism with irony. After beginning this entry in a serious tone, he ridicules patriotism and its disastrous effect of war through his use of the expression "auf die Hühneraugen treten." This ironic tone is later refined and developed in his essay "Über den Patriotismus" (first mentioned in his diary entry of 23 August , 1880). While the motives one might have for feeling patriotic are praiseworthy, Schnitzler believes that the effects are detrimental, for if everyone loves only his own country, contempt and hatred for other nations are inevitable: "Patriotismus ist eigentlich nur Bescheidenheit. Der Mensch sieht in lobenswerther Resignation ein, daß von einem allgemeinen Glück der Menschheit nicht die Rede sein kann. So beschränkt er sich denn darauf, einen kleinen Kreis zu lieben, in einem kleinen Kreise gutes zu wirken. Es ist nur beklagenswerth, daß ein Patriotismus dem andern auf die Hühneraugen tritt und die Leute ihr ganzes Quantum Liebe auf einem Fleck verausgaben."[4]

In November 1880, on the promptings of his friend Eugen Deimel, who had moved to Munich to work for the liberal newspaper *Der freie Landesbote*, Schnitzler submitted two essays for publication by that paper. The second of these, published on 15 November 1880, was entitled "Über den Patriotismus." In his autobiography, *Jugend in Wien*, Schnitzler calls his essay "a type of philosophical dialogue about, or more correctly, against patriotism."[5] As the article is not generally available the full text is included in Appendix 3.[6] Here Schnitzler develops his critique of patriotism from his diary entry of 28 April 1880, cited earlier. The most important condemnation of patriotism occurs early in the essasy when Balduin says: "O wie armselig ist doch, was wir unsere schönsten, erhabensten Gefühle nennen, wenn wir ihnen mit der Schärfe der Logik auf den Grund zu kommen suchen."[7] Here Schnitzler clearly implies that patriotism has negative consequences, for the feelings it involves, although appearing at first glance to be praiseworthy, are revealed in the light of logic to be devoid of value.

At first reading, "Über den Patriotismus" appears actually to be in favor of patriotism rather than against it, especially when Balduin, who had been speaking against patriotism, concludes with an apparent justification for its existence. It is important to remember that Schnitzler published the essay under his real name, during a time in German history when patriotism was almost a hallowed concept. To attack it directly would have caused great public outcry—if the article had not fallen victim to censorship beforehand. For that reason, he employs here a veiling technique that he uses throughout his literary career: namely to allow the view contrary to his own to apparently have the final word, but only after he has refuted the opposition earlier in the text. I say apparently because he uses the ambiguity of the German word "Egoismus" (which embodies both the negative "egotism" and the positive "egoism") to openly praise the virtues of a strong "ich," but secretly to condemn the vice of egotistical chauvinism. When referring to patriotism, Schnitzler intends the term to mean egotism, but he can protect himself from critical attacks by asserting that he meant it as egoism. He decries the effects of patriotism but explains its genesis as a consequence of human nature:

> "Sehen Sie, Balduin, daß Sie mit einem Male dem Patriotismus das Wort sprechen! Denn der ist's, der da ruft: 'Einer für Alle!'"
>   "Nicht doch," erwiderte Balduin. Er sagt: "Einer, d.h. ich für die paar Leute, durch deren Wohlsein es selbstverständlich auch mir selbst gut gehen muß, daß [sic] ich ein Glied des grossen Körpers bin.... Auch ist es durchaus nicht verachtenswerth, daß das Bewusstsein des Ich am stärksten in uns ausgeprägt ist; da wir ja schließlich doch immer nur wir selber bleiben."[8]

Schnitzler's conclusion is of special significance, reflecting a very early recognition of what will become a fundamental aspect of his views on the causes of war, namely, that egoism is an ingrained human trait not subject to change, nor should it be, for the very existence of the individual depends upon the strength of his ego. Schnitzler attacks the shady business of politics and criticizes the use of catch-phrases and empty words or, even worse, misused words in the service of political propaganda. When the narrator enters Balduin's small attic-room, he says: "Sie lesen den Leitartikel und lächeln dabei so harmlos! Man sieht doch gleich, daß Sie sich bisher nicht mit Politik beschäftigt haben."[9] Balduin (whose ideas more closely resemble Schnitzler's than do the narrator's) replies that he is not interested in politics now either, and that only the word "patriotism" intrigues him. The modern reader, aware of Schnitzler's reputation as an apolitical writer, might attribute Balduin's lack of interest in politics to Schnitzler. A superficial reading of the essay even supports this view, for the political content of the article Balduin is reading is never discussed. Two important facts might be overlooked, however, that illustrate the political background and relevance of the essay. First, Schnitzler mentions briefly that the article is about the "most recent events in Paris and Cherbourg." Second, the essay was published not in Austria, but in Munich, Germany. The importance of both these facts emerge when one considers the political events that took place in France during the summer of 1880—a mere three months before the publication of Schnitzler's essay—and their relevance to Germany.

In August 1880 the French premier, Léon Gambetta—generally considered a moderate by Bismarck and his policy makers who, since the Franco-German War of 1870, closely observed the direction of French politics—gave a rousing patriotic speech in Cherbourg, in which he called for French rearmament.[10] Gambetta's speech did little to alter the political realities and served primarily as an exercise in inflammatory political rhetoric. In this respect Schnitzler's article questioning the concept of patriotism is ironically political, for it deals with the very substance of Gambetta's speech and its reception in Germany. In effect Schnitzler criticizes Gambetta's militaristic patriotism echoed by the German nationalists in Austria.

The ambiguous role of Balduin in Schnitzler's essay is an example of Schnitzler's advice to the reader to curb the tendency to connect the ideas of a character with those of the author. He warns against such an activity in the foreword of his *Buch der Sprüche und Bedenken* (1927). While on the one hand intentionally placing another roadblock in the way of critics who might attack him for his opposition to the popular concept of patriotism, Schnitzler on the other supplies the scholar with a key to the interpretation of his works when he writes:

Einer der Gründe, die mich zur Herausgabe dieses Buches bestimmten, ist wohl auch der Wunsch, allerlei Irrtümer, absichtliche und unabsichtliche, über mein Verhältnis zu den sogenannten ewigen und zu manchen zeitlichen Fragen zu berichtigen; Irrtümer wie sie sich leicht ergeben, wenn man z.B. Sätze, die ich irgendeiner erdichteten Figur in den Mund gelegt habe, als Ausdruck meiner persönlichen Überzeugung oder, wenn man gelegentliche artistische Spielereien, die dem Dichter wohl erlaubt sein müssen, als Ausdruck meines innersten Wesens aufzufassen, sich den Anschein geben möchte.[11]

It is somewhat curious that Schnitzler felt the need to issue such a statement, for, as Heinrich Schnitzler and Therese Nickl write, Arthur Schnitzler frequently received inquiries about his works, and he almost always rejected such requests because he believed that a literary work should speak for itself and not require any commentary.[12]

Indeed, in Schnitzler's own words, "Nur still geschwiegen Autor—und keine Erwiderung! Die einzige, die du allen Angriffen entgegenstellen kannst hast du schon vorweggenommen:—dein Werk. Wenn es dauert, hast du recht behalten."[13] This view is later shared by another controversial pacifist author—Erich Maria Remarque. Asked once why he never intervened in the heated debates on his pacifist novel *Im Westen nichts Neues*, Remarque is reputed to have said: "Because I didn't consider it necessary.... Once a work is finished, the author has nothing further to say about it, even if there is a risk of being misunderstood. If this is the case, then this work has not succeeded, and talking about it serves no purpose. But I am only misunderstood where people went out of their way to misunderstand me."[14]

Because Schnitzler's warning to be careful in attributing the views of a fictional character to the author himself appears in the introduction to a collection of aphorisms which might aid in the interpretation of his literary works, it might be seen as an encouragement to do so—not haphazardly, but in a cautious manner.

2.2 Schnitzler's Experience in the Military

With its defeat at the hands of Prussia in 1866, the Austrian army suffered a blow to its prestige, and indeed to its very existence. Because the rising tide of nationalism in Hungary increasingly threatened the unity of the newly formed Empire, the government sought new ways to strengthen the military. One measure was compulsory service introduced in 1868, modeled on the Prussian system. While most young men were required to serve for three years, university students (comprised largely of sons of the upperclass and aristocracy) were "allowed" to serve only one year under the ironic title of "Einjährig-Freiwillige."[15]

William M. Johnston writes that Franz Josef "prized his army as an instrument of unity, a last remaining link with the past."[16] He hoped that by drawing large numbers of men from all areas of the Empire together, national unity could be maintained. However the institution of a military draft created perhaps more problems than it solved. Alfred Vagts writes of the period around 1890: "From the standpoint of national cohesion, the weakest army was the Austro-Hungarian, with its recruits drawn from ten linguistic nationalities."[17] The linguistic differences eventually forced the military to form separate regiments. Nevertheless, German remained the official language of command, which caused much resentment among Magyar (Hungarian) officers.[18] Communication between the different nationalities was poor at best.

Given the high density of the military population in such European cities as Vienna in the final decades of the nineteenth century, conflicts between civilians and soldiers were common enough, but reservists added to the problems. Former conscripts represented a link between the army and civilian life, and military values filtered down into society. The law of universal conscription accomplished a giant leap forward in the militarizing of Austrian society. The army was very conspicuous in the cities, and was much revered by the general populace, which emulated the colorful uniforms as well as the code of honor—notably with regard to the duel. Military values became social values.

Schnitzler's opinions of the Austro-Hungarian army and the military in general were formed in this period, during his year of military service between 1882-1883, beginning on 1 October 1882. Because he was a medical student he was assigned to hospital service rather than the infantry or the cavalry. Although his duties did not generally consist of combat training (he did go on occasional maneuvers), Schnitzler's diary entry two months later reflects intense antipathy (note again his use of the term "zuwider") of anything military: "Im allgemeinen wie vorauszusehen ist mir das ganze Militär, alles was drum und dranhängt, ungeheuer zuwider. Überhaupt kommt man zu gar nichts."[19]

Because Schnitzler was assigned to a medical unit and served only one year rather than the standard three that were the lot of the uneducated classes, his army experiences were certainly not as negative as they might have been had he been attached to an infantry or artillery unit. Perhaps for that reason Schnitzler chose years later to retain his military commission after the lapse of his required period as a reserve officer. Moreover, Schnitzler's connection to the army medical corps permitted him to regard his military role as potentially beneficial rather than detrimental to humanitarian values. Pragmatically, Schnitzler also probably looked forward to the retirement pay awarded retiring reserve-officers. In 1901, however, as a result of the "Leutnant Gustl" affair, Schnitzler's military commission was permanently revoked.

Despite his somewhat ambivalent view of his own role in the army upon his discharge at the end of his year of service, Schnitzler's diary reflects his distaste for the military and a sense of relief that this phase of his life is over: "Mittwoch. Nm.—Wieder Civilist—Ohne nachhaltige Eindrücke bin ich aus meiner Militärgewandung herausgeschlüpft. Höchstens daß es jetzt um ein paar Thatsachen und ein paar Menschen mehr gibt, die mir zuwider sind. So schließ ich mit einem Abschnitt meines Lebens nach dem andern ab..."[20] Despite Schnitzler's claim that his impressions of the year were not lasting, the wording here belies the statement. Once again he uses the term "repulsive" in reference to the military. This was to be his attitude for the rest of his life.

2.3 Bertha von Suttner and
Liberal Opposition to Militarism

The 1880s marked an important period in the rise to pre-eminence of the German army and the relative decline of the Austro-Hungarian army. One of the primary reasons for this was the rapid advance of technology and the industrialization of Europe, especially Germany and Britain. Austria-Hungary, on the other hand, remained curiously aloof from these advances, bound up in its own history and tradition. More than ever before, the Austro-Hungarian military stressed the "code of honor," the dashing cavalry, and the gallant exploits of Field Marshal Radetzky back in 1849, when the Austrian Empire was still winning wars. With its head turned backwards, the Empire ambled slowly towards an appointment with the Great War of 1914-1918 and its own demise. By 1889 Austria-Hungary had seen twenty-three years of peace, but the growing military and the expansion of militarism into civilian spheres cast an ever darkening cloud over the Dual Monarchy, and indeed over all of Europe.

Also in 1889 an important pacifist novel was published by the Austrian baroness, Bertha von Suttner. *Die Waffen nieder* represents not only a statement against war through the depiction of the major battles of the nineteenth century, but also liberal opposition to the expanding militarism that threatened to end the decades of peace in Austria. Irwin Abrams writes that Suttner had difficulty finding a publisher for her work. Most editors shared the opinion of one who said: "In spite of all these merits, however, it is quite out of the question to publish the novel in a military country."[21] When it was finally published, Suttner's work became an international best-seller, being translated into sixteen languages by 1914. For this work Suttner received the Nobel Peace Prize in 1905. Abrams notes that the work itself was more popular than the organized peace movements, illustrated through the fact that the Social Democrats used the novel as a propaganda tool, "although most of them had little use for the middle-class peace societies."[22]

The novel traces the conversion to pacifism of a fictional Austrian countess (Martha von Tilling) who, like Suttner herself, comes from a military family. Martha's first husband, a young lieutenant, dies in the Italian campaign of 1859, leaving her to raise their newborn son. She then marries another officer, a former Prussian named Tilling, who is also converted to pacifism through a discussion with Martha about her philosophical readings, together with his own experiences in war. When Tilling is wounded in the Austro-Prussian War of 1866, Martha sets out to find him on the battlefield. Suttner's narrative gives a vivid depiction of the gruesomeness nature of war, exposing at the same time the propagandistic character of prowar rhetoric. The war is followed by a cholera epidemic which kills virtually all of Martha's family. Her militarist father, a retired general who had always favored war, finally, on his deathbed, curses it. Tilling returns safely from the war, retires from the army, and the couple decide to devote the remainder of their lives to furthering of pacifism—beginning with the education of their own son toward peace. Nonetheless at the outbreak of the Franco-Prussian war, Tilling is trapped in Paris, arrested, and mistakenly shot as a spy.

Suttner's technique for weaving the intellectual arguments of pacifism into the narrative in the form of polemical debate closely resembles the approach taken later by Schnitzler. The substance of Suttner's polemics also anticipates Schnitzler's view of war. For example, Abrams's introduction to the English translation of Suttner's novel might serve equally well as an introduction to Schnitzler's *Der Gang zum Weiher* (1921-1926): "Throughout the telling of these events, the authoress weaves in dialogues that present all the intellectual arguments against war, exposing both its glorification by the officer class and the philosophical and religious arguments put forward in its behalf. The Baroness sees the causes of war in the misguided policies of the diplomats..."[23]

The extent of the militarizing of Austria-Hungary is made clear through the words of Suttner's character, Minister Andererseits (so named because his indecisiveness causes him to include in every sentence a string of contradictions)—a caricature of the wishy-washy, dangerous politician. He argues that only through military escalation can peace be assured: "In der Tat... , es liegt zutage: die Wehrtüchtigkeit, welche wir erreicht haben, ist etwas Großartiges und dürfte alle Friedensbrecher abschrecken. Das Landsturmgesetz, welches alle tauglichen Staatsbürger vom 19. bis 42., die einstigen Offiziere verpflichtet, erlaubt uns, beim ersten Aufgebot allein 4 800 000 Soldaten aufzustellen."[24]

On the other hand, the minister continues, the financial burden placed on the civilian population by such a military buildup is severe to the point of being crippling. His next "andererseits" is the most disturbing, since it reveals the warlike attitude of the civilian populace and the effectiveness of the government's propaganda policy: "... es ist aber andererseits erhebend, mit welchem opferfreudigen Patriotismus die Volksvertreter stets und allerorts die von dem Kriegsministerium geforderte Mehrbelastung bewilligen; sie erkennen die von allen einsichtigen Politikern zugegebene, durch die Wehrhaftigkeitsentfaltung der Nachbarstaaten und durch die politische Situation bedingte Notwendigkeit, alle anderen Rücksichten dem eisernen Zwang der militärischen Kräftigung unterzuordnen."[25]

The powerful grip of the militarist state on the populace through the institution of universal conscription is made evident through the reluctant participation of Martha von Tilling's son in military exercises, and if necessary, in war.[26]

Arthur Schnitzler, although not yet a pacifist in 1882, also expressed liberal opposition to militarism. In his autobiography, *Jugend in Wien*, quoting from his own diaries, he writes of his early opposition to conscription, at the same time indicating a desire to review past wars, perhaps with the intent of analyzing their causes ("das Gemachte nachzuweisen"): "Ich ... entrüstete mich über die "Illiberalität der allgemeinen Wehrpflicht" und fand es eine "dankbare Aufgabe"—der mich zu unterziehen mein Wissen und meine Beharrlichkeit kaum gewachsen wären—'an allen Kriegen die jemals geführt wurden, das Gemachte nachzuweisen.'"27 In a diary entry of 2 June 1880 Schnitzler poses the rhetorical question: "Darf man eine Zeit erhoffen, in der kein Krieg mehr sein wird?"28 This significant question, posed so early in his life, is to be an important aspect of many of Schnitzler's future works.

In the 1890s Schnitzler followed very much in Suttner's footsteps in his opposition to militarism, and eventually, war itself. Schnitzler first met Suttner in 1891. It is highly probable given the popularity of *Die Waffen nieder*, that he was familiar with her novel.

3

Absolutism and Civil Unrest. Schnitzler's Literary Experimentation 1890-1899

3.1 Schnitzler's Campaign Against the Militarist Institution of the Duel

"Der Krieg ist ein erweiterter Zweikampf. Jeder sucht den andern durch physische Gewalt zur Erfüllung seines Willens zu zwingen."
Karl von Clausewitz

The duel is a frequent theme in both Schnitzler's dramatic and narrative works. For the young Schnitzler dueling was an accepted fact of life; his father had made sure that his son was trained well in the art of fencing, should the need ever arise for him to defend his honor in a duel. In his autobiography *Jugend in Wien* Schnitzler tells of his early views on the duel during his year of military service from 1882 to 1883. While serving in the army as an "Einjährig-Freiwilliger Mediziner," Schnitzler continued to attend lectures at the University of Vienna, and it was here that he had his first exposure to the duel which was as much a part of student life as it was of military life. Notably Schnitzler emphasizes that as a student his willingess to duel was not based on any principled approval of the custom. Rather it was his youthfulness, his "esprit de corps," and his defensiveness about his Jewishness which made him willing to duel: "Es war vom Duell die Rede, und wir alle, ohne uns gerade als prinzipielle Anhänger dieser Sitte zu fühlen, betonten aus unserem Studententum heraus und mehr noch als Einjährig-Freiwillige und künftige Reserveoffiziere unsere Bereitschaft, erforderlichenfalls ritterliche Satisfaktion zu geben."[1]

More importantly, for Schnitzler and his small group of friends the duel was an integral part of their Jewishness. Strong anti-Semitism at the university on the part of German Nationalists made scuffles between Christians and Jews quite common and duels often ensued. As a result, Schnitzler writes, many Jews became expert swordsmen. Consequently, fearing the threat of their superior weapons skills, anti-Semites under the name of the "Waidhofener Verband der wehrhaften Vereine deutscher Studenten in der Ostmark"[2] issued an unofficial decree, which several years later became official as the "Waidhofener Beschluß,"[3] declaring Jews "satisfaktionsunfähig"—without honor and unworthy of dueling. For Schnitzler in 1883 the duel was a matter of personal and religious honor.

At this stage, he showed no sign of his later condemnation of the militarist institution of the duel. Indeed, the fact that he retained his military commission as a reserve officer after he was no longer required to do so indicates a tacit approval of dueling within the military. After completing his studies and no longer being exposed to the pressures of daily student or military life, Schnitzler was able to distinguish between the obligation in the military to duel and the militarist obligation in civilian life; it is the latter that he soon would condemn. It is therefore no anomaly that Schnitzler did not surrender his commission until he was deprived of it because of the *Leutnant Gustl* affair in 1901.

In the 1890s Schnitzler's attitude toward the duel became more critical, although his sense of Jewishness remained intact. For Schnitzler the writer, the duel held a particular fascination because of the complex reasons for its continued existence in the early part of the twentieth century. In a questionnaire about the duel, Schnitzler wrote that he had no objection to a duel between two people who truly desire to shoot one another. The right of the two individuals to decide their own fate should not be abridged. It was the "Duellzwang," the obligation forced on society by militarist ideology which Schnitzler criticized in his works: "Hier erst setzt die Frage ein; nicht um das Duell, sondern um den Duellzwang handelt es sich. Und zwar nicht um den augenfälligen Zwang, gegen den einzuschreiten eine verhältnismäßig einfache Sache wäre, sondern um die vielfachen Formen des uneingestandenen, unaufrichtigen, gefährlichen Zwanges, der in unseren gesellschaftlichen Zuständen begründet ist."[4]

Whereas the duel was an acknowledged aspect of military life, the obligation in civilian society to duel remained unrecognized. Schnitzler believed that both the duel and war were supported by the false concept of honor. In his essays on war written during the First World War, Schnitzler crystallized his critique of the false notion of honor, at the same time demonstrating the parallel between the duel and war. In both the army and civilian life of a militarist state, the individual is taught that one's honor can be offended by another. In the same way, governments believe that their national honor can be offended by another country. In the first case the offended party challenges the offender to a duel, in the latter, war is declared to regain lost honor. Schnitzler fundamentally rejects the notion that the honor of an individual or a country can be offended by another. Honor, he believed, can only be lost through one's own actions. In a diary entry made after the War, Schnitzler predicts that (what will be) the Second World War will result from the same false perception of honor: "Hugo Ganz regt zu einem öffentlichen Aufruf an Barbusse [a renowned French pacifist author] u.a. an, gegen die ehrenrührigen Forderungen des deutschen Friedensvertrags, die den nächsten Krieg hervorrufen werden. Halte das für aussichtslos. Wichtiger wäre es, den falschen Begriff "Ehre" zu revidieren—und das Gefühl allgemein zu machen, daß die eigne Ehre niemals durch einen andern verletzt werden kann."[5] The last four lines from above might be seen as an indication of Schnitzler's intention in the past and the future to criticize both the duel and war in his literary works.

Schnitzler differentiated between the obligation for the military officer and that for the civilian to engage in a duel. The officer class, he felt, consisted of individuals who knowingly and voluntarily subjected themselves to a career that imposed certain values and modes of behavior on its members; the obligation to duel was part of this unwritten code in the Austro-Hungarian army. It is important to note that Schnitzler was speaking of a professional officer class, not of conscripted soldiers. The duel was a recognized facet of military life in Austria at the turn of the century. In society at large, however, the right of the free individual to determine his own fate is to Schnitzler the key issue in his condemnation of the compulsion to duel.

Although the duel in Austria, as in most European states, had been outlawed since the sixteenth century, duelists in fin de siècle Austria-Hungary were seldom punished.[6] An unwritten code similar to that affecting military officers obliged civilians of the upper social strata to engage in duels over matters of honor. Schnitzler notes that civilians unintentionally came into daily contact with situations that might force them to engage in a duel. In essence, the military code of honor was applied equally to the upper classes of civilian society, the army's officer corps, and reserve officers. In this sense one can truly speak of the duel as a militarist institution, especially as it applied to the civilian populace.

Although the judicial duel, as a means of selection in a Darwinian sense, had been fought since the first century B.C.,[7] the militarizing of the duel resulted from the rise of the "standing army" in the nineteenth century. In 501 A.D. the duel was legally codified as trial by combat by the Burgundian King Gundobald. Unlike later duels fought solely for honor, these earliest duels were fought to determine guilt or innocence. God was considered the judge, and if the accused should die in combat he was automatically declared guilty of whatever crime he had been charged:

> Die verschiedenen, ursprünglich noch variierenden Bräuche wurden im Jahre 501 vom Burgundenkönig Gundobad zum erstenmal in einem Kodex zusammengefaßt, dem sogenannten "Loi Gombette."
>
> Die Zweikämpfer mußten auf schwarz verhängten Sitzen Platz nehmen, sich einem religiösen Ritus unterwerfen und vor allem schwören, sich keiner Zaubermittel zu bedienen.... Dann erst eröffnete der Marschall mit dem Ruf: "Lasset die guten Kämpfer ins Feld!" das eigentliche Duell. Der Herausforderer warf seinem Gegner einen Handschuh—den Fehdehandschuh—vor die Füße, den dieser aufzuheben hatte, zum Zeichen, daß er die Herausforderung annahm.[8]

From around the end of the fourteenth century the duel fought solely for honor began to slowly replace the judicial duel.[9] "Personal honor," always a part of the "Kampfordal" practice, became a value emphasized by societies in order to ensure certain modes of behavior determined by the ethical codes of those societies. Honor was considered an important possession of each person, the loss of which constituted a serious offense.

With regard to dueling, the concept of honor was most dangerous in that it was something of which another person could deprive one through insult. Only through combat could this sense of personal honor (or the chivalrous defense of the honor of a sister or wife) be restored. At the beginning of the sixteenth century the first "courts of honor" were established in France. The concept spread to Italy where the terms were precisely defined whereby a man of honor would be obliged to engage in a duel. Legal attempts such as that by Richelieu in 1616 in France to abolish the duel by executing duelists were doomed to failure because the individual regarded honor as his personal property. Despite the threat of severe legal penalties, men—and occasionally women too—continued to fight, and the duel persisted.

In 1843 the Prussian cabinet established an "Ehrengericht" to determine under which circumstances military honor had been enough offended to warrant the fighting of a duel. The duel evolved into a symbol of class distinction and upper-class authority in both Prussia and Austria in the mid-to-late nineteenth century. The establishment of a code of honor to govern both military and social behavior further served to enforce the differentiation of social classes. In its trappings of knightly honor the "noble" and "manly" institution of the duel was adopted as the means for settling disputes between members of the same class or military rank. In the late nineteenth century the duel also became a tool of anti-Semites when Jews were declared "satisfaktionsunfähig," meaning that they had no honor to defend and were not considered worthy of engaging in combat.

With the approach of the nineteenth century, several governments, professing to be civilized, placed stricter bans on dueling; by 1900 the duel had all but been abolished in most European countries. In Austria and Germany, however, the tradition persisted. Egon Eis demonstrates how deeply ingrained in the German military the duel was, even as late as 1937, when he cites an army manifesto on the protection of honor. During the Nazi period in Germany, honor was an integral facet of the totalitarian militarist regime:

> Die Herausforderung zum Zweikampf ist das äußerste Mittel zur Wahrung der Ehre. Es darf nur dann angewandt werden, wenn

die schwer verletzte Ehre durch keine Entscheidung des Vorgesetzten wiederhergestellt werden kann. Für einen Offizier kommt nur Zweikampf mit Pistolen bis zur Kampfunfähigkeit in Frage.[10]

The code of honor (primarily unwritten regulations governing the behavior of military personnel)[11] of the Austro-Hungarian army thus became the unofficial code of honor[12] of civilian behavior as well. This situation suited the Monarchy and the aristocracy quite well, because the high social status afforded the officer caste reinforced the dominance of the aristocracy over the lower classes. In addition, the infiltration of military values into society aided in maintaining military preparedness should war break out. In many ways the militarizing of society in most European countries was to the advantage of the respective governments, and so militarism flourished.

In Austria, the military code of honor stood in defiant contrast to the token civilian law banning the duel. The punishments inflicted on those who were ever convicted by civil courts for dueling were mild in comparison to the complete rejection by society and punishment within the military of those who refused to engage in a duel if the code of honor demanded it.

The social role of the duel in the military was only part of the reason for its continued existence. Long periods of peace were thought to have negative effects on the morale of the soldier. The duel therefore satisfied the need for an outlet of physical aggression and also provided a means for toning up the soldiers' courage and weapons skills. In essence, the duel represented a peacetime alternative to war, and duels between civilians and officers were fairly common occurrences. The attrition rate of the Austrian officer corps was effectively reduced through the civilian supply of duelists. This militarization of the duel is an aspect of Schnitzler's literary attacks on the institution, made evident through the fact that in almost all cases where a duel is fought in his works, a soldier initiates the duel against a civilian. A possible explanation for this might be found in William Johnston's observation that in cases where an officer killed a civilian, Franz Josef never failed to grant a pardon.

The duel has frequently been called a "war between individuals" and conversely, war has been referred to as a "duel between nations." Karl von Clausewitz called war "ein erweiterter Zweikampf," in that both parties seek to impose their will on the other through the use of force. Bertha von Suttner in *Die Waffen nieder* (1889) speaks of war as a "Völkerduell" (p. 278). Later, during the First World War Bertrand Russell would add the subtitle "A Method of Abolishing the International Duel" to his work *Why Men Fight* (1915), and Andreas Latzko in *Menschen im Krieg* (1916) writes, "...in diesem Duell der Munitionsindustrien" (p. 140), referring to the First World War and the rise of the military industrial complex. There are obvious parallels between the compulsion to duel and military conscription, and between the institution of the duel and the institution of war. The Danish critic, author, and friend of Schnitzler, Georg Brandes, attacked the notion that war was a natural phenomenon that could not be abolished. Like Schnitzler and Suttner, Brandes believes that courage can be shown in peaceful ways, and that one's honor can be offended only by one's own actions. He draws distinct parallels between the duel and war. If the former could be abolished, so certainly can the latter—not through compulsory military service or arms escalation, but rather through the fundamental rejection of the notion that war is a necessity:

> If the duel could die a natural death one may dream of a day when war will die. But just as the duel could not be eradicated by decapitating duellists, as attempted by Richelieu, so militarism cannot be uprooted by conscription, long military service and a profusion of munitions.
> Think of all the prejudices that had to be destroyed before the duel disappeared!...And yet quietly, unobtrusively, without cries or regrets, it has been eliminated by most of the civilized nations of humanity.... There is no more reason to praise war than there is to praise the duel...[13]

It is clear from Schnitzler's autobiographical documents that he was as strong an opponent of conscription as he was of the compulsion to duel. His early diary entries and subsequent essays opposing war reflect a much stronger concern about conscription than any autobiographical material about the duel. Yet the duel appears more often in Schnitzler's works than does war or conscription. It is true that when Schnitzler wrote the plays *Liebelei* and *Freiwild* he had been influenced by the duel of a friend, Paul Goldmann.[14] But, according to Rena Schlein, Schnitzler's initial interest in the duel stemmed from a hypothetical problem he had posed in 1891: "[Er begann] sich mit der Frage zu befassen, ob 'falsche Ritterlichkeit' zum Tode eines Unschuldigen führen könne."[15] Schlein attributes Schnitzler's fragment "Ritterlichkeit" (1891-1912) to this question. Schlein writes that for almost twenty years Schnitzler toyed with the idea of writing a drama focusing on whetherr "eine käufliche Frau des Duells wert sei."[16] Implicit in the notion of chivalry is the idealization of the qualities of bravery, courtesy and honesty. According to the code of chivalry, a knight was required to defend the offended honor of a woman.

In questioning the notion that the honor of a "käufliche Frau" is worth defending, Schnitzler scrutinizes once again the very concept of honor. His real concern is not, however, with the question of whose honor is worth defending and whose is not, but rather with the question "can one's honor really be offended by someone else?" Schlein does not discuss adequately the broad moral implications of the "käufliche Frau." It is possible that Schnitzler's works attacking the duel were intended as political allegories about war and later, conscription. This is all the more likely because Schnitzler believed that both the duel and war resulted from a misinterpretation of the concept of honor. If this were the case, then the "käufliche Frau" for whom the duel is not worth fighting might symbolize the false ideals or ideas that a government places (according to Schnitzler) before its people in order to justify a war. Perhaps Schnitzler was even questioning whether or not certain governments were worth defending.

It is not difficult to imagine what Schnitzler's response would have been to a questionnaire on the subject of military conscription. All one has to do is replace the word "Duellzwang" or "Duellforderung" with "Wehrpflicht" or "Krieg" in Schnitzler's answer to the "Rundfrage über das Duell" (cited below), and the result might well be found among the essays on war: "Hier kommt es jeden Tag vor, daß Leute auch ohne Absicht in Kreise geraten, wo Anschauungen herrschen, in denen der Duellzwang notwendig inbegriffen ist. Solange Leute als feig gelten werden, die eine Duellforderung ablehnen und solange Leute den Vorwurf dieser sogenannten Feigheit als diffamierend empfinden werden, solange wird auch der Duellzwang bestehen."[17]

In *Why Men Fight* (1915) Bertrand Russell demonstrates that a similar social compulsion is at work during wartime, whereby a pacifist suffers a fate similar to that of a man who refuses to duel.[18]

Russell hypothesizes that a man who will not fight in the War, and as a result is dismissed from his employment and scorned by his friends (both male and female), will feel the penalty quite as hard to bear as a death sentence. Like Schnitzler, Russell sees the roots of this compulsion to fight, in the deception of whole nations by false ideas, myths, and propaganda furthered by the state. Like the duel, war is surrounded with glamor and tradition, and self-sacrifice is lauded as "heroic." Mothers sending their sons off to the battlefield are also considered heroines—another aspect of the myth of the desirability of war.

Russell, like Brandes, compares war to the duel, pointing to the virtual extinction of the duel as a small step forward in the civilizing process of mankind. It is unlikely that Schnitzler ever saw Russell's book *Why Men Fight* (originally given as lectures in 1915), and Russell certainly did not know of Schnitzler's writings on war in 1916, yet the similarities between the two men's ideas are astounding. Even the choice of analogy reflects the same direction and depth of thought.

Russell believes that any progress toward the eradication of war will depend on the modification of institutions that govern human habits: "If political contest within a World-State were substituted for war, imagination would soon accustom itself to the new situation, as it has accustomed itself to the absence of dueling. Through the influence of institutions and habit, without any fundamental change in human nature, men would learn to look back upon war as we look upon the burning of heretics or upon human sacrifice to heathen deities."[19]

Schnitzler too rejects the old notion that wars are inevitable, simply because human nature is unchangeable. He also feels that the institutions that govern people must be changed in order to prevent war: "Der Einwand, daß Kriege immer dauern werden, weil die Menschen in berechenbarer Zeit nicht anders werden, ist hinfällig. Man hätte diese selbe Einwendung hinsichtlich der Inquisition, der Hexenverbrennung, der Folter, machen können, und es ist ganz unzweifelbar, daß die Menschen als solche heute um nichts besser sind als sie vor Hunderten von Jahren waren.... Nicht die Menschen sind zu bessern, sondern die Organisationen...."[20]

Both writers cite similar instances of practices that have become outdated. But notably absent from Schnitzler's list is the duel—perhaps because duels continued to take place in Austria up until the outbreak of the First World War. Nevertheless, it is clear that Schnitzler viewed both the duel and war as institutions of militarist ideology. The duel theme appears in many of his dramatic and narrative works, throughout his literary career. It is present, for example in *Liebelei* (1894), *Freiwild* (1896), *Leutnant Gustl* (1900), *Der Weg ins Freie* (1908), *Das Tagebuch der Redegonda* (1908), *Das weite Land* (1910), *Fink und Fliederbusch* (1916), *Casanovas Heimfahrt* (1917), *Der Sekundant* (1927-1931), and in the fragment "Ritterlichkeit" (1891-1912).

In the narrative work, *Spiel im Morgengrauen* (1926), Schnitzler uses the suicide of the protagonist, Lieutenant Willi Kasda, to criticize the false perception of honor. Unable to pay his gambling debts, Kasda believes that his honor as an officer and a gentleman has been irretrievably lost and there is no alternative but to kill himself. In fact, it is not the loss of his own personal honor (although he is trained to believe this is the case) that drives him to suicide, but the loss of the false notion of honor of the military itself. Rolf Allerdissen notes the complete absence of a personal system of values in the officer caste—a void filled by the values of the military:

> Dabei bemerken Offiziere der k.u.k. Armee wie Gustl und Willi Kasda die sinnentleerte Hohlheit der eigenen Position gar nicht. Leutnant Gustl fand in der Offizierskaste und ihren Normen sogar Ersatz für das Fehlen eines eigenen Wertsystems und gewann auf diese Weise eine neue Identität. Willi Kasda hingegen wirkt geradezu rührend in der naiven Schlichtheit, mit der er auf Leopoldines Frage nach einer Sicherheit für das gewünschte Darlehen...antwortet: "Ich bin Offizier, gnädige Frau."[21]

Of all Schnitzler's works involving the duel motif, *Freiwild* (first staged in 1896 and published in 1898) is probably the most pointed in its critique of the institution of the duel. Schnitzler attacks the compulsion to duel, the concept of the code of honor, and addresses the problem of human aggression. He also compares the military compulsion for Oberleutnant Karinski to duel with the more nebulous militarist compulsion for Paul Rönning to submit to the duel.

The conflict arises from the natural human instinct of aggression when Karinski irritates Paul to the point where the latter strikes the officer. This aggression leads to a problematic situation because Karinski sees himself bound to seek revenge through challenging Paul to a duel, yet Paul refuses to accept the challenge. Through refusing, Paul is rejecting the accepted Austrian pattern of social behavior. He has unwittingly placed himself in a position where he is expected to willingly place his life in jeopardy; for, according to the code of honor, Karinski cannot regain his honor until he avenges himself in a duel.

Paul, faced with the only alternative of fleeing the country and becoming in effect a refugee from the institution of the duel, decides to stay and confront Karinski. In fact Paul is addressing the struggle between the militarist-based determinism of the authoritarian society, and what he feels is his right to exercise his free will to go or stay as he chooses, without having to risk his life in a duel.

Because of his inability to deal with Karinski in a more peace-able manner (first he strikes Karinski in anger and finally arms himself with the intention of shooting the officer), Paul loses the moral advantage he held at first over Karinski and must suffer the consequences of his actions. Karinski is the victim of an upbringing that led him to consider the military his only possibility for a career. In addition to this deterministic view, Schnitzler implies that Karinski lacks the decisive-ness and breadth of imagination to give up his military career and find some other job for which his temperament is better suited. Karinski believes that his position in the military places him above civilians in the social hierarchy and regards his commission as a First Lieutenant as a hunting license, with other human beings merely his prey. In an earlier outburst in which he exhibited his extreme lack of self-control, Karinski severely beat a civilian, and now he pursues Anna as an affront to Paul. Karinski's friend, First Lieutenant Rohnstedt poses an important question about the military profession: "Was fängt so ein Mensch in ewiger Friedenszeit mit seinem Temperament an? Wo soll er hin damit? Es ist ja wahr, solche Leut' wie der Karinski sollen Soldaten sein, aber für solche Soldaten gehört der Krieg, sonst haben sie überhaupt keine Existenzberechtigung."[22]

Here Schnitzler employs carefully veiled irony to criticize the popular notion held by contemporary society that the only career for an overly aggressive man is the army. Rohnstedt is quite serious in this belief when he poses the question, but the fact that the logical conclu-sion of his argument would be the justification of war, indicates faulty reasoning on his part. If for moral or humanitarian reasons Rohnstedt is concerned about such people as Karinski finding a place in society, he should logically be more concerned about the overall welfare of society. Yet if Rohnstedt maintains that the army is really the only possible profession for such aggressive people whose very existence depends on war, he is inverting his moral priorities; this is so because logically the next step would be an attempt to justify war on the basis that even though many would suffer, a few might profit. In an aphorism written during the First World War, Schnitzler suggests that the military could get by quite well without war, engaging instead in occasional maneuvers. Only the diplomats, he says, need war desperately (*AuB*, 230).

Karinski is the victim of both the militarist compulsion to duel and the weakness of character that first led him to pursue a military career, and that now places him in conflict with civilians. As an officer, he believes himself superior to civilians and treats them accordingly. He is unable to cope with the responsibilities of an officer in peacetime. He drinks heavily, causes brawls, and makes a spectacle of himself by pursuing another man's girlfriend. When he is insulted by Paul, Karinski reacts in accordance with the military code of honor by challenging Paul to a duel. Tradition and unwritten law predetermine almost every step Karinski is to take.

Paul, on the other hand, is a victim of Karinski's (and society's) false sense of honor. He is unaware of the obligation to duel and is thus taken by surprise. In fact when he slaps Karinski, the possibility of having to duel never occurs to him. When he is challenged, his initial reaction is one of disbelief; he rejects the notion that he can be obligated to follow a course of action he deems morally wrong. Paul's friends tell him that society will shun him, for he is now "satisfaktionsunfähig." He is branded a coward and is deserted by all his friends. Still, he holds fast to his belief in the right of the individual to exert his free will. Even when Rohnstedt implores him to duel for Karinski's sake (for the officer will otherwise kill himself) Paul declines. Only when Rohnstedt warns him that Karinski might resort to murder does Paul see that he has been backed into a corner—not only by Karinski, but by the militarist mores, customs and traditions of the Austro-Hungarian society. The institution of the duel renders him defenseless in a life and death battle, just as conscripted soldiers in the trenches during the First World War would be defenseless against the shells exploding around them—rendered defenseless as Schnitzler writes, by the institution of conscription.[23]

3.2 Early Historical Drama:
Revolution and Feudal Wars

During the 1890s Schnitzler experimented with the historical drama as a medium for analyzing two types of war (revolution and feudal war) and as a means of presenting a veiled commentary and attack on contemporary conditions in Austria. *Der grüne Kakadu* (1898), a "Groteske in einem Akt," is set on the eve of the French Revolution in Paris on 14 July 1789. Schnitzler uses the technique of a play within a play to illustrate the difficulties facing social critics in an authoritarian state—difficulties such as censorship and persecution. The political satires played out in the pub "Zum grünen Kakadu" are a critique of the government and French aristocracy. Truth and fiction blend. When Grasset attempts to persuade the innkeeper to join the revolution, the latter refuses, placing a higher value on his own well-being and that of his family than on a revolution to free the bourgeoisie from the tyrannical aristocracy. "Mein Lieber, ich liebe die Freiheit wie du—aber vor allem habe ich meinen Beruf."[24] He is not only manager of the pub, but also the director of the subversive plays. Still, Grasset accuses the innkeeper of cowardice in not joining the revolution.

The exchange between the two characters is especially significant because the innkeeper's reply reflects an attitude crucial to understanding Schnitzler's interpretation of his own role as a writer during the First World War,[25] which I shall later discuss at length. Like the innkeeper (a former theater director), Schnitzler is well equipped to produce serious social and political critique, and by placing it in the context of a fictional dramatic work (like *Der grüne Kakadu* or the "Dramatische Historie," *Der junge Medardus* [1909]), avoid censorship or persecution. The innkeeper's words here might well be Schnitzler's own, representing his approach both before and after the First World War:

> **WIRT:** Ach, mein Lieber, mir genügt das, was ich in meinem Fach leisten kann. Es macht mir Vergnügen genug, den Kerlen meine Meinung ins Gesicht sagen zu können und sie zu beschimpfen nach Herzenslust—während sie es für Scherz halten. Es ist auch eine Art, seine Wut los zu werden.[26]

The banning of his play *Freiwild* in Vienna in 1896 [27] had awakened Schnitzler to the threat of censorship. Perhaps the idea of placing social and political critique within the framework of a dramatic or narrative work appealed so much to Schnitzler after writing *Freiwild* that he adopted it as a technique for expressing his own dissatisfaction with contemporary conditions in Austria. Through the innkeeper's veiled critique of society, Schnitzler is illustrating his own technique for similarly criticizing. The "Grüne Kakadu" is even visited by a police commissioner who threatens to ban what he considers to be politically offensive cabaret plays. The innkeeper feigns innocence:

> **WIRT:** Herr Kommissär, ich kann auf diese Anschuldigung nur mit der höflichen Einladung erwidern, sich die Sache selbst einmal anzusehen. Sie werden bemerken, daß hier gar nichts Aufrührerisches vorgeht, schon aus dem Grunde, weil mein Publikum sich nicht aufrühren läßt. Es wird hier einfach Theater gespielt—das ist alles.[28]

The innkeeper is entirely correct in his reply to the bureaucratic commissioner. It is not the content of the plays alone but their reception by a particular audience which incites violence. His audience of the aristocracy is not composed of the people who are likely to engage in the social upheaval, for they represent the status quo. In fact, the plays are a warning to the aristocracy of the potential consequences of their suppression of the bourgeoisie, but the upper class is generally too blind to see the truth behind the plays.

Veiled in parallels in this historical drama, Schnitzler is criticizing the contemporary Austrian upper class for the error of its social and political dominance over the lower classes. In this vein Hartmut Scheible speculates that Schnitzler intended in *Der grüne Kakadu* to draw a parallel between the French Revolution and the situation in contemporary Austria:

> Mag der Gang der Geschichte für Schnitzler, den liberalen Verächter der Politik, unerkennbar sein: indem er die Handlung exakt auf den Abend des 14. Juli 1789 datiert, bleibt zumindest ihr Ergebnis eindeutig. Kein anderes Datum hätte für Schnitzlers Gegenwart aktueller sein können: denn die bürgerliche

Revolution, in Frankreich schon Geschichte, stand, da sie 1848 gescheitert war, in Österreich noch bevor. Schnitzler stellte wiederholt fest, daß das Zeitalter des Absolutismus noch nicht vorüber sei.[29]

In an aphorism written in 1918 Schnitzler discusses the necessity for a revolution of the Austrian proletariat. He compares the failed Austrian Revolution of 1918 to the French Revolution. The former failed, he says, because its primary motive was one of revenge against former oppressors. The latter had at least as its primary motive the freeing of the human spirit.[30]

Schnitzler had always been skeptical about the possibility for eradicating revolution: "Revol. wirds geben, so lang Denken mit Fühlen sich nicht verträgt, d.h. solange es Menschen gibt."[31] The degree to which this is true is demonstrated in *Der grüne Kakadu* through the emotionally-based blindness with which the revolutionaries transform the nonpolitical murder of the Duke at the hands of Henri into a political assassination. Henri believes that Léocadie has been deceiving him with the Duke, whom he kills in a fit of jealous rage. The murder is eagerly perceived by the revolutionaries as an act of political heroism, and Henri becomes a symbol of the revolution—an unlikely role for a man who up until now has sought to escape the impending turmoil through romantic pursuits and plans to retreat to a peaceful life on a farm. The political circumstances coincidentally surrounding this decidedly unpolitical act serve to politicize both the act and the man.

Henri's rationality is overcome by jealousy, and so he commits murder over a woman he has idolized. In the larger social sphere, this personal conflict finds a parallel in the aggressive passions of the masses who seek the ideal of freedom through violent revolution against the aristocracy, symbolized by the Duke. Ironically, the act of violence committed by Henri, which would under normal circumstances be considered a severe, punishable crime, is viewed in the context of the revolution as a heroic deed.

The concept of political "necessity," implied in *Grüne Kakadu* and more forcefully in later works on war, is one Schnitzler attacks most vehemently throughout his life:

Politik, das ist die Freistatt, wo Verbrechen, die sonst Gefängnis
oder Tod zur unvermeidlichen Folge hätten, wo Verrätereien, die
sonst zu flammender Empörung aufriefen, wo Lügen, die sonst
im allgemeinen Hohngelächter untergingen, nicht nur von diesen
sonst natürlichen Konsequenzen bewahrt zu bleiben pflegen,
sondern wo all diese Verbrechen, Verrätereien und Lügen als
durchaus natürliche, wenn nicht gar rühmenswerte Bestätigungen
der menschlichen Natur angesehen werden. ...[32]

In a relatively unknown poem from his *Nachlaß* Schnitzler bit-
terly attacks governments that hypocritically punish murder and
nonetheless condone it when it is to political advantage. The innocent
sounding title, "Ballade von den drei Brüdern," stands in stark contrast
to the brutal content of the poem, adding to its irony and poignance:

Drei Brüder rasten durch das Land
Zu morden, zu rauben, zu sengen.
Der Erste, welch ungeschickter Fant,
Gar bald vor seinen Richtern stand
Und mußte als Frevler hängen.

Die beiden andern, die wußten klug
Ihr Schicksal ins Große zu wenden;
Ein jeder, voran seinem johlenden Zug
Voran eine wehende Fahne trug
In blutbefleckten Händen.

Hier wehte sie rot, weiß wehte sie dort
Und unter so prangenden Zeichen
War Raub nicht Raub mehr und Mord nicht Mord.
Nur die Erschlag'nen—was ist auch ein Wort—
Die hießen auch weiterhin Leichen.

Doch da sie hinraffte politische Not,
So mußten sie's eben verwinden.
Und von den zwei Brüdern in weiß in rot,
Sei Sieg ihr Ende, sei's Heldentod,
Wird einst die Geschichte künden.

Den ersten indes hat längst mit Fug
Ruhmlos die Hölle verschlungen—
Der ohne hochtöndender Worte Flug
Auf eig'ne Faust die Leute erschlug
Und keine Fahne geschwungen.[33]

Beyond criticizing the hypocrisy of war, Schnitzler is showing the political misuse of language. Whether a human being is killed on the battlefield ("die Erschlag'nen") or murdered, he is just as dead, and the value of the lost life is just as great ("Die hießen auch weiterhin Leichen"). Even the two brothers, although volunteers in the war, become victims of political necessity. Like the third brother who dies in shame, a convicted murderer, their own fate does not matter to them, for they do not live to enjoy the fame that will be attached to their names—a gesture of self-serving political expediency on the part of the respective governments. The brother on the winning side will be famous as a "Sieger," the one on the losing side shall gain fame as having suffered a "Heldentod."

The red and white flags, apart from symbolizing blood and loss of innocence respectively, illustrate the emptiness of the causes over which wars are fought. Further, the two flags might allude to the Austrian colors. Here they also represent the two opposing nations to which the mercenary brothers sell their services.

Der grüne Kakadu was Schnitzler's first attempt to illustrate in the framework of a historical drama the social and psychological climate preceding a war (here a revolution). For his next drama, Schnitzler looked further back into the past to examine feudal war. In this work, *Der Schleier der Beatrice*, Schnitzler steps up his critiquue of contemporary social values that he believes lead to war.

The last dramatic work written by Schnitzler in the nineteenth century, *Der Schleier der Beatrice* ("Schauspiel in fünf Akten," 1898-1899) plays in Bologna, Italy at the beginning of the sixteenth century. In view of Schnitzler's professed interest in the study of past wars, the historical setting can neither be considered coincidental, nor regarded as having being selected for purely aesthetic reasons.[34] Having dealt with the subject of revolution in *Der grüne Kakadu*, Schnitzler turns now to a different type of war, namely a feudal war between Italian city-states, fought only to expand the authority of a ruler. The impending war in *Der Schleier der Beatrice* (hereafter referred to as *D e r*

Schleier), like all wars in Schnitzler's works, forms the framework for all other action. But unlike traditional background themes, war serves an extremely important function in *Der Schleier* (as it does in all of Schnitzler's works in which it appears), for it is the catalyst for most of the action.

News of the impending war spreads when word reaches Bologna that Duke Cesar Borgia of Romagna will attack the city within twenty-four hours. The action of the five-act play focuses on this brief period during which the people of Bologna prepare for almost certain death. The work examines the various ways in which the artists, the peasants, and the noblemen face the situation. Some flee from Bologna, some seek to escape reality by falling victim to decadent and frivolous pursuits, some seek solace in what they believe to be love, while others arm themselves to protect their "Vaterland."[35]

Several factors suggest that Schnitzler chose the setting and war-background for *Der Schleier* among other reasons as a parallel for the situation facing Austria-Hungary and Europe at the turn of the century. Schnitzler, like many artists and intellectuals of his period, was able to see through the dreamlike trance in which Europe found itself. Some, like Bertha von Suttner in 1889, even predicted a great European war within the foreseeable future. The joyous, hedonistic trance in which Europe staggered blindly into the First World War is paralleled in *Der Schleier* in the words of the sculptor, Ercole: "Wo bin ich hier? Bald scheint mir selbst, was draußen sich zuträgt, nicht mehr wahr! In diesen Zweigen ruht laue Luft, die nichts vom glühenden Ernst des Tages weiß."[36]

The poet, Filippo, lives a sheltered life in his enwalled house, intentionally shutting out the din of the social and political events that surround him and that will ultimately affect him:

ERCOLE MANUSSI (ist durch die Tür auf die Terrasse getreten): In Flammen steht die Welt! Was kümmert's Euch?
Der eine lümmelt auf der Bank, der andre
Hält seine Laute zärtlich in den Armen,
Und über Rosen schreit' ich zu Euch hin.
So wißt Ihr nichts?
FILIPPO: Umfriedet ist mein Garten,
Die Fenster sind verhängt, den Lärm und Unsinn,

Der durch die Straßen fegt, lass' ich nicht ein;
Es finden seine Boten doch den Weg.[37]

Filippo's actions reflect Schnitzler's decision as a writer to remain silent on and appear uninvolved in political turmoil in Austria, before, during, and after the First World War. Yet Schnitzler refutes the contention that a writer who appears not to concern himself with political affairs is necessarily naive about them, when he has Filippo add: "...es finden seine Boten doch den Weg."

Schnitzler attacks contemporary society's approval of war through the love relationship between Orlandino and Rosina. The young Orlandino is the naive victim of a militaristic upbringing that has left him with a purely romantic image of war. He recognizes the positive value society attaches to war and heroism, and so he uses political rhetoric in an attempt to impress and seduce Rosina. Clearly he has never really considered his own death seriously, and the concepts he praises are of little if any importance to him. Rosina sees through his ploy, however, and reveals the stupidity of war and the hollowness of society's approval of it. She successfully rebuffs him with an equally flippant reference to the effects of war. Ironically, the two naively use war as a weapon in their game of love:

> **ORLANDINO:** Ich habe nur diesen einen Wunsch mehr auf Erden! Denkt, es ist eine vaterländische Tat, einem jungen Helden die letzte Nacht zu versüßen! Rosina, vielleicht schon morgen um diese Stunde bleichen meine Gebeine auf dem Sand vor Bologna!
> **ROSINA:** Orlandino, hättet Ihr nur das nicht gesagt! Es ist ein abscheulicher Gedanke! Ich müsste immer an Eure Gebeine denken! Nein, nein, laßt mich! Ich hätte nicht das geringste Vergnügen!
> **ORLANDINO:** Herzlose, o höchst herzlose Rosina![38]

Not long after this encounter, Orlandino and Francesco are about to duel over a petty insult, when Orlandino cries out patriotically: "Ah, ich will meinen Degen am Vorabend großer Taten nicht durch einen läppischen Streit entweihen! Mein Leben gehört nicht mehr meiner Laune, sondern meinem Vaterlande! .... "[39] This apparently patriotic attitude is revealed as false through the devious misuse of terms such as "Held" and "Vaterland" in the earlier cited exchange between Orlandino and Rosina. Were Orlandino an earnest, mature adult, his heroic words might be taken more seriously, but given his evident lack of maturity, they come across as naive and hollow; more a critique of the concept of "Vaterlandsliebe" than praise thereof. Given the feudal nature of the Italian city-states, it is not inconceivable that some sense of allegiance was felt to one's town, but the concept of "Vaterlandsliebe" as expressed here by Orlandino was almost certainly a later development in Italy. Hugo von Hofmannsthal later raises a similar question as to the use of the comparative terms "Heimatliebe" and "Vaterlandsliebe" in Schnitzler's *Der Gang zum Weiher*, set in Austria in 1750. Schnitzler (who was well acquainted with the history and culture of sixteenth century Italy) uses these modern terms in an historical setting to criticize contemporary society.

Orlandino also suffers from the weakness of human character that permits manipulation of the masses by the state, he naively looks forward to a death that he has been raised to believe will be a glorious, heroic event. Just as Orlandino has no real conception of death, Beatrice, too, sees it as something romantic and positive. Until she stands face to face with it, death is for her a meaningless concept. But her last-minute loss of courage and refusal to commit suicide are not inconsistent with human nature or behavior, according to Schnitzler's later theory of the "Phantasielosigkeit der Völker," expressed in an essay on war in February 1915.

"Phantasielosigkeit der Völker," cited by Schnitzler as one of the causes of war (*AuB*, 201), goes beyond the general concept of "imagination." It encompasses the ability or rather the lack thereof, to retain an event from the past (or project an event from the future), not in terms of mere words, picture images or specific detail, but in all the sensual and intellectual complexity of an action taking place in the present.

Schnitzler postulates that over the course of history, man has developed an inner defense against the horrors of the world. The price of this defense mechanism is the inability to truly conceive of death. Schnitzler differentiates between merely imagining a concept and truly perceiving it: "Könnte man sich den Tod vorstellen, so wäre das Leben gewissermaßen unmöglich. Und ebensowenig wie den Tod stellt sich jemals der Mensch Ende, Trennung, Leid wirklich vor. Was er gewohnt ist, als "Vorstellung" zu bezeichnen, ist Erinnerung, und zwar nicht einmal Tatsachenerinnerung, sondern Wort- oder Bilderinnerung. Daß alles was geschieht, schon im nächsten Augenblick Erinnerung ist, macht das Dasein erst möglich."[40]

Some of what we call insanity, Schnitzler says, is the ability to hold onto a present moment and not allow it to become the past. "Phantasie" in its highest form is the suspension of time as we know it through the flexibility of the imagination, enabling it to sense an event from the past or the future as though it were in the present.

The despotic leaders of nations make the greatest use of the "Phantasielosigkeit" of the masses by turning concrete political or historical facts into abstractions. In order to retain the support of the people during wartime, a government does all it can to play down the intrinsic value of the individual life—to eliminate the concept of the "individual" effectively from the consciousness of the people.

In his literary works and later in "Und einmal," Schnitzler attacks absolutist rulers and the notion of divine right. As an absolutist ruler, the Duke of Bologna exercises his divine right to reverse his stance on both personal and political issues. In the case of Beatrice and the impending attack by Borgia, the political and personal spheres are inextricably intertwined. Before he falls in love with Beatrice, the Duke's thoughts are of his beloved Bologna and the tyrant Borgia: "...doch gewiß ist eins: Daß auf der Welt für mich und Cesar Borgia / Nicht Raum genug ist, und daß er der Stärkre."[41]

He is ready to leave Bologna if it will lessen the damage Borgia intends to inflict on the city. But later, obsessed with Beatrice, the Duke forsakes his obligation to his people. Blinded by his love, he becomes indifferent to all else. Ironically it is only through the shutting out of the larger political sphere to concentrate on the selfish, egotistical personal sphere, that the folly of war is revealed. The Duke tells his people of the unfavorable (for them) reordering of his priorities:

> Gleichgültig seid ihr mir alle und was euch bedroht,
> Gleichgültig meine Stadt; die Schlacht von morgen
> Ein sinnlos blutiges Gezänk, da mir
> So wenig Abscheu gegen Cesar blieb,
> Als Liebe für Bologna und für euch!
> Mein ganzes Leben ist zusamm'gepreßt
> In dieses eine:—Wo ist Beatrice?[42]

In order to further world peace, Schnitzler would later write (March 1916), "es genügt beinahe, daß jeder sich selbst, daß er seine Angehörigen, daß er seine Heimat (wir vermeiden hier absichtlich das Wort Vaterland), liebe ...."[43] In the case of the Duke and Beatrice, however, love means but a temporary escape from reality. The impending war represents inescapable destiny, but each character exercises in varying degrees some measure of free-will in his or her response to the inevitable. Because of his position of power and authority, the Duke's options range beyond those of the other characters; he may suspend morals and laws at will, and because of this, according to Reinhard Urbach, he alone survives to face the uncertain future.[44]

Clearly there are parallels between the historical setting of *Der Schleier* and the events at the beginning of the twentieth century in Europe: the impending war, absolutism, and militarism as fostered by the state. Schnitzler writes in his diary on 15 September 1914 of the relevance of *Der Schleier* to the period of the First World War: "Nm. las ich mir allerlei durch (Ruf, Medardus, Beatrice etc.) was ev. für die Vorlesung in dieser Zeit sich eignen könnte.-"[45] Hermann Bahr, too, sees contemporary and future significance in *Der Schleier* in this letter to Schnitzler from 1904:

> Ich denke jetzt so oft an Deinen "Schleier der Beatrice," an die schaurig große Stimmung jener letzten Nacht, die den blutigen Borgia schon vor den Toren weiß... und morgen wird er kommen und mit ihm kommt der Tod. Sind wir nicht selbst jetzt in solcher Nacht einer Welt, die morgen versinkt? Aber da wollen wir doch die paar letzten Stunden, bevor der Borgia kommt, endlich einmal nicht entsagen, nicht mehr uns fügen, nicht mehr nach dem Gebot der Väter fragen, sondern nachholen, bevor es zu spät ist, und endlich nichts als wir selbst sein und, den Tod im Leibe, endlich, endlich leben!...[46]

As will later become evident, Schnitzler rejected the notion of a "versunkene Welt," believing that war alone does nothing to improve human character.

4

Schnitzler's Rejection of Austrian Militarism
and
His Early Critique of War: 1900-1913

4.1 Viennese Society and the
Austro-Hungarian Officer

During the first decade of the twentieth century, Schnitzler wrote several works involving the military and militarism in contemporary Vienna.[1] Most notable is the monologue novella, *Leutnant Gustl*—one of his most controversial works, precisely because of its critique of militarism. The common thread connecting these pieces is an attempt by Schnitzler to analyze critically the relationship between the Austrian military as an institution of the aging aristocratic order and representatives of the rising middle class and landed gentry who come into conflict with it, often as reserve officers.

The rise of the "Bürgertum" in the economic and political spheres of Austrian life filled the military ranks at the close of the nineteenth century with lower-ranking officers. The rapid industrialization of Europe (even though less pronounced in Austria than in Germany or England) in the early years of the 1900s added to these social changes a rapid growth in weapon technology which helped complete the internal transformation of the Austro-Hungarian army. Military commanders were too preoccupied with the internal conflict between the old aristocratic order and the rising middle class to foresee the profound changes modern technology would make in military life and in the nature of warfare. This transformation was not accompanied by any appropriate modernization of the outdated military bureaucracy, i.e., changes in rules, discipline, or in the highest levels of command. Military procedure remained as it had been through much of the nineteenth century. The incompatibility of the new soldier with the archaic army caused numerous conflicts, both within the military and in civilian life.

Schnitzler addresses such problems as anti-Semitism, which he first encountered in the military in the early 1880s, and the conflict between civilians and middle-class officers who enlisted mainly because they were unable to find a profession in civilian life. He also criticizes those who see the military as a means to vent legally their aggressive tendencies. By the turn of the century anti-Semitism pervaded all levels of society and it was especially evident in the military. Even as early as as 1882-1883, during his year of military service, Schnitzler noted the severity of anti-Semitism in the army: "Auch unter den militärärztlichen Eleven, wie beinahe in allen Freiwilligenabteilungen—und wo nicht sonst!—fand eine—sagen wir auch hier 'reinliche Scheidung' zwischen christlichen und jüdischen oder, da das nationale Moment immer stärker betont wurde, zwischen arischen und semitischen Elementen statt..."[2]

In *Leutnant Gustl* Schnitzler attacks anti-Semitism in both civilian and military settings. Gustl notices during a concert that many members of the audience are Jews, and he thinks to himself: "Nicht einmal ein Oratorium kann man mehr in Ruhe genießen..."[3] Typically, Gustl bases his recognition of Jews on stereotypical physical characteristics such as their "big noses." Gustl's prejudice is even more evident in the following observation. Here, his chain of thought leads from mere jealousy of a man whom he sees in the company of Steffi (a woman whom he fancies), to his general hatred of Jews. For Gustl the anti-Semitic movement is not radical enough: "Muß übrigens ein Jud' sein! Freilich, in einer Bank ist er, und der schwarze Schnurrbart ... Reserveleutnant soll er auch sein! Na, in mein Regiment sollt' er nicht zur Waffenübung kommen! Überhaupt, daß sie noch immer so viel Juden zu Offizieren machen—da pfeif' ich auf'n ganzen Antisemitismus!"[4]

Gustl's condemnation of the Jewish reserve lieutenant brings out another aspect of the modern Austrian military that Schnitzler seeks to condemn: the condescending attitude of career soldiers toward reservists. With the introduction of compulsory military service in

1868, university students (comprised largely of sons of the aristocracy and the landed-gentry) were legally exempted from the standard three years of arduous military service and were instead required only to serve as "Einjährig-Freiwillige Offiziere." For some career officers of the "Bürgertum" who spent their lives working their way up the professional and social ladders, it seemed unjust that those sons of the aristocracy could serve one year and later retain their ranks as officers in the reserves. Gustl reveals this antipathy when he spots some young reserve officers by night: "Sind das Freiwillige da drüben?...Ekelhaft, bei der Nacht schau'n sie aus, wie Offiziere..."[5] He resents the proviso that a reservist need serve only one year to achieve the same rank as a career officer.

A Jewish reserve officer himself, Schnitzler must have identified quite strongly with his Jewish reserve lieutenant mentioned in *Leutnant Gustl*. That he produced the novella over the span of only six days—most uncharacteristic for an author who otherwise spent years writing and rewriting his works—supports the likelihood of his strong personal involvement with the issues of anti-Semitism and militarism.

Schnitzler does not directly address the Hungarian question, or the problem of nationalities within the Austrian-Hungarian army.[6] He focuses instead on the example of the Viennese in order to represent the Austro-Hungarian army. His viewpoint is not confined to Viennese society, however.

While appearing to focus on individuals, he is in fact characterizing general personality types in a militaristic society. Although he is primarily interested in presenting a psychological study of his characters, history and politics are nevertheless integral aspects of his works. Schnitzler thought of the human psyche as basically unchanging, but he saw hope for the eventual elimination of war through the modification of political institutions and social mores. He believed firmly in free will, but felt that man too frequently allowed other people and events to determine his actions. He therefore criticizes those aspects of society that he feels need to be changed. At the same time he warns that man should abandon the naive belief that the human psyche is capable of substantial change. In *Leutnant Gustl* the volatile sociopolitical climate of a declining order is the spark that ignites psychological conflict.

There are two distinct realms of conflict in *Leutnant Gustl*. First, Gustl, as representative of the rising middle class, comes into conflict with the declining aristocratic order in the military. Second, because of the militarization of society, he encounters conflict with civilian life. Gustl finds himself at odds with two civilians: a baker and a doctor. The social hierarchy places the baker on a lower level than an army lieutenant; hence the baker is considered "satisfaktionsunfähig"—his inferior social standing makes him unworthy to engage Gustl in a duel. The doctor, however, is obliged to duel with Gustl. As an academic he is of comparable social standing despite the obvious differences in upbringing, education, and intelligence.

The doctor's compulsion to duel with Gustl represents one of the two forces Schnitzler criticizes in both *Leutnant Gustl* and *Freiwild*: the military obligation of the officer to duel and the militarist compulsion for the civilian. In *Freiwild* Karinski is driven by the military's code of honor, as is Gustl in his duel with the doctor. Both officers tacitly accepted this possibility when they enlisted in the army.

Although the Austrian government was officially opposed to the duel, the lax enforcement of the law banning duels tended to support the hypothesis that the government secretly supported it.[7] The state found it could not prevent the military from breaking the anti-duel laws. Eventually, in an attempt to save face, the government contradicted its own laws and adopted the military's unofficial pro-duel stance. Klaus Laermann describes the process leading to the governmental tolerance and eventually acceptance of the military duel: "Aus dieser ursprünglich gegen die staatlichen Duellverbote gerichteten Anschauung....hatte sich am Ende des 19. Jahrhunderts in Preußen sowie in Österreich ein staatlich weitgehend tolerierter, wenn nicht gar legitimierter Duellzwang herausgebildet."[8] The militarization of Austrian society was at least partially accomplished by the introduction of reserve officers in the army since 1868. The more nebulous and sinister militarist compulsion manifests itself in *Freiwild* through the infringement upon the personal freedom of the civilian (Paul) to decline the officer's (Karinski's) challenge.

In *Leutnant Gustl* Schnitzler attacks another militaristic aspect of the duel. Beyond the military obligation to duel, which Gustl readily accepts, there is the bizarre militarist compulsion to kill himself in order to restore his honor, because the baker is not worthy of dueling against him. This recalls Karinski's predicament in the face of Paul's refusal to duel. On being commissioned, neither officer considered the unusual possibility that circumstances might arise that would dictate

suicide. The contradictory nature of the code of honor is thus exemplified. In a militarist state military precepts are ironically often counterproductive to the welfare of the army itself.

Gustl is representative of the new Austro-Hungarian army officer
at the turn of the century. He uses his status as lieutenant to engage in
duels and vent his aggressions on civilians. In keeping with the code
of honor, Gustl believes that his rank as an officer elevates him to the
same social class as the doctor. He is unaware, however, that he is
being manipulated by the state.   Gustl never realizes that it is the
honor code of the military and its support by a militarist government
that are to blame for his predicament. Alfred Fritsche is thus not quite
correct when he interprets Gustl's words regarding his obligation to
commit suicide ("Ich muß! Ich muß! Nein, ich will!") as being a brief
recognition of the responsibility of the army for his forced suicide:
"Nur kurz läßt Gustl den Zweifeln an der Armee als staatlicher
Institution freien Lauf."[9]   In fact Gustl never sees the truth behind the
obligation to duel or to commit suicide.

Instead Gustl blames civilians against whom, he believes, soldiers are defenseless.[10]   He does not realize that civilians of certain
social classes (here, the doctor) are bound by similar rules to which
they have never consented (unlike the soldier, who in entering service,
accepts the obligations of the army).   Gustl reveals an awareness of
only the superficial causes for his quandary. Using words that reflect
the enmity between civilians and officers, Gustl blames civilians for
the compulsion to duel:

> Darauf möcht' keiner kommen, daß ich mich hab' totschießen
> müssen, weil ein elender Bäckermeister so ein niederträchtiger,
> der zufällig stärkere Fäust' hat ... Aber wenn ich jetzt wen immer
> fragen tät', jeder möcht' mir die gleiche Antwort geben.... ganz
> wehrlos sind wir gegen die Zivilisten. Da meinen die Leut', wir
> sind besser dran, weil wir einen Säbel haben...und wenn schon
> einmal einer von der Waffe Gebrauch macht, geht's über uns her,
> als wenn wir alle die geborenen Mörder wären...[11]

Gustl is saved from suicide by his instinct of self-preservation
and the timely death of his intended opponent. The night before Gustl
is to kill himself the baker dies of a heart attack, making it impossible
(unless Gustl himself were to publicize it) for anyone else to find out

about the demeaning incident at the theater. Gustl places a higher
value on his life than on the rules of the military, for according to military convention he is required to commit suicide whether or not the
affair is made public (technically his honor has not been regained).
His decision reveals both the absurdity of the military rules and the
falseness of the code of honor; after all, his death could neither serve
the military nor restore his sense of honor. In selectively adhering to
one military code (the obligation to duel) while rejecting another (the
obligation to commit suicide), Gustl also reveals his own hypocrisy.

Unfortunately, Gustl acts purely on instinct rather than on an ide-
ological rejection of militarist determinism. This is proved by his
unabated desire to duel with the doctor despite his close brush with
death over the incident with the baker: "..na wart', mein Lieber, wart',
mein Lieber! Ich bin grad' gut aufgelegt... Dich hau' ich zu
Krenfleisch!"[12]

Ironically, the cause of Gustl's duel with the doctor is the latter's
recognition that Gustl is the type of person who enlists in the army to
find an outlet for his aggressions. Gustl's difficulty in remembering
the cause of the duel and his response to the doctor's accusations illustrate the insignificance of incidents deemed infringements on the code
of honor—and thus expose the falseness of the code of honor:

>...dieser junge Mensch,...—wie heißt er denn nur? ...Meiner
>Seel', der ist an der ganzen Geschichte schuld gewesen! Der hat
>von den Manövern geredet; und dann erst ist dieser Doktor
>dazugekommen und hat irgendwas g'sagt, was mir nicht gepaßt
>hat, von Kriegsspielerei oder so was—aber wo ich noch nichts
>hab' reden können.... und ich hab' von einem patriotischen Fest
>erzählt...und dann hat der Doktor gesagt—... "Herr Leutnant, Sie
>werden mir doch zugeben, daß nicht alle Ihre Kameraden zum
>Militär gegangen sind, ausschließlich um das Vaterland zu vertei-
>digen!" So eine Frechheit! Das wagt so ein Mensch einem
>Offizier ins Gesicht zu sagen! Wenn ich mich nur erinnern
>könnt', was ich d'rauf geantwortet hab'?[13]

Gustl's militant response confirms that he represents the very type of
person the doctor describes. Schnitzler had long been aware of the
emotions and drives that motivate certain behaviors deemed by society
as the expression of its highest values ("patriotism" and "heroism").[14]

The publication of *Leutnant Gustl* on 25 December 1900 in the liberal Viennese newspaper, *Die Neue Freie Preße*, brought swift response from military circles. Because Schnitzler was a reserve officer, the military considered his publications within its jurisdiction. A board of officers known as the "Offiziersehrenrat" was responsible for, among other things, determining when military honor had been sufficiently offended to warrant a duel. Its decisions were based on the military code of honor which combined strict written rules of conduct with unwritten traditions. This awkward arrangement made it difficult to effectively challenge judgments of the board.

Leutnant Gustl also brought instant responses from several critics. The most notable was a denunciatory article by Gustav Davis, editor of the conservative paper *Die Reichswehr*, read mostly in military circles. Davis writes of Schnitzler and *Gustl*:

> Die Armee steht hoch über diesen vierundzwanzig Spalten Schimpf und Spott. Die Offiziere, die "nicht ausschließlich zum Militär gegangen sind," um das "Vaterland zu verteidigen," gehören ganz Herrn Schnitzler. Es wird sie ihm Niemand streitig machen. In der Armee gibt es solche Offiziere nicht, weil man sie eben nicht duldet.
>
> Der Schlag hat Ihren "Bäckermeister" getroffen, Herr Doktor, und nicht—die Armee. Gehen Sie heim nach dem Lande der "süßen Mädl," lassen Sie sich vom Johann "kalt abreiben" und bedecken Sie sich und diese literarische Schmutzgeschichte mit dem "Schleier der Beatrice"! [15]

Davis's article led to Schnitzler's court-martial and the loss of his military commission.

Schnitzler soon received a letter from the "k.k. Landwehrergänzungsbezirkskommando Nr. 1," which sought to determine whether he was the author of *Leutnant Gustl*.[16] Schnitzler replied on 6 January 1901 that he had written the novella but that his literary activities were no concern of the military. Before the army received Schnitzler's reply, it issued a second letter on January 8, again demanding to know whether he had authored the work and why he had not responded to the first letter. Schnitzler's reaction was typical. In Schinnerer's account: "Schnitzler considered an answer superfluous and did not reply. Several weeks later he was notified by the

"Ehrenrätlicher Ausschuß der Landwehroffiziere und Kadetten in Wien" that proceedings had been instituted against him and he was commanded to appear before the board."[17] Schnitzler wrote back, declining the invitation. He was then given the option to appear in person or respond in writing. He replied by mail but was then told that he had to appear anyway. The date of the hearing was postponed twice, and again Schnitzler was commanded to appear personally or send an attorney in his stead. In his letter of 25 April 1901 Schnitzler mimics the military jargon, using against the army its own language of logical precision:

> Mit Bezug auf die an mich gerichtete Aufforderung zur Schlußverhandlung in der meine Novelle Leutnant Gustl betreffenden ehrenrätlichen Untersuchung persönlich zu erscheinen oder einen geeigneten Verteidiger zu entsenden, habe ich nur wiederholt zu bemerken, daß mir nicht bewußt ist, inwiefern obgenannte Novelle als eine jener Unterlassungen oder Handlungen gedeutet werden könnte, die einer ehrenrätlichen Behandlung zu unterwerfen sind, und daß daher für mich auch heute, wie im Verlauf des ganzen Verfahrens, kein Anlaß zu irgend einer Äußerung zu dieser Angelegenheit vorliegt.[18]

Schnitzler knows full well that according to the army's interpretation of the term honor, the publication of *Leutnant Gustl* constitutes enough of a transgression to warrant his court-martial. He is not contradicting himself, however, when he writes that he can see no justification for an "ehrenrätliche[n] Behandlung" because he is thinking in terms of his own definition of honor. Because he does not recognize the army's claim that his literary activities are within its jurisdiction, Schnitzler denies the accusation that he has offended the honor of the military. Furthermore, he believes that one's honor can only be offended by one's own actions, and in publishing *Leutnant Gustl* he was acting as private citizen, not within a military capacity. At worst he could have offended only his personal honor. As far as Schnitzler was concerned, the military had damaged its own integrity through the abuse of the term "Ehre." The intent of this letter is not merely a defense against the charge, but also an attack on the army—a challenge to clarify its case against him and explain its own interpretation of the concept of honor.

Schnitzler received notification from the military board on 14 June 1901 that he had been relieved of his commission because the publication of *Leutnant Gustl* had insulted the image of the Imperial Austro-Hungarian army, and Schnitzler had not undertaken any steps to defend his personal honor against the attacks of Gustav Davis of the *Reichswehr*. The second reason given by the board for the action taken against Schnitzler is astounding, even ironic: a condemnation of Schnitzler for not challenging Gustav Davis to a duel. While some critics deplored the action of the court for its harshness, others felt that the punishment had not been severe enough. Some even took advantage of the situation to publish anti-Semitic deprecations of Schnitzler and his works.

In 1932 Joseph Roth's *Radetzkymarsch*[19]—one of the best known and most critical novels on the Austro-Hungarian military—would expose similar tendencies in the Austrian army to those that surface in *Leutnant Gustl*.[20]

In his drama, *Der einsame Weg* (1903) Schnitzler pursues his analysis of the Austro-Hungarian officer corps and the problems brought about during the extended period of peace since 1866 by the influx of large numbers of young men who see the army as an escape from boredom, a way of finding adventure, and a means to vent their aggressions. Felix Wegrat (the son in a family of the landed gentry) becomes an officer in the Austrian cavalry, because it is the "most reasonable thing" ("das Vernünftigste")[21] he can do. Lacking the direction to pursue a civilian profession, Felix is a prime candidate for the military. The true reason for his selection of the army as a career—a desire for adventure and danger—comes to light when Felix bemoans the peaceful state of politics in Europe. He wishes he had lived in a time when there was less order in the world, and more adventure.[22]

Unlike Gustl, who sees the army as his ticket to engage in all those activities prohibited a civilian, Felix partially understands the restrictions of military life. When his sister Johanna tells him admiringly that he is free and can move around as he wishes, he replies: "Doch nur innerhalb gewissen Grenzen."[23] Nevertheless, Felix naively believes that his freedom would have been greater had he been born in times of less social order. Naturally the freedom of the individual is much more restricted during such periods of frequent wars. When he finds that the military restrains him and cannot at this time afford him the excitement he craves, Felix is disillusioned. Stefan von Sala, an old friend of the Wegrat family, expresses the prevalent notion that army life during peacetime does not supply an adequate release for aggressions. He replies ironically to Dr. Reumann's (the Wegrats' family doctor and close friend) comment that Felix's father would probably have preferred his son to pursue a more peaceful profession: "Es gibt ja heutzutage gar keinen der friedlicher wäre."[24] Given the political tensions and the threat of war that existed even in 1903, there is pointed irony in Sala's words.

Even the aging Sala reflects the desire of his times for intrigue and adventure when he plans an expedition to Asia. He tells of the terrible fate of an earlier expedition, not in order to scare Felix, but on the contrary, to entice him with a colorful portrayal of the danger. That only eight of the twenty-four members of the last expedition ever returned, should normally still one's desire to participate in such a dangerous undertaking. Instead, Felix is all the more interested in going along. Still, he fears that a scientific expedition might not be exciting enough for him. Felix's naive desire for adventure even in light of the death of those who went before him parallels the support of Europeans for war in 1914, despite the obvious fact that war brings death and destruction. Indeed, Schnitzler implies that there is a connection between the expedition and war in terms of the dangers involved as well as the blindness with which people regard war merely as an exciting adventure.

Sala tempts Felix by explaining the military possibilites of the expedition: "Überdies treffen wir an der Grenze mit einer rußischen Abteilung zusammen, die unter militärischer Bedeckung reist. Auch hier gedenkt man übrigens der Sache einen politisch-militärischen Anstrich zu geben."[25] Later, Sala is even more specific about the potential for action when he tells Felix: "Aber es ist sehr leicht möglich, daß es allerlei geben wird, wobei junge Männer wie Sie sehr gut am Platz sein werden.... Vor sieben Jahren unter Rolston war mancherlei zu bestehen was nicht im Reiseprogramm vorgesehen war. Und in der Ebene Karakum am Flusse Amu Darja gab es eine regelrechte kleine Schlacht."[26]

This pseudo-scientific expedition would satisfy Felix's desire for adventure and serve as a reasonable substitute until a real war should break out, especially in light of the fact that "ein Herr vom Generalsstab, einige Genie- und Artillerieoffiziere sozusagen in offiz-

iöser Eigenschaft" would be going along. Dr. Reumann reveals
Schnitzler's view (as he would later directly express them in his essays
on war) when with bitter sarcasm he points out that for those who die
in battle, there is no glory: "Für die, die dort liegen geblieben sind,
wird sie groß genug sein, Ihre kleine Schlacht."[27]

Schnitzler attributes to his characters, motives for going on the
expedition, which he has drawn from the underlying reasons that contemporary Europeans desire war: namely, boredom, desire for adventure and danger, and ignorance about the realities of war. But
Schnitzler was aware that it is not always the underlying cause that
propels an individual from thought to action. Furthermore, without
personal motives in a situational context, his characters would remain
hollow representations of personality types. Consequently it emerges
that Sala's great desire to undertake the expedition stems from the fact
that he is dying and is desperate to experience as much of life as
intensely as possible before he passes away. Ultimately he chooses
suicide rather than face the final torturous moments, waiting passively
for death to take him. On the other hand, Felix decides to go on the
expedition to escape from his difficult domestic situation. When he
learns that his real father is not Professor Wegrat but Julian, Felix is
unable to forgive Julian for having left his mother. Faced with the
choice of staying behind and possibly attempting the difficult process
of reconciliation, Felix chooses the easier path of running away on a
daring and risky expedition. In *Der einsame Weg* Schnitzler describes
the tense period of peace before the First World War—a time of almost
eager anticipation of the storm that would supposedly "cleanse"
Europe. Through the haunting words of Sala, Schnitzler captures the
attitude of his times: "Es scheint mir überhaupt, daß jetzt wieder ein
besseres Geschlecht heranwächst,—mehr Haltung und weniger
Geist."[28] It is precisely this lack of spirit and weakness of intellect that
lead to the First World War and are objects of criticism in Schnitzler's
subsequent historical dramas dealing with war: *Der Ruf des Lebens*
and *Der junge Medardus*.

4.2 On War and Heroism in the Historical Dramas

In 1905, with war closer on the horizon, Schnitzler turned his
eyes to history for his drama *Der Ruf des Lebens* (hereafter referred to

as *Der Ruf*). The setting is Austria in the middle of the nineteenth century, and the plot revolves around an impending war.

Thirty years earlier (ca. 1821), during the Italian revolts, the prospect of peace had shattered the dreams of Schnitzler's protagonist, an Austrian Colonel, of finding glory in battle. Now once again he longs for war, but this time his reasons are more complex. Drawing analogies to other professions, the Colonel offers an opinion shared by many that war is necessary to justify a soldier's existence: "Keinem andern kann ja sowas passieren wie unsereinem. Es gibt keinen Doktor, dem sie dreißig Jahre lang, Puppen für Kranke in die Betten legen,—keine Advokaten, die an gemalten Verbrechern ihre Kunst probieren,—und sogar die Pfaffen predigen öfters vor Leuten, die wirklich an Himmel und Hölle glauben....Bei Gott, ich weiß nicht, was ich am Ende noch angestellt hätte, Max, wenn's nicht endlich doch dazu gekommen wäre!"[29] The inapplicability of his analogies negates the Colonel's argument and reveals his misperception of war. He fails to see that the primary role of the army is to act as a deterrent to war—a prevention rather than a cure. A more correct version of the Colonel's analogies would involve a soldier making war to justify his existence, a doctor furthering the spread of disease, and a lawyer encouraging the commission of crime. The Colonel is unable to see the error of his perception.[30]

The Colonel knows nothing abut the reality of war and speaks naively. Possibly he wants to go to war to seek adventure and become a hero, but a more likely motive is to escape from a disastrous domestic situation. He knows about his friend (also an officer) Max's affair with his wife, and he already intends to kill her. Having committed murder, however, his life will be as good as over, and he wants to take Max with him into battle in order to gain revenge and at the same time die himself. All of these motives based on a false sense of pride are egotistical, the more so in that the Colonel is responsible for the lives of his men. He hopes to regain his lost pride (read honor) through glory in battle. Whereas in earlier works involving marital infidelity Schnitzler's characters would seek to restore lost honor through dueling, in *Der Ruf* the duel is replaced by war. The Colonel wastes no words in telling Max that the two of them must make utmost use of the opportunity to go into battle: "Ich habe keine Zeit mehr, einen Zufall abzuwarten, der mir Beweise in die Hand spielte, und käm' einer in dieser Sekunde selbst, er hälfe nichts mehr. Denn wir hätten kein

Recht mehr, um unser Leben zu spielen, da es ja nicht mehr uns gehört, sondern dem Kaiser, dem Vaterland—oder einem Wahn...Wie immer—wir dürften den Einsatz nicht zurückziehen, selbst wenn wir das Spiel mit einem Male abgeschmackt fänden."[31]

This speech is very enlightening. The patriotic compulsion, so real to the youth of the nation, to sacrifice one's life for the "Vaterland" becomes a convenient and useful pretext to the Colonel. Although perhaps unwittingly, he reveals that it is the same thing to give one's life for the "Kaiser" as for a "Wahn"; both are simply deceptions and neither is worth the loss of human life. As a pretext for the suicide mission, the Colonel uses the obligation of his regiment to restore the good name of the "blaue Kürassiere." Legend has it that thirty years earlier the "blaue Kürassiere" had turned cowardly in battle, fleeing and losing their lives in shameful defeat. The regiment still lives with the stigma and is pledged to die to the last man, before it will ever retreat. The old soldier Moser (former leader and sole survivor of the "blaue Kürassiere") tells his daughter about the battle incident which brought shame to the "blaue Kürassiere." This is the experience of a soldier who, having survived an earlier war, can see through political rhetoric:

> Ich führte die dritte Eskadron. Am Fuße des Hügels von Lindach standen wir zu Pferd und warteten. Seit vier Uhr morgens saßen wir zu Pferd und warteten. Nichts andres hatten wir zu tun, als zu warten.... Und da mit einem Male packte es mich.... Angst... entsetzliche Angst!... Denn in diesem Augenblick wußt' ich mit einem Male, daß sie uns all das, was uns auf den Fleck gebannt hielt hundert Ewigkeiten lang, nur vorlügen...Ehre und Vaterland nur vorlügen, um uns sicher zu haben!...Wer lohnt's mir? Wer dankt mir's?...Und so rast' ich davon, die andern mit mir, mir nach...vor mir...und so ist es gekommen, daß heut die jungen Leute in den Tod ziehen, die ich nicht kenne, und daß ich noch lebe mit neunundsiebzig und sie alle überleben werde—alle—alle....[32]

Moser implicitly attacks not only the military and governments ("sie") that seduce and coerce young men into sacrificing their lives, but also the society that supports such a system. The most terrible result of the seduction of a people by its government is, as Moser says, the fact that decades later, innocent young men continue to be sent to their deaths. Only nine years after Schnitzler wrote the play, young men were sent off by the millions to fight the First World War, once again to die for "Ehre" and "Vaterland." Moser here anticipates Schnitzler's condemnation of war and the state-propagated interpretation of such terms as "Vaterland," "Ehre," and "Patriotismus" in his essays and aphorisms on war, entitled "Und einmal wird der Friede wiederkommen...." (1914-1919).

Moser's observation that society learns nothing from war illustrates an aspect of one of the causes of war Schnitzler describes in his diary entry of 28 April 1880: "Traurig aber ist es, daß immer, so lang die Welt steht, ein Nachwuchs der schlechten Elemente hervorwuchern [sic] und schließlich der Krieg, mit vorurtheilslosem Blicke betrachtet, nutzlos gewesen sein wird."[33]

At the outbreak of the First World War, an actor in the Munich *Kammerspiele* staging of *Der Ruf* refused to continue in the role of Albrecht, a soldier with pacifistic tendencies, asserting that the play was unpatriotic and anti-Austrian. As a result, performances were temporarily banned by police censors. When the attorney for the theater, Dr. Leo Fromm, requested Schnitzler's position on the play, he admitted that Albrecht's words might be seen as unwarlike, but not unpatriotic or anti-Austrian. With deliberate sarcasm, Schnitzler describes how the scene between Albrecht and Max might be interpreted by those blinded by the patriotic fervor of the moment:

Sollten jedoch desequilibrierte Köpfe, an denen es in dieser großen Zeit gewiß nicht mangelt und auf die ein kluger Theaterdirektor natürlich Rücksicht nehmen müßte, die Haltung des Albrecht von Holzwarth (der immerhin für sein Vaterland zu sterben versteht wie ein anderer) als bedenklich verurteilen, so könnten sie sich dadurch beruhigen lassen, daß gerade in der einzigen Szene, die dem Albrecht im Verlaufe des ganzen Stückes zugeteilt ist, sein Partner Max nicht nur die gerade entgegengesetzten, also höchst kriegerische und jedenfalls durchaus vaterländische Ansichten ausspricht, sondern überdies, was für den Gesamteindruck gewiß nicht unwesentlich, das letzte Wort behält.[34]

In this scene of *Der Ruf*, as in his early essay "Über den Patriotismus," Schnitzler allows the opposing viewpoint to have the final word, but the refutation appearing earlier in the polemic carries more weight and thus negates the opposing viewpoint. In both cases Schnitzler protects himself from criticism by citing the thorough presentation of the contrary position and its significant place at the end of the argument.

At the end of the letter to Fromm, Schnitzler clarifies his own interpretation of a patriot: someone who in times of both peace and war unselfishly serves his country simply by doing his job to the best of his ability. The false patriot (like the actor who refuses to play Albrecht) is one who, to further his own career or embellish his image, selfishly hinders others in their professions.[35] Schnitzler even gives Fromm permission to publish his letter—but only if in its complete, unabridged form. Fromm declined. In light of Schnitzler's general refusal to state his opinions publicly, it is noteworthy that he was willing in this instance to do so. When one examines his use of terminology, however, it becomes clear that Schnitzler intentionally chose words that he interpreted differently from his contemporaries. He used the popular word "Vaterland" which he had already rejected in 1908 (*Der Weg ins Freie*) in favor of "Heimat," and talked of fulfilling one's "duty" (implying some form of military service) but meaning simply "to do one's job."

In the controversial scene between Max and Albrecht (Act II, Scene 3), Schnitzler cites the typically youthful desire for adventure, as an important factor in the perpetuation of war. Max is eager to go on the suicide mission. Albrecht, however, is able to perceive what Schnitzler will later write in an aphorism: namely, that the individual only desires war as a pretext for danger, adventure, fame, and honor:[36] "Solltest du gar *freudig*-? Ich glaube das ist zu viel verlangt...von dir und von uns allen. Freudig meinethalben in Abenteuer, in Gefahren, aber doch freudig nicht in den sichern Tod!"[37] Albrecht rejects the notion that the past wrong of the "blaue Kürassiere" can justify the death of the present group bearing that name. The importance for peace of refusing inherited guilt anticipates Schnitzler's first prerequisite for a world without war, as expressed in an essay in March 1916: The question of guilt in all previous wars must be put aside in order to prevent the perpetuation of animosity between peoples.[38] Schnitzler's condition for peace in turn resembles the first of Kant's "Präliminärartikel zum ewigen Frieden": "Es soll kein Friedensschluß für einen solchen gelten, der mit dem geheimen Vorbehalt des Stoffs zu

einem künftigen Kriege gemacht worden. Denn alsdenn wäre er ja ein
bloßer Waffenstillstand, Aufschub der Feindseligkeiten, nicht Friede,
der das Ende aller Hostilitäten bedeutet,..."[39]

Schnitzler may not have read Kant when he wrote his essays on
war;[40] and if he did not reach his conclusions independently, there is a
good possibility that he received inspiration from Bertha von Suttner's
Die Waffen nieder, which he had probably read before the turn of the
century. Following the Austro-Prussian War of 1866, von Suttner's
heroine, Martha, writes: "Die Feindseligkeiten werden eingestellt, aber
die Feindseligkeit dauert fort. Der Samen für künftige Kriege ist
gestreut und die Frucht des eben beendigten Krieges enfaltet sich weiter..."[41] Suttner, like Kant and Schnitzler, recognizes the need to set
aside the question of guilt in past conflicts in order to prevent future
wars.

As Schnitzler says in his letter to Fromm, Max does get the last
word. But it is Albrecht who is aware of the connections between war
and rhetoric, deception and truth, and life and death. Albrecht is the
only survivor of the mission, but ironically he too falls victim the militaristic necessity and the false code of honor. Unable to face the shame
of being the sole survivor, he commits suicide. The fact that Albrecht
will go down in history as a hero reflects the twisted nature of the
political institution that drives a man to suicide and lies about his death
in order to acclaim him a war hero.[42]

After *Der Ruf* Schnitzler treats war in the historical drama *D e r
junge Medardus* (1909; hereafter referred to as *Medardus*). The play is
loosely based on Napoleon's expulsion from Vienna exactly one-hun-
dred years earlier. By choosing to write about an event so distant in
time from his own period, Schnitzler gained three advantages: he was
able to criticize contemporary political figures in the cloak of history
and through this disguise to avoid likely censorship; the historical dis-
tance from the events made him better able to evaluate them and place
them in context; he sought to show by analogy, the danger of a war he
felt was impending. Those able to learn from the past might be able to
avoid the same errors.

On 9 May 1880 Schnitzler writes in his diary that because political history has a tendency to repeat itself, the end of the nineteenth
century would see "ein ähnliches Schauspiel (...) wie das Ende des
18."[43] In 1809 the "play" was the Franco-Austrian (Napoleonic) War.
In 1914 it would be the First World War. The prelude of *Medardus*

contains much detail that might as easily reflect the public reaction to the First World War as it does the ousting of Napoleon from Vienna in 1809. Schnitzler sensed the growing belligerence between European nations in 1909 and this same atmosphere is present in *Medardus*.

In *Medardus* Schnitzler attacks state-sponsored indoctrination of youth to favor the military profession, to admire soldiers, and to believe in the necessity—even the desirability—of war. Dialogues between both leading and minor characters echo the early diary entries of 1880 on patriotism and war and anticipate some of his aphorisms and essays. In the prelude Anna recalls the French soldiers marching into Vienna—not with horror over the occupation of her city but rather in naive admiration of their uniforms. When Anna sighs over Medardus's imminent departure with his militia unit, Agathe's (Medardus's sister) response reflects both her reliance on a benevolent fate and the misorder of her priorities, fostered by the state. She places her faith in God's will and in the same breath pays homage to a graven image won through violence: "Er wird sicher zurückkommen, wenn's Gott will, heil und gesund, und am Ende gar mit einem Orden auf der Brust."[44] It never occurs to her that Medardus's medal would mean that some other young man would not be returning home "heil und gesund." Agatha reflects society's state-fostered admiration of soldiers when she says that were Medardus to stay at home, he would not be the same man whom Anna loves.

Only men who are weaklings or malingerers are left behind in the civil defense force. The effectiveness of state propaganda in promoting the cause of war is illustrated in the fact that all the men so desire to prove their valor on the battlefield, that they draw lots to see who will remain behind in the "Bürgermiliz." Should Medardus die on the battlefield, adds Agathe, "es ist wohl nicht das Schlimmste, jung dahin zu gehen, und für was Hohes, Heiliges!"[45] Schooled like Bertha von Suttner's character, Tante Marie (*Die Waffen nieder*), to worship the military, Agathe believes completely in the state's concepts of patriotism, heroism, and what is in fact the perversion of Christian values. Early in the prelude Schnitzler's genuinely patriotic figure, the saddlemaker Eschenbacher, discusses war, patriotism, and the compulsion to serve in the military, with Frau Klähr.[46] Here he pokes fun at the state's false patriotic ideal:

ESCHENBACHER: ...Ich kann das eine so wehmütige
Gelegenheit nicht finden, daß ein junger Held in den Krieg zieht.
Meiner Seel', ich möcht' ihn fast beneiden.
FRAU KLÄHR: Du, Jakob?
ESCHENBACHER: Es ist doch zum mindesten eine
Abwechslung.
FRAU KLÄHR: Ja freilich. Du nimmst es so.
Ich hätte mir's denken können.
ESCHENBACHER: (sehr gutmütig) Bin dir wohl nicht patrio-
tisch genug, Schwester? Wenn ich dir nun sagte, daß mein mil-
itärisches Gewand frisch aufgebügelt ist und der Säbel blank
geputzt...
FRAU KLÄHR: Wär' lieber dein Herz bei der Sache!
ESCHENBACHER: (ernst) Es wär schon dabei, wenn die
Menschen so wären, wie's die Sache verlangt...[47]

Frau Klähr tells of an unfortunate shoemaker who kills himself,
so distraught is he at having to remain behind as a result of the drawing
of lots.[48] Eschenbacher's sarcastic reply regarding the shoemaker
anticipates Schnitzler's aphorism (*AuB*, 187) to the effect that one best
serves one's country by performing in one's profession, not by becoming a zealous nationalist:

ESCHENBACHER: Ja, es gibt schon solche auch. Aber ob's
eben die klarsten Köpfe sind...? Und die besten Schuhmacher?
FRAU KLÄHR: Wärst du doch eben mit mir gewesen! Das
Treiben in den Straßen, Bruder! und die Begeisterung überall!
ESCHENBACHER: Ja, ich kenn' welche, die aus lauter
Begeisterung ihre Arbeit stehn und liegen lassen und überhaupt
nur mehr spazierengehen.[49]

The dialogue between Plank and Bernburg, students in the militia, is a development of Schnitzler's polemical form first employed in
"Über den Patriotismus." While the participants are now only minor
characters, the arguments are more clearly stated. Through the character Plank (an experienced soldier with pacifistic tendencies), Schnitzler
presents a realistic view of warfare without the trappings of patriotic
rhetoric that blind the nation's youth. Although cut from the script for

Reinhardt's planned staging of the work—presumably to prevent the play from being rejected by censors—Plank is present in the final published version of the play. He warns Bernburg, the naive young man who desires adventure but knows nothing of war:

> **PLANK:** He, Bernburg, du hast so besondere Lust in den Krieg zu ziehen? He? Du hast Lust, dir ein Bein wegschießen zu lassen? Oder einen Arm? Oder eine Kugel mitten durch die Stirn? Du hast Lust, dazuliegen mit blutenden Wunden—, schäumende Pferde über dich sprengen und dir den Hufen in die Gedärme treten zu lassen?... Oder juckt's dich gar, verwundet und lebendigen Leibes mit den Toten in eine Grube geschmissen zu werden und in ihren Verwesungsdüften zu krepieren?[50]

In a naturalistic manner comparable to that of Bertha von Suttner in *Die Waffen nieder*, Schnitzler portrays warfare at its (for that time in history) worst.[51]

Bernburg appears to have learned nothing from Plank's speech on the realities of war. Later he reveals his mercenary tendencies when he confesses that his allegiance can be bought. Not only does he deny a sense of standard patriotism (service to the government of his country), but he even denies allegiance to the land itself: "Wo ist mein Vaterland? Dort, wo sie meine Gaben und meine Kräfte nützen können! Nicht wo ich zufällig geboren bin."[52]

Through Medardus's development into a literary hero, Schnitzler reveals the absurd and false meanings attached by the state to the terms heroism, patriotism, and honor. Medardus's motive is personal and apolitical. He wants to kill Napoleon only to avenge the death of his father, a soldier who died froze to death, while waiting for Napoleon to review the defeated Austrian troops earlier in the war. Although he hears that peace has been declared and Napoleon is no longer his country's enemy, nothing changes for Medardus. His desire to kill Napoleon has no connection with current political circumstances. Even in the face of the argument that since Napoleon is now an ally of Austria and killing him would constitute an act of treason, Medardus is not swayed.

In *Medardus* Schnitzler also criticizes the state's manipulation of language. For Medardus, words that in varying situations acquire different meanings—especially words holding the power of life and death—are meaningless. Despite his indecisiveness, Medardus remains true to the idealism of his original intention and thus sacrifices his life. Ironically, the very words he condemns are used to describe him, when Rapp tells Etzelt at the very end of the play: "Es ist der Wille des Kaisers, daß Medardus Klähr mit allen Ehren und in geweihter Erde begraben werden, als dieses Krieges letzter und seltsamster Held."[53] Napoleon's message reflects a double irony, because he alone recognizes Medardus's actual heroism. Like Albrecht in *Der Ruf*, Medardus is called the "last and strangest hero of the war." Medardus resembles Schnitzler's concept of a true hero in the sense that he is willing to die for something he believes in, even if his motive is revenge. His choice of death is based upon his own convictions; this is better than facing a life based on empty words and the false ideals of the state. Medardus fails to realize, however, that his death will prevent his avenging his father. His death therefore represents his defeat.

When *Medardus* was performed for the first time in Berlin on 24 October 1914, almost three months after the beginning of the First World War, Medardus was strongly criticized for not displaying the decisive nature of a "true" hero.[54] The German press took the opportunity to attack both Schnitzler personally and Austria for its supposed shortcomings in its support of Germany. Feeling an increasingly strong sense of attachment to Austria (the people, not the government), Schnitzler took great offense at such criticism. In a letter dated 22 December 1914 to his sister-in-law, Elisabeth Steinrück, Schnitzler takes the counteroffensive. The critics were attempting to impose the traits of a military hero on a literary hero:

—als wär es wirklich und wahrhaftig das Wesen des Helden (—des für das Drama brauchbaren Helden wohlgemerkt) schon im ersten Akt zu wissen, was er im letzten Akt für einen Heldentod sterben wird und sich in der Zwischenzeit wie ein eigensinniger scheuklappiger Narr zu gebärden, der nichts vor sich sieht als sein Ziel, während er doch erst dadurch interessant wird, daß er dieses Ziel immer wieder aus den Augen verliert, daß er zaudert, daß er schwankt, daß er irrt—daß er das Leben mehr liebt als den Tod—daß er also im Sinne germanistisch-reporterhafter Weltanschauung überhaupt kein "Held" ist.[55]

Schnitzler reaffirms his reluctance to preach, but he also implies that *Medardus* contains veiled political criticism. This is all the more likely because in the same letter he stresses the presence of the First World War in his works, past, present, and future:

> Du schreibst "daß diese ungeheuern Umwälzungen irgendwie auch auf mich werden wirken müssen," als wollt ich mich dagegen auflehnen, als würd ich von der Weltgeschichte, die wir miterleben, gewißermaßen nichts wissen wollen, als bedeute mir persönlich all das Große und Grauenhafte, was sich begibt eine Störung in egoistisch literarischem Sinn—, als hätt ich die Absicht, diese Zeit nicht auf mich wirken zu lassen.... ich wage zu behaupten, daß ich [sic] manchen der Sachen, die ich schon vor dem Krieg geschrieben und in fast allen die ich entworfen...-—eine Ahnung, oder besser ein Vorverstehn dieser Epoche herauszuspüren ist;—und in dem was noch kommen wird—oder soll,—kann ganz natürlicher Weise der Nachklang der Dinge, die wir mitleben, mitleiden—nicht fehlen; wenn er auch nicht jedem gleich deutlich werden dürfte.[56]

In his closing words Schnitzler acknowledges the use of the veiling techniques that make his social and political critique appear ambiguous.

4.3 "Die Hirtenflöte" : The Conflict of Reason and Emotion

In the same year that he completed *Medardus*, Schnitzler wrote another work involving war, "Die Hirtenflöte" (1909). The main theme is the conflict between emotion and reason, represented by the two leading characters. Erasmus is a wise man who, having seen the world, takes up astronomy. His naive young wife Dionysia goes off into the world at his behest, to "find her self." She may return with no questions asked, but only after her every curiosity and desire has been satisfied. As Maja D. Reid points out, the names of the two protagonists are appropriate in terms of an apparent experiment by Schnitzler to test the compatibility of opposite character types: "Erasmus is the rational, spiritual, and purely intellectual type, while Dionysia is portrayed as irrational, sensual, and capable of emotion. ... Erasmus himself experiments by sending his wife into the world, but Schnitzler in turn uses the experimenter as a figure in his own experiment."[57] The concept of an experiment of opposites is wholly in keeping with the didactic intent in many of Schnitzler's works. For Schnitzler believed that revolutions would continue to be fought as long as reason and emotion cannot coexist peacefully—in other words, forever. As shown by Erasmus and Dionysia all attempts to reconcile these opposing forces fail. Whenever Dionysia's action is motivated primarily by emotion rather than logic, conflict results.

Schnitzler demonstrates in "Die Hirtenflöte" the effects on different social levels of the opposition of emotion and reason. The higher the social class, the more explosive the conflict. With each adventure Dionysia advances up the social ladder, falling in love with a man of a successively higher social class. Each step up is accompanied by an escalation of the level of resulting violence. Dionysia supplies the emotional dimension to the relationships with her various lovers. A conflict arises, however, between her emotionality and their rationality—especially as to their work. Some concession on the part of both is required to restore a balance, lest one become all-consuming. Succumbing to emotion Dionysia becomes at first greedy, next apathetic, and finally evil.

Dionysia leaves her husband, first for a shepherd whose flute music has enchanted her. One day, out of spite and emotional excess, Dionysia breaks the flute in two. Several months later, having forgotten the incident entirely, Dionysia asks the shepherd to play something for her. When he reminds her that she destroyed the flute a long time ago, she admonishes him for not having held onto it more tightly. In terms of the allegory, the flute might be regarded as a phallic symbol—all the more so since this instrument is traditionally associated with Pan, god of the forest and fertility. But the flute also represents the means by which the shepherd makes his living.

Without his music to keep them together, the sheep wander off aimlessly and are lost. Giving in to Dionysia's every whim, the shepherd sells even his last lamb. Because he devotes all his energy to amorous pursuits (the emotional), the shepherd loses his livelihood. Dionysia in turn loses respect for a man who is unable to balance his priorities.

In her unintentional social ascent Dionysia is next taken in by a wealthy capitalist squire ("Gutsherr") and lord of a castle that is surrounded by his factories and the dismal homes of poor workers. Schnitzler portrays the suffering of the lower classes, victimized by big-capitalist profiteers,[58] having Dionysia visit the miserable home of a factory worker. While criticizing the inhumanity of industrialism, Schnitzler explains the rationale of capitalism. Dionysia returns to her new husband, the squire, in the belief that he is ignorant of the suffering. She is certain that only lower-ranking bureaucrats could be responsible for the perpetuation of such abject poverty and is shocked to hear a logically-presented defense of the capitalist free-enterprise system. Differences in innate abilities, her husband tells her, make social equity impossible: "Der Gutsherr klärte sie auf, daß selbst innerhalb der einfachsten, scheinbar gleichmäßigsten Verhältnisse das Schicksal der einzelnen je nach persönlichen Eigenschaften und allerlei Zufälligkeiten sich höchst verschieden zu gestalten pflegte, und riet ihr, sich um dergleichen Dinge fernerhin nicht zu kümmern."[59] The squire's speech might be regarded as a rejection of communism as an alternative to capitalism. It reflects Schnitzler's pessimism about the possibilities for social improvement even through political change.[60]

Dionysia follows her heart and attempts to alleviate the poverty wherever she can, but she soon learns that her help is uneven and at times unfair. Realizing that to be effective in bringing about social change, the causes—namely the organization of the state—not merely the effects of the problem need to be treated, Dionysia gives up her philanthropic aid completely: "..., und wenn sie auch hier und dort von einem Tag auf den andern ein Schicksal günstiger zu gestalten imstande war, sie begriff bald, daß sie die Ordnung des Staates, ja die Gesetze der Welt hätte ändern müssen, um vollkommen nur für die Dauer zu helfen."[61]

Ironically, Dionysia's idealism backfires. Her earlier good intentions produce the opposite effect of that desired. For the first time, the workers realize that they have been exploited by the squire. They resent having been given a taste of the better life, only to have it taken away again. What begins as small-town strife in the form of strikes, demands for better working conditions, and shorter hours, soon assumes the dimensions of a revolution when the people's reason gives way to emotion: "Die Bewegung, ... verbreitete sich durch das ganze Land, so daß bald nicht nur die Arbeiter gegen die Fabrikherren, sondern auch die Armen gegen die Begüterten, die Abhängigen gegen die Freien, die Bürger gegen die Adel in Aufruhr standen."[62]

With the help of the army, the active revolution is quelled, but underground resistance continues. Disenchanted with her squire's tyranny, Dionysia leaves him and falls in with a group of former coal-miners who are planning to take over a town in the name of the revolution. In the resulting battle she is wounded; while recuperating in the hospital she falls in love with an admiring Count whose army uniform impresses her.[63] He has a high military rank in accordance with his aristocratic social standing. Word soon arrives that the army of a neighboring country has been mobilized on the border and the Count is called up to head his regiment.

Obeying his heart rather than his head, the Count assents to Dionysia's request to accompany him into battle. Although the war assumes a relatively insignificant role in the main plot, its portrayal indicates Schnitzler's tendency toward pacifism. He is condemning war in general, not merely this particular one, because none of the specific causes of the war between the two nations in the story is mentioned. The outcome is inconsequential too; the victorious army simply returns to its own country and life continues as it had before. Underscoring the senseless loss of life in war, the Count is killed just as the white flag of peace is waved.[64]

Dionysia returns to the hereditary castle of her late "husband" as a grieving widow and mother-to-be. Following the birth of her son, she takes her final step up in social class. She becomes the Prince's concubine and alienates herself from the relatives and friends of the Count, who see her as an adventuress and a whore. Worse still, the Prince is already married—and to a woman who is loath to relinquish either her husband or her position.

The country is divided in loyalty between its now despotic Prince and his former wife; civil war threatens. To protect Dionysia from his people, the Prince resorts to tyranny, executing anyone who should speak out against Dionysia. As Dionysia's (the aspect of emotion) hold over the Prince (the aspect of reason) increases and she becomes an egocentric murderess, the political situation worsens. Furthermore, Dionysia begins to hate the Prince just as she had grown to resent the shepherd for giving in to her every whim. In what is as yet the most unhappy triumph of the heart over the mind, Dionysia loses her son and almost her life when the citizens rebel against her. Dionysia flees when the Prince is obliged by his people to sign her death warrant. Only through the expulsion of the hedonistic influence of pure emotion can the country be saved—at immense cost, however, to the state and its people.

The story comes full circle on the return of Dionysia to her first husband, Erasmus. Realizing that she cannot live with a man, who with his cold intellect regards her wanderings as mere detail, unimportant to his experiment, Dionysia again leaves Erasmus, this time for good. Schnitzler comes here to the same unhappy conclusion as he had in his diary entry of 28 April 1880: reason and emotion are irreconcilable forces in both the mind of the individual and the organization of the state alike. Worse yet, given the volatile social and political circumstances in "Die Hirtenflöte," the results can range from the destruction of a marriage to the devastation of countries through war.

The idyllic title of this short story betrays nothing of its socio-economic and political critique. Although no dates or places are named, numerous allusions to technology, strikes, and laborers' rights make it likely that the action takes place in Europe in the late nineteenth century. Schnitzler portrays the transition from feudal absolutism to capitalist absolutism. On the one hand, he shows how the suppression of the middle and lower classes by the aristocracy inevitably leads to revolution. On the other hand, he explains the logical basis for the capitalist free-enterprise system. He illustrates the phases of industrialization, from the pastoral period via feudalism to the industrial era of capitalism into which the feudal age blends. He shows how absolutism is as widespread in the modern industrialized period as it was in earlier times.

Although the primary cause of conflict is the psychological struggle discussed above, "Die Hirtenflöte" is Schnitzler's first work in which capitalism and industrialism are cited as contributing factors to war and revolution. He does not condemn capitalism per se, nor does he offer an alternative to it. He implies, however, that revolution is the result of the exploitation of the lower classes. He also warns of the dangers of well-intended idealism.

Finally, Schnitzler criticizes the authoritarianism of absolutist monarchs. Yet he illustrates that ultimately even a tyrannical monarch must answer to the will of a people acting together to rid themselves of absolutism. Within ten years of the writing of "Die Hirtenflöte," both Austria and Germany would abolish the monarchies that helped bring about the First World War. Schnitzler's works during the first decade of the twentieth century anticipated World War One and the ultimate demise of the Austro-Hungarian monarchy.

5

The First World War and the "Weltruin": 1914-1919

5.1 Schnitzler's Troubled Reaction to the Outbreak of the War

On 25 July 1914 on vacation in Switzerland Schnitzler noted tersely in his diary that an Austro-Serbian war is imminent. Two days later he writes of "Kriegs- und Beruhigungsnachrichten." Indeed, ever since 6 October 1908 when the Dual Monarchy annexed the provinces of Bosnia-Herzegovina, there had been talk of an Austro-Serbian war. Although Austria retained a policy of nonintervention during the Balkan wars of 1912 and 1913, there had been some tense times in Vienna—most notably during October 1912 and the Scutari crisis of May 1913. Throughout this period Schnitzler's diaries reflect an informed interest in the political events in the Balkan region. Schnitzler's attitude is almost belligerent, and years later he ashamedly admits that in 1913 he had actually favored Austria's attacking Serbia.

On 2 August 1914 Schnitzler records in his diary simply that Germany has declared war on Russia, but by 5 August, with England joining in, the magnitude of the event had sunk in. Returning from a leisurely walk with his wife, Olga, Schnitzler is devastated by the news of a war that he believes heralds the ruin of civilization: "Mit O. im Wald. Herrliche Luft!—Im Hotel Nachr. von der Kriegserklärung Englands an Deutschland!—Der Weltkrieg. Der Weltruin. Ungeheure und ungeheuerliche Nachrichten.... Mit O., Leo, Bella, St. Moritz. Über die Ereignisse. Wir erleben einen ungeheuren Moment der Weltgeschichte. In wenigen Tagen hat sich das Bild der Welt völlig

verändert. Man glaubt zu träumen! Alle Menschen sind rathlos."[1]
Without hesitation, the Schnitzlers make plans to return to Austria.
Soon after his arrival in Vienna, Schnitzler begins to write informal
essays and aphorisms against war (mentioned first in his diary on 8
September 1914), the earliest of which reflect the prowar influence of
the press (in spite of his position against the political manipulation of
the media).

An incident on 20 August 1914 characterizes Schnitzler's
refusal to take a public stand on the War.[2] The theater director, Rainer
Simons, asked Schnitzler to contribute a patriotic play appropriate to
the times. Schnitzler declined. On 28 November 1915, Moriz
Benedikt, editor of the *Neue Freie Presse* also asks Schnitzler to write
something on the War, to which Schnitzler replies: "Lasst [sic] sich
nicht drucken."[3] He was probably thinking of his antiwar essays,
which could never have been published in Austria during the War.
Realizing that to speak out openly against the War would almost certainly mean the end of his literary career and possibly subject him to
arrest, Schnitzler felt that the only alternative was to remain, at least
apparently, silent. "Apparently" because Schnitzler's literary works
constitute a statement against the War. Furthermore, with one exception early in the War, his essays and aphorisms are clearly antiwar.

Schnitzler's diary entries from this early period (August-
October 1914) reflect his ambivalent patriotic stance in the first weeks
of the War. He was so overcome by his strong sense of attachment to
his country and its people, that at first he actually defends "German"
politics. His diary on 10 September 1914 reveals his frustration over
the "uninformed" reaction in the United States to the outbreak of the
War: "Bedenkliches (privat) aus Amerika, wo die Stimmung auch
gegen Deutschland sein soll. Man möchte verzweifeln."[4] It is noteworthy that Schnitzler does not differentiate Germany from Austria—
a distinction that he makes more and more frequently, as the war pro-
gresses and his sense of an "Austrian heritage" strengthens.

One of the most remarkable example of Schnitzler's initial
defense of Austria's and Germany's position in the War can be found
in one of his earliest essays on war. Clearly influenced by the government's successful media propaganda, Schnitzler maintains that
Austria and Germany had been the innocent victims of French,
Russian and British aggression.

Ironically, in the same essay in which he condemns the Allies on the basis of information obtained primarily from the Austrian press,[5] Schnitzler warns Austrians against believing everything they read in the papers, "... so wie wir wünschen, daß unsere Feinde nicht alles blind glauben, was in ihren Zeitungen steht."[6]   Although it was not characteristic of his attitude toward the First World War, Schnitzler's initial reaction shows that he was subject to the war fervor that pervaded Europe in 1914. Gripped by this fervor, many of Europe's most respected poets and artists became aggressive patriots. However, Schnitzler's essay of October 1914 reveals a change of attitude from emotionalism to rationality.

To document Schnitzler's views on war, I shall first examine his diary and correspondence, followed by an analysis of the essays and aphorisms. The only article devoted to war in Schnitzler's early and central works was written in September 1914 by Theodor Reik. Subsequently, only scant and largely uncritical attention has been paid to the subject. Although highly perceptive in other respects, Reik's article is blind to the irony in Schnitzler's works. He cites the case for war in numerous plays, invariably ignoring the countering opinions presented by protagonists or secondary figures. One might hope that Reik was trying to preempt criticism of Schnitzler's writings for being antipatriotic and antiwar, by stressing that the opposite was intended. But in all likelihood, Reik was caught in the fervor of war and wanted to contribute to the volumes of prowar feuilletons that flooded the newspapers in the last months of 1914.

Reik states that Schnitzler uses the incidence of war in his works primarily for aesthetic purposes, specifically to heighten the sense of tragedy or comedy in the personal fates of his characters. But Reik goes beyond the aesthetic when he attributes to Schnitzler a premonition of the First World War in the social decay of Austria during the decade before 1914:

> Hellsichtiger als andere, hat Schnitzler erkannt, daß Österreich über kurz oder lang ein Krieg bevorsteht. Er hat die drückende, gewitterschwüle Atmosphäre des letzten Jahrzehnts miterlebt, und kein Aufrichtiger in diesem Lande der sozialen Unaufrichtigkeiten (wie Schnitzler es einmal genannt hat) hat diesen Druck, diese stete Ungewißheit ableugnen können. Auch er konnte sich den Fragen seiner Zeit nicht entziehen, wenn-

gleich sie sich ihm gedämpfter und ins typisch Menschliche erhoben aufdrängten.[7]

Reik shows remarkable perception of the intricate manner in which Schnitzler weaves the theme of war into his works without allowing it to dominate. But Schnitzler's same rational perspective in his postwar works leads less astute critics to call Schnitzler's works outdated and irrelevant to the times— the cry of the "versunkene Welt": "Vielleicht liegt ein echt österreichisches Schicksal darin, daß man die Größe und Schwere seiner Probleme nicht erkannte, weil seine Bücher und Dramen seltsam kluge und gelassene Worte enthalten, weil sie, auch dort, wo Kanonen donnern, ruhig bleiben, auch dort, wo Begeisterung emporjauchzt, den Blick für die Zusammenhänge nicht verlieren.[8] Despite its shortcomings and misinterpretations Reik's article is a valuable contribution to the field in the sense that it recognizes Schnitzler's opposition to the militarizing of civilian life, as well as the significance of war and the military in his works.

Schnitzler's response in his diary to Reik's article reflects amused pleasure over Reik's recognition of the importance of war in his works. It also indicates the significance of war as a theme in his projected oeuvre: "Neulich Reiks Artikel 'A.S. und der Krieg' im Berl. Tagbl.; sehr hübsch, wo er auf die vielen Kriegsbeziehungen,—ja '-ahnungen' in meinen Sachen hinweist;—es fällt mir ein[,] daß in fast all meinen nächsten in Betracht kommenden Stoffen der Krieg mit- oder doch im Hintergrunde spielt. (Verführer,—ein Glas zu viel—Weiher— Geschwister.)"[9]

Much has been written on the matter of "Arthur Schnitzlers Protest"—an open letter from Schnitzler, published in Zürich on 22 December 1914, in which he defends himself against a libelous attack by Alexander Kuprin of Moscow.

On 10 September 1914 Kuprin published an open letter to Schnitzler in the Moscow newspaper, *Russkoe slovo*, rebuking him for remarks attributed to Schnitzler in an apparent interview which had appeared shortly before. Schnitzler had purportedly made defamatory remarks about numerous famous non-German authors:

Darüber zu reden, daß Kunst, vor allem aber die höchste unter den Künsten, die des Wortes, nichts mit Nationalität, Politik und

persönlichen Zwistigkeiten zu tun hat, mit Ihnen darüber zu
sprechen—das ist ganz so, als wollte man einem Taubstummen
und Blinden die grüne Farbe erklären. Doch Sie haben sich in
Ihrem lächerlichen Schreiben erlaubt, Tolstoj, Dostojevskij,
Shakespeare, Anatole France und Maeterlinck in einem zu
beschimpfen!....[10]

Schnitzler immediately drafted a reply. His diary entry of 23
November 1914 reveals the importance that he attributes to the rectifi-
cation of this unjust attack:

Arthur Kaufmann kommt mir mittheilen (über Bella
Wengerow—Frau Moller) daß in russ. Zeitungen ein erlogenes
Interview von mir steht, in dem ich u.a. geäußert, Tolstoj sei ein
Faselhans; Maeterlinck martre seine Bauern, Anatol France habe
mich bestohlen—und ich halte Hauptmann für größer als
Shakespeare!—Einen (allzu großen) Theil des Nachm. verbringe
ich (nach teleph. Gespräch mit Zweig, der auch gegen einen
unter seinem Namen gefälschten Brief in Amerika "Wien in
Verzweiflung" einschreiten will) mit Abfassung einer Abwehr.[11]

Schnitzler sends the response to Stefan Zweig with the request
that he forward it to the French pacifist, Romain Rolland, for translation into French and publication in the *Journal de Genéve,* Rolland's
pacifist forum in Switzerland. On December 3, 1914, Zweig writes
back to Schnitzler, acknowledging receipt of the document and con-
firming that he has sent it to Rolland for translation by him personally,
to avoid the possibility of a mistranslation.[12]

In his article, Schnitzler denies that any such interview had taken
place. He also criticizes the "false patriot" who could fabricate such
lies merely to "prove" his own value to society. Schnitzler concludes
his letter with a plea for reason in the face of the insanity that had
engulfed Europe: "So lassen wir es denn lieber genug sein;—und
später, wenn der Friede wieder da ist, wollen wir uns schmerzlich
daran erinnern, daß einmal eine Zeit war, in der wir einander über die
Grenzen hinüber die Versicherung zurufen mußten, daß wir zwar jeder
unsere Heimat geliebt haben, daß wir aber trotzdem Gerechtigkeit,
Urteil und Dankbarkeit niemals verlernt, daß wir, um es einfacher zu
sagen, niemals gänzlich den Verstand verloren haben."[13]

Kuprin apologizes to Schnitzler in a letter published in the Moscow paper *Brzevye Vedomosti* on 17 January 1915 but concludes with a reminder that there are a number of German authors who have indisputably engaged in just such activities as those for which Schnitzler had been falsely accused.

This "Protest" represents an important statement from Schnitzler for two reasons: it indicates that he was willing to risk unfavorable public opinion in order to maintain his moral integrity, and it demonstrates publicly Schnitzler's opposition to nationalistic chauvinism. He is careful to use the word "Heimat" rather than "Vaterland"—a clear statement that his allegiance lies not with a government but with the nation, its culture and its people.

At the beginning of the First World War, Schnitzler was working on the three plays, *Stunde des Erkennens, Große Szene* and *Das Bacchusfest*, comprising the *Komödie der Worte* cycle. Even during the first days of the War Schnitzler continued working on *Stunde des Erkennens*. *Das Bacchusfest* had already been sent for typing on 1 August 1914 to Schnitzler's secretary, Frieda Pollak. All three works were virtually complete before August 1, when war broke out, and Schnitzler looked forward to staging and publishing them. He soon realized, however, that as far as the public was concerned, their appearance would be most untimely.

In 1937 Josef Kainz wrote that a critique of society's misuse of language was a fundamental aspect of *Komödie der Worte* and Schnitzler's works in general: "Dergleichen Wortkomödien, wie sie die Menschen voreinander aufzuführen pflegen, zu enthüllen, die Unwahrheit großer Worte und konventioneller Phrasen mit ironischer Skepsis aufzuweisen, stellt sich Schnitzler seit jeher zur Aufgabe; die Themen Lüge und Entlarvung gehören zu den Hauptanliegen seiner Dichtung."[14]

The abuse of language is a common feature in the problems of the personal relationships portrayeed in *Komödie der Worte* as is the political manipulation of nations by their leaders in *Der Ruf des Lebens* and *Der Gang zum Weiher*. The people's lack of imagination ("Phantasielosigkeit der Völker") revealed through their inability to perceive this misuse of language, contributes to both forms of deception. A crucial element in an individual's perception of past events is the varying ability to relate words and images to reality—in effect, to perceive the past as though it were the present. Martin Swales discusses the conclusion of *Stunde des Erkennens* in light of the declaration of the heroine Klara: "Worte lügen," highlighting the significance of present perspective on the interpretation of memories: "Words do not articulate the truth—because words are so rarely located in a situation that allows of truthfulness. When the individual recalls his own life, he does so from a present perspective which conditions his interpretation of the past, conditions his memory."[15]

Swales points to a connection between the superficially unrelated themes of personal and social deception. He likens the conflict between Eckold and Klara to a war, a "battle in which the past is used as one of the principal weapons": "And because of the passion and stridency of its basic intention, because Eckold is out to wound, and Klara to defend herself from his attacks, the content of what is being said, i.e., the past that is being recalled, is only important as ammunition in the present battle."[16] Extrapolating this personal conflict to the social and political sphere, entire peoples are propagandized with embellished reminders of past conflicts in order to facilitate present and future wars.

Despite initial success in Vienna *Komödie der Worte* suffered bitter attacks by critics and journalists in Germany: "Unter den zahlreichen Rezensionen kann eine aus der *Kölnischen Zeitung* als repräsentativ genommen werden, die sich angesichts der *Komödie der Worte* die Frage stellt, ob 'nicht gerade jene letzten Dokumente eines Wiener Literatentums Beweis dafür seien, daß unser trefflicher Bundesbruder in diesem Weltkrieg auch einer inneren Reformation an Haupt und Gliedern bedarf, um fortan in einer neuen deutschen Weltkultur bestehen zu können...'"[17]

In a letter to Georg Brandes Schnitzler takes the counteroffensive against critics whom he claims have found a new political criterion by which to judge the quality of literary works: the World War. He demonstrates the hypocrisy of those who attack his works on moral grounds, while ignoring or supporting the immorality of war. Their perception of morality is in fact an infringement on the concept of morality itself: "Und wie es diesen Herren gerade paßt, wird man dafür zur Rechenschaft gezogen, daß das betreffende Werk irgendwie an den Krieg erinnert oder daß es das nicht tut.... *Die Komödie der Worte*...hat das Sittlichkeitsgefühl dieser Herren aufs Tiefste beleidigt. Daß unter Sittlichkeit nach wie vor nicht etwa Wahrheit oder sonst etwas Vernünftiges oder Positives, sondern ausschließlich Unterdrückung des

Geschlechtstriebes verstanden wird, brauche ich nicht erst zu erzählen."[18] In Brandes, Schnitzler had an ally in his opposition to the War. There were others among his literary and pacifist contemporaries.

5.2 Schnitzler's Relations with the European Peace Movements and Independent Pacifists

Although Schnitzler never joined any organized pacifist movement, his association with numerous important members of such groups bears witness to his own stance on the matter of pacifism.[19] Among Schnitzler's notable allies were Andreas Latzko, Romain Rolland, Bertha von Suttner, Fritz von Unruh, and Stefan Zweig, a veritable "who's who" of European pacifists.

In his eulogy of Bertha von Suttner Schnitzler's admiration for the famed Nobel Peace Prize-winning (1905) pacifist authoress and her ideal of peace is evident in the glowing praise with which he begins the essay: "Gerade in den letzten Jahren ihres Lebens war es mir beschieden, mit der merkwürdigen Frau einige wenige Stunden zu verbringen. Und da habe ich gefühlt: sie wäre eine wundersam helle Erscheinung gewesen, auch ohne das Leuchten jener Idee, die ihr eigentliche Größe gab und die ihrem Namen die Unvergänglichkeit geben wird."[20]

On 29 October 1913 when Suttner visits Schnitzler to interview him for Clement Deltour's *Nos contemporains*, Schnitzler recalls in his diary having been introduced to her about twenty years earlier by his journalist friend Paul Goldmann.[21] The conversation soon turns to the subject of war and peace, and Schnitzler's pessimistic but pragmatic sense of realism contrasts with Suttner's hopeful idealism: "Über die Friedensfrage. Sie glaubt, in 100 Jahren gibts keine Kriege mehr. Ich glaube in 100 000.-"[22]

On 22 December 1913, Arthur and Olga Schnitzler, visiting Baroness von Suttner for tea, make the acquaintance of another Nobel Peace Prize-winning (1911) pacifist, Alfred Hermann Fried (see also Schnitzler's letter of 19 March 1919 in Appendix 1). Schnitzler is impressed with Fried's intelligence but not by his naive belief in an early realization of his ideal of world peace: "Das Gespräch bewegte sich vielfach auf dem dadurch gegebenen Gebiet (Friede). Fried scheint eher klug als gescheidt, und nicht groß genug für seine Idee.

Er glaubt wie die Suttner, daß in wenigen Jahren die Kriege erloschen sein werden."[23]

On 10 March 1914 Suttner visits the Schnitzlers for tea; in his diary Schnitzler refers to her as a good person, but one blinded to reality by her belief in the eventual victory of reason: "Über die neuen Kriegsdrohungen. Sie ist eine gute, aber doch wohl im Grunde sehr banale Person—wie es Menschen die berufsmäßig 'an etwas glauben müssen'—und gar 'an den Sieg der Vernunft'— ergehen muß."[24] Schnitzler last saw Suttner on 3 April 1914, shortly before her death. Ironically, her final letter to Schnitzler, dated 14 May 1914, only two-and-a-half months before the outbreak of the War, asks the Schnitzlers to attend a planned peace conference—which of course never took place.

By the beginning of the First World War Schnitzler was well acquainted with the French author and pacifist, Romain Rolland.[25] Between 18 October 1910 and 25 December 1912 Schnitzler read all ten volumes of Rolland's epic work *Jean-Christophe* (1904-1912). Early in the War Schnitzler learned through a mutual friend, Stefan Zweig, of Rolland's pacifist and war relief efforts from his adopted home base in Switzerland. Apart from his work with the Red Cross Rolland had undertaken the publication of articles in the *Journal de Genève*, attacking political propaganda—a matter close to Schnitzler's heart, especially now during the early months of the War.

On 14 December 1914 and again on 7 January 1915, Schnitzler wrote to Rolland[26] about the falsified "interview with A.S." published in Russia at the outbreak of the War. A month earlier Zweig had served as a courier for the transmission of his "Protest" to Rolland with the request that he translate and publish it in French.

Zweig, responding to a letter from Schnitzler dated 2 December 1914 (*Arthur Schnitzler: Briefe 1913-1931*, pp. 59-60) writes:

Wien, 3. Dezember 14 [1914] Sehr verehrter lieber Herr Doktor! Ich danke Ihnen viele Male für Ihren lieben Brief und das schöne Dokument Ihrer gerechten Gesinnung. Ich glaube, daß auch ein so gelegntiches [sic] Wort nur durch den Geist und die Güte, die es bezeugt, in diesen Tagen zum Manifest wird und zweifle nicht, daß es überall (außer bei jenen Menschen, mit denen eine innere Verständigung über alles für uns unmöglich ist) die vorteilhafteste Wirkung im Gefolge haben wird. Ich habe es

Romain Rolland gesandt und ihn gebeten, die Übersetzung ins
Französische womöglich selbst vorzunehmen, damit auch nicht
ein Wort in seiner Bedeutung oder bloß in seinem Tonfall durch
schlechte Nachbildung verändert werde. Ich bin sicher, daß er
sich eine Freude daran machen wird, Ihnen und vor allem der
uns gemeinsamen Sache der gegenseitigen Aufklärung dienlich
zu sein. In wenigen Tagen werde ich mehr darüber wissen....
Stefan Zweig.[27]

Schnitzler also wrote directly to Rolland, remarking with irony
that journalists and diplomats should be the ones sent into the trenches.
On Monday, 10 January 1915, Rolland writes to his mother: "Chère
maman ... Schnitzler m'a de nouveau écrit pour me remercier d'avoir
publié la traduction de sa protestation. Il propose, ironiquement, de
faire envoyer dans les tranchées les journalistes et les diplomates... Ah!
si c'était possible...la guerre ne durait plus longtemps."[28] A letter from
Zweig to Schnitzler describes censorship during the War with some
measure of sarcasm:

Wien 16. Januar 1915.
Lieber verehrter Herr Doktor, den Ausschnitt aus dem "Journal
de Genève" sandte ich Ihnen schon vor paar Tagen durch
Stringa. Von Romain Rolland habe ich plötzlich keine Briefe
mehr. Die Censur hat anscheinend unsere—doch zweifellos,
staatsgefährliche und an den Fundamenten Österreichs rüttel-
nde—Correspondenz unterbunden und abgedrosselt. Ich
schreibe ihm über Italien und wende mich übrigens heute noch
an Die [sic] Briefcensur direkt, um ihr den Begriff Romain
Rolland aufzuklären.
Hoffentlich gelingts!
Viele viele Grüße Ihres getreuen Stefan Zweig.[29]

By publishing his article in Geneva Schnitzler became a member
of the loosely knit society of European intellectuals combating the
spread of war hysteria.
    In an attempt to unite the intellectuals of Germany and France,
Rolland wrote to Gerhart Hauptmann, imploring him to speak out
against the War. Hauptmann, himself blinded by war-fervor, rejected
Rolland's plea and even defended German militarism. Partially

because of his anger at Hauptmann's response, Rolland's antiwar essays, *Au-dessus de la mêlée*, became colored with the same chauvinism he sought to combat.[30] When Schnitzler obtained a copy of Rolland's collected essays on war, he was disappointed by the famous pacifist's hypocrisy: "Las Rollands 'Au-dessus de la mêlée'—seine gesammelten Aufsätze, wurde ganz traurig. Dies ist nun der klugste—gerechteste—gütigste—?! Ist ers?— Chauvinist im Grunde wie die andern;— allein (im concreten) Deutschland—nicht nur die Schuld auch den Willen zu diesem Kriege;— Thatsachen nicht wissend—verschweigend— stilisirend!— Dies wird das wichtigste sein, wenn man einander nach dem Kriege wird finden wollen: **KEIN WORT** vom vergangnen—besonders über die 'Schuld'-frage sprechen."[31] Schnitzler contemplates demanding an explanation from Rolland on his blatant antagonism toward German intellectuals.

Among his essays and aphorisms on war is an as yet unpublished five-page essay (Appendix 4) on Rolland's *Au-dessus de la mêlée*.[32] Here Schnitzler cites Rolland's attacks on Thomas Mann as a further example of Rolland's chauvinism: "...Er zitiert immer wieder den Artikel von Thomas Mann aus der N.R. [*Neue(n) Rundschau*] "Gedanken im Kriege." Ich denke nicht daran ihn zu rechtfertigen, aber er ist ein Feuilleton, für den keineswegs das intellektuelle Deutschland verantwortlich gemacht werden darf. Wieviele Artikel solcher Art sind wohl in dieser Zeit in Frankreich geschrieben worden, für den herrlichen Krieg zur Befreiung des geknechteten Elsaß-Lothringen—!"[33] Nevertheless, Schnitzler was impressed by many of Rolland's ideas on war and peace, and they certainly encouraged his own essayistic work on the subject.

Five years after the War, in August 1923, Schnitzler travels to Zweig's home in Salzburg expressly to meet Rolland for the first time. Unfortunately, the long awaited meeting is somewhat of a disappointment because of Schnitzler's poor French and Rolland's frail health.[34] Although Schnitzler saw Rolland only once again,[35] his diaries contain evidence that the Frenchman still played an important role in his writings years after the War. Three of Schnitzler's unpublished diary entries indicate that he possibly intended to publish his essays on war ("Und einmal") and his aphorisms on politics[36] as an addendum to *Au-dessus de la mêlée* and as a tribute to Rolland.

On 14 July 1925 Schnitzler writes in his diary of working on "aphoristisches (-Politik, für das Rolland-Buch)"[37] and on 19 July

1925 he talks of the great time expenditure the Rolland book is demanding of him: "Nm mit aphoristischem beschäftigt (für das Rolland Buch)—dergleichen nimmt mir ungebührlich viel Zeit."[38] Finally, on August 5, 1925 Schnitzler writes: "Dictirt (fur [sic] das Rolland Buch Liber amicorum, und die Lessingth-Blätter[)]."[39] In the absence of any further mention of the "Rolland book" I can only speculate that the same reticence that prevented Schnitzler from speaking out publicly on politics during the war also caused him to refrain from doing so in a time of ever-increasing anti-Semitism in the mid-twenties. Schnitzler's profound respect for Rolland is made clear through the very fact that he was working on the "Rolland book." Certainly, the materials contained in "Und einmal" would constitute an admirable corrective to Rolland's *Au-dessus de la mêlée* in the annals of pacifist literature.

Although Zweig later claimed to have been a pacifist from the start of the War, his words and actions during the first months of the War do not bear out this assertion. Recent scholarship by D. A. Prater[40] and C. E. Williams[41] has uncovered documents indicating that Zweig was as much affected by the fervor of war as most Europeans. Indeed, Schnitzler records in his diary on 7 September 1914: "Zweig sagte, wenn er Deutscher wäre, hätte er sich freiwillig gemeldet."[42] Although Schnitzler entrusted Zweig with his "Protest" sent to Romain Rolland, he never seemed to warm completely to Zweig's professed pacifism. It is not Zweig's intentions that Schnitzler distrusts, but rather "das tiefste seines Wesens."[43] One possible reason for Schnitzler's coolness toward Zweig was that the latter, like numerous other Austrian authors, including Rudolf Bartsch, Robert Michel, and Rainer Maria Rilke, was working in the "Kriegsarchiv," writing propaganda for the Austrian war effort. By 1917, however, Zweig had taken up residence in Switzerland (as had Rolland), where he published anti-war material and saw the world premiére of his pacifist play *Jeremias*. Karl Kraus, one of the outspoken pacifists to remain in his own country during the War, soundly criticizes Rolland, Zweig, Unruh, and others in his journal, *Die Fackel* (15 October 1918), for not speaking out against the War in their own countries: "Die guten Europäer aus Wien, Berlin und Budapest, die sich in Zürich zusammenfinden, werden dort als solche anerkannt, wiewohl sie bisher keinen Versuch gemacht haben, auch daheim diese Gesinnung zu betätigen, wo sie im Gegenteil fürs 'Donauland' zu sterben bereit sind, und es gelingt ihnen sogar, bei den guten Europäern aus Paris, die es schon eher sind, aber auch besser täten, es daheim zu sein, Kredit zu finden."[44]

Schnitzler shares Zweig's abhorrence of those "Kriegsschreier unter den Literaten; die sobald es an sie ging, die Begeisterung verloren und schlottern."[45] And yet Zweig's attempts to appear objective make Schnitzler even more suspicious. On 1 October 1916, Schnitzler writes sarcastically of the "Objektivität" with which Zweig finds "mehr Entschuldigungsgründe für Italien als für Österreich!"[46]

After the war, Schnitzler is visited by Zweig, who has spent one-and-a-half years in Switzerland with Rolland. Schnitzler is struck once again by Zweig's good intentions, but still detects an underlying flaw in his character: "Er hat gute Tendenzen; ist aber gewiß nicht ein 'wahrhaftiger,' oder gar reiner Mensch. Zutiefst in ihm ein Stück Renegatentum."[47] And so once again, Schnitzler's path to a meaningful dialogue on war and peace is blocked by his perception of inconsistency in character of one of the instrumental individuals of the pacifist movement.

Fritz von Unruh was the ideal German nobleman for Schnitzler: "Hier ist ein Mensch, in dessen Anblick und Anhören das Wort 'deutsch' wieder seinen Sinn bekommt, der einem in Lauf der Geschehnisse so verdunkelt und verekelt wurde."[48] Schnitzler observed Unruh's dutiful, even passionate entry into the War as an officer, and his radical conversion to pacifism as the direct result of the injuries he received in battle. Schnitzler reportedly thought of Unruh almost as a son,[49] and was in turn a literary mentor for Unruh. While fifty-six letters from Unruh have been found, all but six of Schnitzler's letters have been lost or destroyed. On 3 October 1917 Schnitzler writes to Unruh, praising the combination of past and contemporary themes in the latter's drama, Ein Geschlecht, and noting the effectiveness of this combination in forestalling censorship—a technique that he too employed in his works. "Nun habe ich 'Ein Geschlecht' gelesen und seine legendenhafte Art und Kraft, die in edelschönen Versen aus dem Leid der Gegenwart zum ewigen Leid der Menschheit und so zu Gott emporschwebt, hat mich sehr ergriffen,... Auch wüßte ich nicht, was der Aufführung eines Dramas im Wege stehen sollte, in dem, wenn auch begleitet von den unheimlichen Geisterstimmen der Gegenwart, uralte Schicksalsmelodien von Anfang bis Ende durchklingen, mit denen sich die Zensur wohl schon abgefunden haben könnte."[50]

Ein Geschlecht, Unruh's first tragedy, written in the trenches in 1916, is set in a cemetery on a giant hill. Before this background, Unruh weaves a mythical tale of the triumph of mother earth over the destructive forces that kill her children. Unruh's intention here is to attack the traditions that perpetuate war, as well as the notion that war is fated necessity:

> **EIN SOLDATENFÜHRER** (zur Mutter): Dieses Volk wirst Du uns nicht vom Zügel reißen!
> **MUTTER:** Was Ihr getürmt, gelenkt im Hin und Her, schuf salzge Augen!
> **EIN SOLDATENFÜHRER:** Doch der Ordnung Thron!
> **MUTTER:** Im Leichenhaus! Es rundet sich die Welt aus tiefster Freude nur ins Gleichgewicht!
> **EIN SOLDATENFÜHRER:** Frau, unsre Macht, die auf der Sitte Grund sich durch Geschlechter hart entwickelt hat schreist Du nicht um! Sie lebt aus altem Recht!
> **MUTTER:** Es wandelt sich auch Recht![51]

Schnitzler publicly followed Unruh's literary/political career with great interest and admiration, but in his diary he was more critical. His letters to Unruh were always diplomatic. Schnitzler rarely said anything unkind, preferring to praise strong areas, while understating weaknesses, perhaps with the intention of prodding Unruh to rethink those areas of his work. On 18 March 1924 Schnitzler attended an anti-war speech held by Unruh[52] and was extremely disappointed by Unruh's "pathetisches Geschwätz." When the two met after the speech, however, Schnitzler was once again overcome with affection and respect for the young German. Two days later, Unruh visited Schnitzler and outlined more clearly the material he had presented in his speech. Schnitzler indicated in his diary that if Unruh could write as well as he spoke, he might be a truly great author.[53]

An acquaintance of both Schnitzler and Unruh, Berta Zuckerkandl (daughter of the publicist Moritz Szeps), plays an important and curious role in Schnitzler's perceptions of the War. This is evidenced in their frequent conversations on politics and the behind-the-scenes maneuvering of politicians and diplomats. On 21 October 1917, for example, he writes of Zuckerkandl's secret diplomatic mis-

84   Adrian Clive Roberts

sion to Switzerland and the resulting revelation of the absurd and cruel
"game" of international politics and diplomacy:

> ...Mit O. zur Hofräthin Z.[uckerkandl]. Sie war 4 Monate in der
> Schweiz. Diplomatische Verhandlungen, von denen sie unter
> tiefstem Siegel allerlei verrieth, ohne daß alles ganz verläßlich
> geklungen hätte. (Der Präsident v. L.[andesberger] äußerte sehr
> richtig über sie, daß sie zu diplom. Missionen gut zu verwenden,
> weil man sie immer desavouiren kann.) Immerhin war der
> Einblick in die Politik lehrreich und grauenhaft. Zu denken
> während an der Oberfläche dieses lächerlich- infame Spiel wei-
> tergeht, in der Tiefe tausende, hunderttausend Unschuldige,
> Unwissende getödtet und verstümmelt werden.... Noch ein Jahr
> Krieg—und das Elend wird so namenlos, als es heute noch fast
> unvorstellbar ist.[54]

Schnitzler's diaries enumerate some prowar, but decidedly more
pacifist works on his reading list, many of which had an effect on his
own writing. In October 1917, for example, Schnitzler reads Andreas
Latzko's famous pacifist novel, *Menschen im Krieg* (1917), and
records in his diary (9 October) his horror at the gruesome character of
war on the Western Front. Although he saw no evidence of great literary value in the work, Schnitzler found confirmation of his own
thoughts about the war; it is possible that Latzko's ideas inspired some
of his aphorisms on war.[55]

Eleven years did not dampen the horrifying effect of battle-scene
descriptions on Schnitzler. On 10 February 1929 Schnitzler finishes
reading Erich Maria Remarque's *Im Westen nichts Neues* (1929), and
notes in his diary: "Las Remarque... mit Erschüttern zu Ende."[56] As
another war becomes increasingly likely, Schnitzler's diary alludes to
conversations with numerous individuals about the First World War.

Schnitzler also reads Georg Friedrich Nicolai's *Die Biologie des
Krieges* (1919), and praises it because, "...es sei nicht das übliche paci-
fistische Geschwefel [sic]..."[57] Nicolai examines the causes of war
dispassionately and scientifically. His book is a response to the
"Manifesto to the Civilized World," published in October 1914 by
ninety-three representatives of German science and art. In this manifesto such renowned individuals as Richard Dehmel, Gerhart
Hauptmann, Max Planck, Max Reinhardt, Wilhelm Röntgen, and

Wilhelm Wundt reject, among other things, the claim that Germany was in any way responsible for the First World War.[58]

One of the most significant portions of Nicolai's work is that dedicated to the genesis of patriotism and the widespread misinterpretation of the term. Here Nicolai found in Schnitzler an interested and sympathetic reader. Nicolai's words echo Schnitzler's definition of patriotism in 1880: "so kann nicht nur jeder Mensch sein Vaterland lieben, sondern soll es auch lieben. Aber er soll nicht vergessen, daß dies eine Sache persönlicher Sympathie ist, und daß die Sympathien anderer Menschen zu anderen Ländern ebenso berechtigt sind."[59] Nicolai believed that false patriotism parts company from patriotism when the latter is used for any other purpose than "die Verwirklichung der Humanität."[60] Nicolai describes how mass suggestion turns patriotism into mere "jingoism." Ultimately, Nicolai sees hope for the prevention of war only in man's gradual acceptance of other cultures and of an ever widening geographical area as his own "Vaterland."

Schnitzler's alternating admiration for and dislike of Karl Kraus have been well documented in past studies, but his reactions to Kraus's pacifism have yet to be discussed. In July 1922 Schnitzler notes in his diary that he has finished reading Kraus's antiwar satire, *Die letzten Tage der Menschheit* (written during the War). He praises the drama in the most glowing terms, criticizing only what he refers to as the limitations that the satirical mode imposes on a literary work.[61] Despite its specific attacks on Viennese society and the individuals who in 1914 led Austria into the First World War, Kraus's work is a brilliant critique of militarism in Europe at the turn of the century and a condemnation of war.

Kraus takes to task journalists who sensationalize the War and big-businessmen who reap financial profit from the suffering of millions. Above all, Kraus criticizes the abuse of language by those in positions of power. In analyzing *Die letzten Tage*, Franz H. Mautner points out the significance of the state's misuse of language in Kraus's critique of war and its causes. The following from Mautner's essay might apply as well to Schnitzler's *Der Gang zum Weiher* or *Der Ruf des Lebens* as to Kraus's *Die letzten Tage*: "He [Kraus] believed in a mystical unity between word and sense, between word and essence, resulting in an unconscious revelation of spiritual and moral abuses through corrupted word usage. Language in daily usage appeared to him to be just as mishandled and tarnished as all other cultural possessions. Certain wartime phrases surface again and again in the drama in order to reflect the social and spiritual situation."[62]

Like Kraus, Schnitzler sympathized with many of the ideals expressed by the pacifist movements, but neither man could see his way clear to identify himself with a group. Schnitzler's diary reflects his interest in the "Paneuropa Movement," founded in 1923 by Count Richard Nickolaus Coudenhove-Kalergi. In a conversation with Coudenhove Schnitzler discusses the pan-Europe concept and other matters, including the politics of the Burgtheater: "Nm *G f Coudenhove* u Frau Roland. Anregendes Gespräch *paneuropäisches* und allerlei andres politisches wozu auch Burgtheater gehort [sic], u Einfluß Piffls. Starke Sympathie für Coudenhove."[63] But in 1929 when approached by Coudenhove to serve on the "Ehrenkomitee" of the Paneurope Movement, Schnitzler expresses his skepticism as to the possibility for a united Europe in the foreseeable future:

> Darf man sich schon als einen Paneuropäer bezeichnen, wenn man die Idee Paneuropa sympathisch, einleuchtend, erhaben findet? Oder erst, wenn man eine Wirklichkeit Paneuropa in absehbarer Zeit für erreichbar hält? Oder erst dann, wenn man ein erreichtes Paneuropa als ein durchaus erstrebenswertes Ziel betrachtet?....
>
> Vielleicht haben diese Zweifel ihren Grund nur in der Erwägung, daß in Paneuropa jedesfalls die gleichen Menschen leben werden, die in den bisherigen Einzelstaaten existiert haben und daß wir nach den bisherigen Erfahrungen der Weltgeschichte auch an ein Paneuropa, ja selbst an eine vollkommen überstaatliche Menschenvereinigung, keine allzu kühnen Hoffnungen knüpfen dürfen.[64]

During this period, Schnitzler's increasing number of references to pacifism is accompanied by a growing concern over "Hetzpolitiker[n]" and "Hakenkreuzler." At least twice Schnitzler refers to Hitler. In his diary on 10 September 1924 Schnitzler mentions Hermann Bahr's "Schwärmen" for the "Hitlerei," and on 30 September 1930 he writes of a conversation with Shalom Asch who tells of the terrible damage being done outside Germany by "die Hitlerei." The diary entry ends with the ominous words: "Der künftige Krieg."[65]

5.3 The Myth of "Die große Zeit" and Schnitzler's Rejection of War in "Und einmal wird der Friede wiederkommen..."

"Große Zeit, das ist diejenige, in der die Entdeckungen und Erfindungen, die in der kleinen Zeit gemacht worden sind, zur Tötung und Verstümmelung von Menschen sowie zur Vernichtung der in der kleinen Zeit entstandenen Werte und Werke ausgenützt werden."[66]

With these words written during the First World War, Schnitzler ironically condemned the catch-phrase that called the period of the First World War "Die große Zeit." At the outbreak of the War, several notable German and Austrian writers, including Richard Dehmel, Gerhart Hauptmann, and Thomas Mann contributed to the flurry of patriotic essays published in newspapers and journals. Despite requests from numerous publishers, Schnitzler chose not to involve himself in the propaganda effort. Instead, he began work on a collection of essays and aphorisms opposing war. His diary entry of 8 September 1914 makes first mention of this project just one month after the start of the War: "Schreibe allerlei Bemerkungen zu dem Thema—'Und einmal wird der Friede wiederkommen.'" (*Tagebuch 1913-1916*, p. 133). Ten years later, on 24 July 1924, Schnitzler is still interested in this collection: "Las unter andern Aphorismen meinen Convolut 'Und einmal wird der Friede wiederkommen—'; viel kluges und gut gefaßtes."[67]

The absence of any systematic organization of the materials suggests that at the time of his death in 1931, Schnitzler still had no plans to publish the works. Stylistically, the essays vary from calmly argued, logical theses to short emotional reactions to daily news items. Though Schnitzler's essays and aphorisms on war reflect the possible influence of Suttner and Rolland, there can be no doubt that the majority of the ideas are Schnitzler's. Many of his opinions on war had been formed by the age of eighteen. Nonetheless a major change occurred during the First World War, as his pacifism developed. After writing his essays against war, he was better able to critically discuss the causes of war in his literary works. The aphoristic writings represent a theoretical base for the practical pacifism in Schnitzler's late works.

In October 1914 Schnitzler's essays still showed patriotic prejudice. Initially he blames Britain and France for starting the war, but he
soon concedes that all countries involved should share the blame.
Schnitzler focuses his analysis and critique of "Die große Zeit" on four
areas: the political, social, psychological, and philosophical causes and
effects of war.

Even within the young system of European democracy, remnants
of absolutism abound, as in the case of conscription, which Schnitzler
attacks: "Der einzige unbezweifelbare Besitz des Menschen ist sein
Leben... Die allgemeine Wehrpflicht aber ist die ungeheuerste
Vergewaltigung an dem einzigen unbezweifelbaren Besitz des
Menschen und überdies zugunsten einer im ganzen und oft im besonderen höchst diskutablen Idee wie Dynastie, Vaterland, Staat. 1915"[68]
Compare a later observation on the role of universal conscription in the
change in the very nature of warfare: "Zu Popper...Darüber, dss [sic]
der Krieg sich seit Jahrtausenden nur quantitativ verändert[.] Ich
bemerkte, daß die allgemeine Wehrpflicht doch auch das *Wesen* des
Kriegs verändert, was er zugab.."[69]

Schnitzler criticizes diplomats whose true motives are only to
gain wealth and power and to advance in their careers. Only rarely do
they bother to attempt to find peaceful solutions to international problems, and frequently their incompetence actually causes conflicts as in
the Balkan Wars of 1912 and 1913.

But it is in his own field, in the realm of the spoken and written
word, that Schnitzler finds the most evidence of governmental misuse
of power. Journalists and "Feuilletonisten" thrive on the propaganda
lies and exaggerations of politicians. Authoritarian governments capi-
talize on the citizens' love for their homeland. Equating state with
country, "Heimatgefühl" becomes "Patriotismus" or "Vaterlandsliebe."
Allegiance is owed the state rather than the country itself. Other terms
such as "Heldentum" and "Ehre" acquire renewed military importance
when they appear in print in the Austria of 1914. The time-worn
clichés of military propaganda are no match for Schnitzler's logical
insight. The dictionary of war, he says, is written by the diplomats, the
military, and those in positions of power. It should be rewritten by
those who are directly affected by war: those witnesses who survive it,
the widows, the orphans, the doctors and the poets (*AuB*, 220).

With the advent of the "Materialkrieg"[70] in the early twentieth
century, the genuine "Heldentod" became ever rarer. Modern technol-

ogy facilitated killing to the point where the individual was rendered helpless in the face of such weapons as the flame-thrower, the tank, shrapnel, the machine gun, and the airplane.[71] Still, effective propaganda led millions to volunteer for infantry duty. Schnitzler analyzes the underlying motives for such an action, and comes to the following conclusions. The individual soldier, if he has not been conscripted into the army, signs up because he naively desires adventure, danger, or action. But he does not consider his own death or injury seriously. If he did, Schnitzler writes, he would certainly seek another, more peaceful outlet. Even those individuals who believe that they are fighting for ideas are only deceiving themselves or being deceived by their government: "Niemals ist wirklich für eine Idee Krieg geführt worden; weder für eine nationale noch für eine religiöse...Aber die Ideen werden immer vorgeschützt, als Banner vorangetragen, sozusagen als Fahnen der Seele. Man kann natürlich jede Phrase zu einer Idee ernennen. Dies gehört zu den Hauptaufgaben des Politikers, der das Gleichgewicht auch dadurch wiederherstellt, daß er aus jeder Idee eine Phrase macht. 1916"[72] According to Schnitzler, all wars are simply struggles for power, and are made possible by "1. durch die Schurkerei der Mächtigen, 2. die Dummheit der Diplomatie und 3. die Phantasielosigkeit der Völker."[73]

Schnitzler's essays on war also reveal a practical political strategy for the prevention of future wars. His first prerequisite for a lasting peace concurs, as I mentioned earlier, with one of Kant's premises in *Zum ewigen Frieden*, namely that peace treaties should avoid placing blame on a single country, for this is merely sowing the seed for future conflict. The second prerequisite is to avoid discussion of individual criminal acts that occur during the war:

Auch hier scheint es zwecklos, Unterschiede zu machen. Es bleibt die gleiche Ungeheuerlichkeit, ob nun sogenannte Zivilisten, Frauen, Kinder aus der Luft durch Bomben getötet und verstümmelt werden, ob man diese Zivilisten zum Hungertode zu verurteilen gedenkt oder ob junge und ältere Leute (ebenso unbeteiligt und ebenso unschuldig wie die Zivilisten und bewußt oder unbewußt zum Kriegsdienst gezwungen) durch Mordwaffen umgebracht und zu Krüppeln gemacht werden. Auch Schurkerei und Heldenmut, Verrat und Patriotismus sind in Kriegszeiten so nahe beisammen, daß im Einzelfall für den objektiven Beurteiler sich eine Differentialdiagnose nur selten stellen läßt und die Entscheidung nur opportunistischen Erwägungen anheimgestellt bleiben muß.[74]

The third prerequisite is to remove all speculation on the possibility that human nature will improve in the foreseeable future. Only when we recognize that it is useless to rely on the improvement of humanity and turn to the task of improving political organizations will real progress toward peace be accomplished. In this sense Schnitzler's works are eminently political in nature.

To achieve this improvement in political and social institutions Schnitzler proposes an organization of states with the sole task of dealing with international disputes, about borders, trade, national honor, and prestige. The honor of a state can never be insulted by another state, he maintains, but only by the behavior of its own government. Problems of trade should be settled through free enterprise. Here, incidentally, Schnitzler once again compares war with the duel: "Die Handelsfragen ließen sich dadurch schlichten, daß der Fleißigere, Tätigere, Begabtere den Vorteil haben sollte. Auch hier kommt es nicht zu Duellen zwischen den Schustern, die einander ihre Kunden streitig machen. Warum sollte es bei den Völkern durch Blut entschieden werden, ob Michel oder John Bull [Germany or England] seine Waren beim Nachbarn absetzt?"[75]

Schnitzler's notion of a peace parliament anticipates the League of Nations and the United Nations, the main difference being that Schnitzler's organization would have more political power. Any decision made by the parliament would be binding. The members themselves should have such a vested interest in peace that war would never be an alternative: "Für diese Parlamentarier dürfte der Krieg so wenig in Betracht kommen, wie etwa einem der bisherigen Parlamente in Streitfälle ein Duell zwischen den Parteiführern als Ausweg auch nur in Erwägung gezogen werden dürfte..."[76]

In the social realm Schnitzler considers the role of peaceful professions in times of war. Unless an author is willing to serve as an agent of propaganda for his government (as, for example, did Hofmannsthal and Zweig), he is considered by most members of his society as superfluous. All topics not dealing with the War directly are thought of as inappropriate. Anything that he writes about after the

War that does not reflect direct influence from the War will automatically be deemed outdated and old-fashioned.

But Schnitzler felt that it is not the role of a writer merely to please his readers; far more it is his duty to reflect the highest achievements of his culture. The average citizen also serves his country best by excelling in his work. The common laborer who strives to achieve his utmost potential at his job is as good a patriot as any general, perhaps better, Schnitzler writes. Once again the propaganda of the state can be seen at work, devaluing peaceful professions in wartime in order to promote militarism. Yet for all his attacks on those in power, Schnitzler's harshest words are for the average citizen: "Und Ihr alle, die Ihr jetzt seufzen und stöhnen und fluchen und nach den Schuldigen suchen und die Schuldigen hängen wollt—seid Ihr nicht alle schuldig, da Ihr doch Eure ganze Existenz, die Erziehung Eurer Kinder, das Leben des Alltags, Eure ganze Weltanschauung darauf gegründet habt, daß der Krieg etwas Erlaubtes, ja etwas Vernünftiges, ja etwas Notwendiges..."[77]

To a large extent Schnitzler blames the individual for the perpetuation of war, focusing on man's lack of imagination ("Phantasielosigkeit" [see chapter 3]). While being mastered by one's imagination leads to madness, the absence of imagination equates with feeble-mindedness ["Schwachsinn"]—a trait prevalent in the masses and in the rulers of nations who frequently have the role of influencing the course of history. Franz Kafka also is reported to have said in 1916, that "dieser Krieg... aus einem entsetzlichen Mangel an Phantasie entstanden [ist]."[78]

In 1912, however, Theodor Reik anticipates both Schnitzler and Kafka in his assessment of the psychology of heroism: "Wie also entsteht ein Held? Auf zwei Arten. Die erste: durch Mangel an Phantasie. Wer keine hat, wird sein Leben hinwerfen...."[79]

In the psychological realm man's basically unchanging nature (according to Schnitzler), prevents him from making war more humane, let alone establishing a lasting peace. The human mind in most cases is so feeble in its ability to translate mathematical figures into real human terms that an axiomatic inversion takes place: the larger the number of killed and wounded reported in a war, the less the populace feels an emotional effect. Realizing the potential for quelling opposition to the War, the state-run newspapers print only staggering numbers of casualties. The reader, totally overcome by the figures, is alienated to the point of becoming incapable of human compassion: "Tausend Verwundete stellen sich für die Phantasie keineswegs so schlimm dar wie ein Verwundeter. Sie bedeuten nicht tausendmal eins, auch nicht eins, auch nicht einen Bruchteil von eins, sondern sogar etwas qualitativ anderes. Es liegt immer im Interesse des Staates, diesen Denkfehler aufrecht zu erhalten, vom einzelnen abzusehen."[80] Because greed, aggression, desire for power, danger and adventure are all human traits that are unlikely to change or disappear, Schnitzler writes, we must channel them into peaceful or at least less harmful outlets than war. But Schnitzler was also a realist. He writes that as long as one individual exists who can gain something from war and has the power and influence required to start it, any attempt to prevent war is futile. Schnitzler believed that the only way to prevent war was to modify social and political institutions so as to make it impossible for such individuals to achieve positions of power. Yet Schnitzler was optimistic about the eventual eradication of war for two reasons: the number of people who stand to gain something from war is constantly declining; the problems leading to war can all conceivably be solved by other means:

> Der Krieg, selbst wenn er mit einem Siege endet, liegt stets nur im Interesse einer verschwindenden Minderheit. Alle Fragen, die angeblich nur kriegerisch zur Entscheidung gebracht werden können, das sind also Grenz- (meist nur dynastische Macht-), Handels- und Ehren- (Prestige-) Fragen, sind stets auf einem andern Wege in Ordnung zu bringen.[81]

Schnitzler also discusses the role of philosophy in the prevention or perpetuation of war. All his life he fought against dogmatism of any kind, but most specifically that in the areas of literary criticism, religion, politics, and psychoanalysis. As to the causes of war, Schnitzler condemned those people who subscribe to the dogma of necessity (compare Bertha von Suttner's *Die Waffen nieder*). In believing that war is inevitable, one submits to the dogma of necessity and automatically relinquishes the notion of free will. Schnitzler rejected the notion of the necessity of war, on the basis that war results from the state's manipulation of human nature:

Das Dogma lautet: Der Krieg ist eine Schicksalsnotwendigkeit; er ist in der Organisation der menschlichen Natur begründet. Dieses Dogma ist falsch. Der Krieg ist nicht in der menschlichen Natur begründet, sondern im Wesen der Staatenbildung und in dem Verhältnis der einzelnen Staaten zueinander. Das Individuum als solches will niemals den Krieg..., ausgenommen diejenigen, für die der Krieg eine Gelegenheit ist, ihrer persönlichen Abenteuerlust, ihrem Ehrgeiz, ihrer Habsucht Befriedigung zu verschaffen ....[82]

Schnitzler's stand on the question of fate versus free will can be clearly documented. Reinhard Müller-Freienfels writes of Schnitzler's increasing belief in free will, manifested in his later dramatic works, particularly in *Der Gang zum Weiher*.[83]

Indeed, in an undated aphorism in "Und einmal" Schnitzler writes of his belief in a basic chain of causality, subject to the possible influence of a thousand parallel chains:

Die sogenannte Schicksalsnotwendigkeit. Wir vergessen immer wieder, daß dasjenige Ereignis, das uns, nachdem es geschehen, als das absolut Notwendige, also im Geist der Geschichte gelegene oder von Gott gewollte (je nach der Weltanschauung) erscheint, bevor es eintrat, auch nichts anderes war als eine von tausend Möglichkeiten. Natürlich mußte es geschehen nach dem Gesetz der Kausalität, aber häufig genug lag die letzte Ursache nicht auf der großen Linie, sondern diese letzte Ursache kam auf einem Seitenweg daher, kann also wohl auch als Zufall bezeichnet werden, ...[84]

Schnitzler in 1927 writes of a balance between the law of causality and free will and of the importance for the individual to take responsibility for his or her life:

Kann man sich wirklich einen Gott vorstellen, der sich einfach damit begnügte, das Kausalitätsgesetz zu schaffen, worauf dann vom ersten Anstoß an, mit dem er die Welt in Gang brachte, die weiteren Geschehnisse unabänderlich und vorbestimmt sich abrollten? Nein, so leicht hat Er es sich nicht gemacht: Er hat

sich einen ebenbürtigen Gegner ins All gesetzt, den freien
Willen,...[85]

It is clear then, that Schnitzler's belief in free will gained
strength after the First World War, but also that his belief during the
War in a chain of causality did not exclude the notion of free will.

Schnitzler points out in "Und einmal" the absence of logic on the
part of those who, on one hand, believe in the fated necessity of war
and, on the other hand, pray to God for victory and the lives of their
loved ones. The irreconcilability of the two notions is expressed by
Schnitzler: "Und warum beten sie denn eigentlich zu Gott? Gäbe es
eine historische Notwendigkeit—und dieser Begriff fügt sich auch in
die religiöse Ideologie—, so müßte sie doch von aller Zeiten Anfang
feststehen. Denn daß solche historischen Notwendigkeiten abwech-
seln, läßt sich weder mit historischer noch mit religiöser Anschauung
im allergeringsten vereinigen..."[86]

The history of the twentieth century supports Schnitzler's theories on the causes of war. Human beings do not change overnight.
And if future wars are to be prevented we must strive to improve our
national and international organizations.[87]

5.4 The War Fragments: "Kriegsgeschichte" and
"Der Oberstabsarzt"

Arthur Schnitzler never completed a literary work about the
First World War, but among his posthumous documents are two fragments for works on the subject.[88] It is not unusual for Schnitzler to
set aside a work only to return to it decades later, but the question
remains as to why specifically the two works on the War should have
remained uncompleted. Renate Wagner suggests convincingly that
the lead female character in "Der Oberstabsarzt" is modeled on
Schnitzler's close friend, Stephi Bachrach and that the personal
nature of the work made him hesitant to publish it. In Schnizler's
diary entry of 2 September 1930 there is an indication that had he
lived longer, Schnitzler might well have completed "Der
Oberstabsarzt." The fact that he sees a war movie and reads a
"trench" novel the same day gives clear evidence of his heightened
interest in the War: "*Marienbad*....—Nm Landsknecht durchgesehn.
Sonderbarer Weise die 4 Mscrpte, die ich (außer 'Zug') mit-

habe—lauter Kriegsstoff: Landsknecht, Oberstabsarzt, Sangerin [sic],
Abenteuerer.—Kino;—ein (altes) Kriegsstück 'Flandern.'—;
genachtm bei 'Winterling.'—Lese (außer "Byron")—Flaherty, 'die
Bestie erwacht'—ein Kriegs (Schützengraben-) Roman."[89] It is clear
that war and the First World War specifically remained a subject of
interest in his literary works.

The "Kriegsgeschichte" fragment (a collection of brief sketches
and scenarios) was evidently drafted in 1915.[90] It consists of a basic
plot, "Wahre Geschichte" (perhaps based on a real-life story, or possibly the term was intended to make the work appear more realistic),
and seven "Variationen." Although the seventh scenario is the only
one that promises to include actual combat or front-line scenes,
Renate Wagner is incorrect in her claim that in his unfinished
"Kriegsgeschichte" Schnitzler's "Interesse [gilt] nicht dem Krieg,
sondern der Situation einer daheimgebliebenen Frau."[91] Schnitzler
felt very strongly that there was more to war than front line combat.
Through his personal relationships with men involved directly in the
war and with their relatives at home, Schnitzler became closely
acquainted with the psychological conditions of war: separation,
divorce, and death. In "Kriegsgeschichte" he intended to portray the
hypocritical morality during wartime. In "Die Daheimgebliebenen,"
an essay written in the same year, Schnitzler attacks critics who find
the subject of marital infidelity in *Komödie der Worte* (first performed in 1915) irrelevant to the times and more morally objectionable than the War itself:

> Der Theaterkritiker weiß auch nichts davon, daß gerade das,
> was er Sittlichkeit nennt, noch niemals so tief gesunken war,
> wie in diesem Kriege. Es ist ihm unbekannt, daß der Ehebruch
> sowohl unter den im Felde stehenden Männern, als unter den
> daheimgebliebenen Frauen ein außerordentlich häufiges
> Vorkommen ist; er weiß nichts davon, daß wegen der unge-
> heueren Ausbreitung der Syphilis eine ganze Reihe von
> Spitälern im Hinterlande hat errichtet werden müssen. Er
> gebärdet sich immer wieder so, als wenn die Frauen daheim
> ausschließlich weinen und die Männer draußen keiner anderen
> Versuchung unterliegen würden, als zu töten und getötet zu
> werden.[92]

Such critics praised the War and were blind to the reality that the symptoms of a decadent society, prevalent before the War, were only compounded by it.

"Kriegsgeschichte" contains no reference to the First World War. That the conflict is an extended one, during which the wounded soldiers could go home to convalesce before returning to the field, tends to support this hypothesis, however. Stronger evidence can be found in Schnitzler's letters expressing dismay over the effects of the War on personal relationships. Schnitzler's other war fragment, "Der Oberstabsarzt," clearly set during the First World War, is also about love and deceit, and the coincidence of theme and dates of production tend to support the notion that "Kriegsgeschichte" takes place during the First World War. Nonetheless the problem he addresses in placing war as a backdrop for social relationships is a timeless one that could apply to any extended war in history.

In "Kriegsgeschichte" an officer goes off to war, leaving his young wife alone in Vienna. He thinks the long absence will be difficult for her to bear. So when a friend is slightly wounded in battle and will convalesce in Vienna, the officer gives him "permission" to have an affair with his wife. In this first portion ("Wahre Geschichte"), the wife agrees to the arrangement and the affair begins. The wife's acquiescence to her husband's peculiar wish is the only portion of the "Wahre Geschichte" changed in the "Variationen" that follow.

Each scenario explores a different aspect of human nature or a particular peculiarity of society. In the first, the extended absence combines with the stress of combat to make the officer doubt his wife's ability to resist temptation. Ironically his fear of her infidelity acts as a catalyst for her extramarital affair. The wife had been resisting the advances of another man until she hears her husband's proposal from the wounded friend. Her husband's lack of faith in her decides her to engage in the affair. She spurns the wounded officer who, upon his return to the field, tells the elated husband of his wife's loyalty.

The second scenario reflects the emancipation of the wife, who misuses her freedom in an attempt to gain revenge. Furious at her husband's assumption that he can control her "inner freedom," she gives herself "dem ersten besten hin, sagt es ihrem Mann, wie er zurückkehrt. Oder sagt es ihrem Manne nicht, er findet sie als eine Art Dirne wieder."[93]

Jealousy is the motif of the third scenario, in which the wife becomes the lover of the friend, who subsequently returns to the front. Now he too is jealous, because he is certain that the woman will find another lover to replace him. The situation accentuates the danger of exaggerated possessiveness. In the fourth scenario as in the third, the friend returns to the front, but he and the officer's wife have fallen in love and wish to stay together after the war. The officer, himself now wounded, returns home only to find that his wife and best friend are a couple. The fifth scenario, returns to one of Schnitzler's favorite themes, the duel. The wife becomes the friend's lover, but then deceives him with yet another. The two men duel over the officer's wife, and the husband returns and "ist niemand."[94]

The sixth scenario is a critique of the double standard between men and women. Here the friend has an affair with the wife, but later has second thoughts about her morality. He complains to the husband who returns from the war, saying: "Deine Frau betrügt dich, du kannst dir das nicht gefallen lassen."[95] Apart from ignoring the fact that the affair was the husband's idea in the first place, the friend condemns the wife for her role in the matter without considering his (the friend's) own guilt. The final scenario stresses the situation of the officer at the front. The friend has an affair with the wife, and yet upon returning to the field, tells the officer nothing of what has occurred. Afflicted with jealousy and unable to find out about what has transpired in Vienna, the officer nevertheless fears for the life of his friend in combat.

Schnitzler's view of the forced camaraderie of soldiers at the front is a stark contrast to Remarque's positive view of the phenomenon in *Im Westen nichts Neues* (1929). The comrades share war experiences, and return home either finding the wife dead or about to die. Although Schnitzler says nothing about the cause of her death, it is conceivable that she dies as a result of the Spanish influenza epidemic, the spread of which was facilitated by soldiers in 1918. The epidemic plays an important role in "Der Oberstabsarzt" and it therefore all the more likely that Schnitzler considered using it in "Kriegsgeschichte" as well. The wife's death is a final stroke of irony: she who has remained behind in the relative safety of Vienna has died, while the the two men who faced death daily at the front survive. Here Schnitzler illustrates that the far reaching effects of the war could be as deadly on the home front as well as on the battlefield.[96]

"Der Oberstabsarzt" is the only work produced by Schnitzler that is clearly set during the First World War.[97] It contains many historical facts pinpointing not only the location of the action, but also the approximate date. The Austrian military hospital is located in Bolzano, and the Austrian troops are about to withdraw, indicating that it is quite late in the war. There has been an outbreak of influenza, killing twenty-four in Bolzano, and cases have been reported in Vienna too. In 1918 an influenza epidemic killed millions worldwide; it is possibly the early phase of this epidemic that strikes in "Der Oberstabsarzt." In the Viennese railway station, an officer tells the heroine Gerty: "Wir rücken vor ...," yet Schnitzler notes: "Begeisterung der ersten Jahre ist fort."[98] This comment reflects the war-weariness that replaced the naive emotional excitement of the early years.

Schnitzler never visited a battlefield, and perhaps he did not feel qualified to write about modern combat. Simply writing about the horrors of the battlefield would in any case be illustrating the self-evident. But if it had to be done, then better by one who had been in the trenches himself. Nevertheless, in numerous places in "Der Oberstabsarzt" Schnitzler injects criticism of the war and militarism. Gerty's brother has been killed in battle, leaving a broken-hearted father and a home devoid of love. On the train to Bolzano, Gerty and Robert (the Oberstabsarzt) are struck by the apparent serenity of the landscape. They feel more distant from the war than they did in Vienna, but this tranquil illusion is shattered by the reality of the wounded and dying in the troop trains upon their arrival in Bolzano. Schnitzler's visits to military hospitals in Vienna[99] and his observation of his brother, Julius, who worked in one, supply much factual background material for the story. A nurse enters the room and, in correct military fashion, says: "Melde gehorsamst," to which Robert replies: "Lassen Sie doch diese Kindereien.."[100] Schnitzler had always rejected military formalities and he felt that they should play no role in the running of a hospital.

The Oberstabsarzt is a complex character who in many ways resembles Schnitzler. Like his character Robert, Schnitzler too supported the initial war effort (though Robert's patriotic response is much more profound and longer lasting than Schnitzler's). After years of operating on wounded soldiers Robert is now ashamed that he ever favored the war. His thoughts echo Schnitzler's condemnation of man's lack of imagination and of a militarist bureaucracy that devours human lives: "Zu Beginn war er auch begeistert. Er schämt sich jetzt. Herzschmerzen, die ihm auch gleichgültig sind. Jämmerliche Intrigen ringsum. Was haben sie eigentlich oben mit ihm vor."[101]   Robert's indifference reflects the war-weariness pervading Europe in the final years of the War by which Schnitzler was quite significantly affected. Robert appears to be a blend of Schnitzler himself, Otto Zuckerkandl (a friend of Schnitzler and an Oberstabsarzt since February 22, 1915), and Rudolf Urbantschitsch (director of the Sanatorium in Vienna and head of a mobile military hospital).   Schnitzler's diary entries from 1915 provide numerous parallels to the characters and situations in the fragment "Der Oberstabsarzt." The model for Gerty can be found in the young Stephi Bachrach—Schnitzler's close friend, with whom it has been conjectured he was in love. Like Gerty, Stephi was an army nurse in Vienna, serving under Rudolf Urbantschitch. Also like Gerty, Stephi had a lover named Rudi at the front in Italy—Rudolph Olden. To complete the analogy, she too was torn between her love for her soldier and her superior, Urbantschitsch.[102]

Robert's precarious relationship with his wife closely parallels Schnitzler's marriage to Olga, who was so jealous of Stephi that she frequently dreamed Arthur was having an affair with her. On one occasion she told him that her dream had seemed more real than reality itself. Schnitzler, whose marriage was already on the decline in 1915, perhaps found an outlet in assigning Robert a similar marriage: "Der Oberstabsarzt in seinem Hause. Er ist froh, daß er seine Frau nicht mehr antrifft.... Seine Frau, die Zärtliche spielend, sein Ekel. Sie tut, als wäre sie eifersüchtig. Spricht von der Schwester Dora, von irgend einer Frau."[103]

The autobiographical character of "Der Oberstabsarzt" cannot be ignored.

5.5 Social Criticism and a
Return to the Duel as a Dramatic Theme

Although *Leutnant Gustl* was written in six days, this was the exception to Schnitzler's standard approach to writing. Most of his works required years or even decades before they were completed.[104] After establishing the initial idea for a work, Schnitzler would file it. A year later he might add to the file and finally begin writing another year after that. He constantly revised and rewrote chapters, even after the work had been published. Seldom was he satisfied enough with any complete work to let it remain untouched, as he did *Leutnant Gustl*. *Fink und Fliederbusch* (hereafter referred to as *Fink*) illustrates Schnitzler's usual procedure. Conceived in 1903 and not completed until 1917, *Fink* benefited from many years of changes and additions to its basic plot about a journalist who secretly works for both a conservative and a liberal newspaper, publishing opposing political articles. By writing the work over the span of fourteen years, Schnitzler was able to integrate contemporary themes with earlier ones. The result is an especially vivid collage of subjects and characters that represents Austria of the then recent past and present. The striking political theme of the play makes it almost unique among Schnitzler's works.

The the play was largely written during the War, concurrently with "Und einmal," and it is likely that the characters in *Fink* are based on the personality types described in that work. Schnitzler modeled several of *Fink's* characters after real Viennese publishers, journalists, and politicians. In turn they also served as models for the personality types portrayed in his theoretical writings. In *Fink*, however, the significant factor is the portrayal of personality types rather than merely specific individuals. Although the idea of centering the plot around Fliederbusch's duel with himself was conceived before the First World War,[105] Schnitzler chose to write the play while the War was in progress, at the same time as "Und einmal."

In the editorial office of the liberal newspaper *Die Gegenwart* at the beginning of the play, there is talk of politics. But Frühbeck, the editor for local news, wants to hear nothing of the subject. People are interested, he argues, only in local affairs. Just how small their concerns are is reflected in the example he gives—the resurgence of phylloxera ("Die Reblaus")—a small insect that destroys grape crops. The irony here lies in the fact that phylloxera, despite its small size, is capable of devastating the economy of entire nations. Small issues, if ignored, can lead to disastrous results for a society. Here Frühbeck reflects the lackadaisical attitude toward politics of not only the Viennese in 1900, but the general European populace in July 1914: "Wer schert sich denn in Wirklichkeit um Politik? Minister, Diplomaten, Börsianer, Fürsten, Abgeordnete, Journalisten, Bank-Präsidenten,—kurz, die geschäftlich Beteiligten. Ja, wenn irgendwo im Namen der Politik gemetzelt oder geschändet wird, dann bilden sich auch die andern Leut' ein, sie interessieren sich für Politik. Aber das ist eben nur Einbildung. Nehmen Sie den Ereigissen ihren trügerischen Parfüm von zukünftiger Weltgeschichte, was bleibt übrig—Die Reblaus."[106]

The duel between Fink and Fliederbusch results from a controversy surrounding a political article by Fink in the conservative newspaper *Elegante Welt*. Fink, more enamored of his rhetorical skill than of the issue at hand, reports on Count Niederhof's address in parliament. Niederhof argues that the aggressors in Strakonitz are really those who employ terrorist phrases to inflame the otherwise peaceful order in Czechoslovakia. Ironically Fink himself lapses into inflammatory rhetoric. His argument strays further and further from the real issue, until he is accusing the unnamed enemy of attacking the very concept of private property and "property in a higher sense." By this he means the very ideals that he feels one must support and be willing to defend to the death: "Vaterland und Glauben." The circular arguments, flight into the abstract, and the appeal to the reader's sense of patriotism make Fink's report so convincing to the feuilleton writer, Obendorfer, that he asks what could possibly be considered offensive about the article. Fink's closing words, a direct quotation from Niederhof's speech, could easily be an extract from the speech of a German or Austrian politician encouraging the war effort in 1916: "Dem Politiker steht Sentimentalität so wenig an wie dem Soldaten! Und wer durfte mit größerem Recht ein Wort wie dieses prägen als ein Mann, dessen Ahnen jederzeit bereit waren, Blut und Leben für Gott, Kaiser und Vaterland—"[107]

Fliederbusch feigns disgust at Fink's article and writes a rebuttal. This time the extreme liberal view is given. The notion of an individual playing at political journalism to satisfy his own desires is intended by Schnitzler, among other things, as a critique of egoistic journalists and critics who are rarely if ever truly involved in the subjects about which they write.

Up to a point Fliederbusch's arguments are rational and cohesive, but soon political clichés appear here as well. Word of the massacre tells of a fourteen-year old boy who has been killed. The chief editor, Leuchter, suggests changing the age to twelve, for the emotional effect the younger age will have on the reader. Fliederbusch then reads: "...vor allem dem— zehnjährigen Knaben."[108] Appealing to the reader's emotions the implication is that a ten year-old boy has more sentimental impact than a fourteen year-old. Schnitzler is demonstrating here the conventions of political propaganda. Similarly in "Und ein-mal" Schnitzler points out this common propaganda technique of play-ing on the public's sympathy—used especially effectively during the First World War to encourage hatred between peoples of the nations involved. The articles of Fink and Fliederbusch, although callously written, represent opposite political extremes that lead to battle. The duel between Fink and Fliederbusch is instigated by a "third party": Satan's (the chief editor of the *Elegante Welt*) son, Egon. Satan and his coworkers represent allied countries that ignite a war and then are will-ing to give only secondary aid to the combatants.

The cause of the duel is thus a difference of political opinion—a false difference, for Fliederbusch does not really support any of the political convictions he presents in the two papers. Wars, too, are fought over supposed differences of political opinions between coun-tries. But Schnitzler writes in "Und einmal," as with the duel between Fink and Fliederbusch, that most of the ideas or convictions for which wars are fought are false. Further, he says that honor cannot be offend-ed by others, but only by one's own dishonorable actions. Because Fliederbusch has disgraced himself through the misuse of his journalis-tic position, it is only appropriate that he duel with his alter ego. The duel in Fink appears to represent both personal and national honor. The characters are divided into two opposing camps, briefly mentioned earlier: the liberal newspaper, appropriately named *Die Gegenwart*, edited by Leuchter, and the conservative paper, *Die Elegante Welt* headed by Satan. The symbolism of the names is self-evident; it is interesting that Schnitzler attributes the evil name to the chief editor of the conservative paper of the aristocracy. The title, *Die Elegante Welt* immediately suggests elitism, and one is reminded of Schnitzler's list of the enemies of the concept of peace outlined in "Und einmal." Among these are "die Snobs (der Krieg, die Courage, das Abenteuer etc. ist irgendwie elegant)."[109]

Count Niederhof (around whom Schnitzler planned at one time to center a play about a politician), a member of parliament, is a politi-cian only for fun, not out of conviction. In an important dialogue with Fliederbusch, the Count agrees to accept Fliederbusch's classification of him as a "sportsman." He is Schnitzler's "snob"—an adventurer who polarizes everyone he meets into two categories: "sportsmen" or "monomaniacs." Unable to accept the notion that an individual can honestly pursue a single lifetime profession without therefore being a "mono-maniac," the Count reduces the choices of the individual in society to two extremes. Niederhof's lack of imagination makes him a prime candidate to be a catalyst in any conceivable conflict. He dabbles in politics, for that is his current interest, but like Fliederbusch, he has no personal convictions. This detached interest with which politicians and diplomats toy with the lives of their peoples is another of Schnitzler's causes for war as outlined in "Und einmal."

Although the Count's political decisions might have a profound impact on the people of Austria, they are not determined by morals, or in the interest of peace. Niederhof resembles the Austrian foreign minister, Count Leopold Berchtold, one of the major instigators of the First World War. As long as Niederhof stands to lose nothing by it, he pursues any passing whim, irrespective of the potential for harm to others. When he decides that he wants to start his own newspaper and employ Fliederbusch to write for him, Niederhof tries to dissuade Fliederbusch from dueling, lest he lose his star journalist. His attempts become all the more earnest when he hears that the duel will involve three exchanges of pistol shots rather than the usual one. As the increased magnitude of warfare in 1914 first made people realize the horror of war, so does this multi-shot duel make Niederhof aware for the first time, of the danger in dueling. When Niederhof had himself fought a duel years before, it had been a calculated risk—as earlier wars were regarded—, undertaken for the "fun" and "sport" of it. The real possibility of death was not taken seriously, if it were taken into consideration at all. Like soldiers from opposing countries, facing one another in the trenches without hatred (an observation made by Schnitzler in "Und einmal"), the Count had felt no animosity toward his opponent. It was simply a case of "him or me." Had Niederhof comprehended the fact that he stood a good chance of losing his life, he almost certainly would not have engaged in the duel.

The doctor, an addicted bettor at the horse races, cites the odds for Fliederbusch's survival as being fairly good. The doctor callously reduces a life and death affair to a game of mere figures—another example of what Schnitzler refers to in "Und einmal" as a "Flucht ins Abstrakte." This speculation for profit based on the life and death of others finds a parallel in the First World War, from which bankers and businessmen derive profit (a subject we shall return to with *Komödie der Verführung*).

The princess in *Fink* is the epitome of Schnitzler's impression of members of the Austro-Hungarian royalty (and the aristocracy in general), who interest themselves only in petty, egocentric pursuits and care nothing for politics. In the following dialogue with Fliederbusch about the *Elegante Welt* the princess betrays her true interests:

> FÜRSTIN: ...Ich hab' Ihr Journal gerne, es ist ein sehr amüsantes Blatt. Besonders die Geschichten aus der Kulissenwelt, die studier' ich immer mit viel Vergnügen. Zuweilen ein bisserl équivoque, aber—Schreiben Sie die vielleicht?
> FLIEDERBUSCH: Nein, Durchlaucht, ich bin für den politischen Teil engagiert.
> FÜRSTIN: So—Politik—? Na ja, muß auch sein.— (Nimmt wieder die Bilder) Das ist die vordere Ansicht vom Schloß. Man sieht's nicht von draußen. Es steht ganz tief im Park drin.[110]

The fact that the palace, a symbol of the monarchy and of the aristocracy, is not visible from the outside, standing as it does deep in the park (another significant symbol as will be seen in *Komödie der Verführung*), symbolizes the exclusion of the masses of the middle-class from the decision-making processes of the monarchy. The misordering of her royal priorities is even more pronounced when the Count invites the princess to the duel between Fink and Fliederbusch. She points to her riding outfit and asks: "Ja, kann man denn so zu einem Duell gehen?"[111] In the same scene Kajetan (a private consultant for the *Gegenwart*) excitedly tells the princess that the duel will involve five pistol shots—yet another increase from the earlier three. By word of mouth, the scale of the duel is expanded, making it seem more and more like an escalating war. Whereas the idea for Fliederbusch's duel is put into motion by a rumor, journalistic rumor also magnifies an event—like reports of battles—for sensationalism. The anarchist Styx most closely resembles Schnitzler in the play. Fliederbusch's last article, which also reflects Schnitzler's ideas on absolutism and elitism, spurs Styx on in his determination to take Fliederbusch's job at *Die Gegenwart*. Styx's intention is to expose the evils of government and society, just as Schnitzler does in "Und einmal" and in "Materialien zu einer Studie über Kunst und Kritik," a collection of aphorisms and essays containing a scathing critique of journalists, "Literaten," and critics.[112]

Although Fliederbusch is able to recognize that people can be classified by personality types, he is able to see only the categories, not the individuals who might fit into them. Styx on the other hand, using words that one could easily attribute to Schnitzler himself, fills in the gaps that methodology alone cannot fill: namely a knowledge and understanding of psychology. Here he speaks of Fliederbusch's short-comings: "Ich—ohne mich an journalistischen Talent mit dem Verfasser messen zu wollen—ich habe jedenfalls eins vor ihm voraus: Ich kenne die Leute, mit denen es ihn gelüstet anzubinden. Ich habe unter ihnen gelebt, ich habe zu ihnen gehört, ich bin—gewissermaßen—als einer von ihnen geboren—".[113]

Because of his father's social prominence, Schnitzler, like Styx, was exposed to the Viennese aristocracy from childhood on. The similarity between Styx and Schnitzler is even more apparent when Styx says that he and *Die Gegenwart* (here, the "present" quite literally) need one another. Styx wants to place his material that is "bursting the cupboards at home" at the disposal of *Die Gegenwart*, just as Schnitzler perhaps secretly desires to make public his collections of essays condemning war, politicians, and journalists. Indeed, in the same way that Styx plays down his journalistic abilities, Schnitzler more than once ironically cites modesty for not speaking out publicly on the war when he is requested to do so. Styx's "Kulturgeschichte" and "Weltgeschichte" would not be appropriate for the conservative *Elegante Welt*, but the liberal *Gegenwart*, he feels, would know how to make use of it. Styx says that he will publish stories, the brutal honesty of which will "make people's hair stand on end." But, like Schnitzler, who during his lifetime never published his essays against war, Styx never prints his revelations of social evils.

Schnitzler declined to involve himself in a direct way publicly with the same question of political opposites addressed in *Fink*. His diary entry of 13 June 1916 reports a visit from Hermann Sudermann, a representative of the Deutscher Kulturbund. Sudermann wants Schnitzler to contribute to a series of lectures to strengthen national consciousness and attempt "in Österreich Versöhnung der nat.[ionalen] Gegensätze etc....ich erwiderte mäßig, mit Sympathie für die Sache, meine geringe Solidaritätsempfindungen und mein mangelndes Propagandatalent betonend."[114] Given the effective way in which Schnitzler satirizes political propaganda in *Fink*, there can be no doubt that lack of talent for such matters was not the cause of his reluctance to contribute to the war propaganda effort. If *Die Gegenwart* is analogous to the liberal *Neue Freie Presse*,[115] it is also conceivable that the *Elegante Welt* (apart from possibly representing a conservative Viennese paper) was inspired by the swing to conservatism in 1914 of S. Fischer's previously liberal journal, *Neue Rundschau*. In the first months of the War, the *Neue Rundschau* published such patriotic feuilletons as Thomas Mann's "Gedanken im Kriege." Schnitzler had been on poor terms with Samuel Fischer since September 1914 when Fischer wrote to Schnitzler criticizing Austria for its shortcomings in supporting Germany and the war effort: "Es ist schade, daß sich die Österreicher, wie es scheint, auch jetzt nicht auf der Höhe der Situation zeigen. Mir wird erzählt, daß Ihr Aushebungssystem nicht so funktioniert, daß alle wehrfähigen Männer auch wirklich mittun, und auch mit der Ausrüstung scheint es bei Ihnen zu hapern. Und verlassen sich nicht die Österreicher ein bißchen zu sehr auf die Deutschen? Hier ist alles sehr zuversichtlich, aber es tut auch wirklich jeder seine Pflicht."[116] Schnitzler's diary entry of 30 September 1914 shows the profound effect Fischer's letter has on him. Schnitzler becomes rather defensive about his silence on the War when his wife criticizes him for not engaging in literary activities appropriate to the times: "Nm. les ich O. [Olga] meinen Brief an Fischer vor... es entwickelt sich eine Discussion, in der sie mir was sie meine "reservirte kühle Haltung" nennt, eine unzeitgemäße Selbstbewahrung u. dergl. vorwirft;—ins concrete übersetzt—daß ich nicht essayistisch auftrete oder sonst irgend eine dem Augenblick gemäße Thätigkeit suche.— Sie tadelt meine Verclausulirungen und Einschränkungen im Brief an Fischer u.s.w."[117] Schnitzler also discusses Fischer's letter with Hugo von Hofmannsthal who visits him that afternoon; Hofmannsthal agrees that Schnitzler's reply is the best that he could send under the circumstances.[118]

Schnitzler even cites Fischer's letter as a possible cause for a dream he has two months later, in which he angrily asks a woman selling wigs, why Austria and the Austrian army are being scorned by Germany at this crucial time in history.[119] While he condemned the political manipulation of the term "Vaterland"—which he equated to the state—Schnitzler professed his own "Heimatsliebe"—a love for the Austrian land and culture. An early example of this bond can be found in *Der Weg ins Freie* (1908) when Heinrich says: "Vaterland... das war überhaupt eine Fiktion, ein Begriff der Politik,

schwebend, veränderlich, nicht zu fassen. Etwas Reales bedeutete
nur die Heimat, nicht das Vaterland...und so war Heimatsgefühl auch
Heimatsrecht."[120] In early aphorisms entitled "Bekenntnis" and
"Vaterland" (both dated 1904) Schnitzler elaborates on his love for
Austria and rejects the terms "Patriotismus" and "Vaterland":

> Ich liebe mein Vaterland nicht, weil es mein Vaterland ist, son-
> dern weil ich es schön finde. Ich habe Heimatgefühl, aber
> keinen Patriotismus...Ich liebe dieses Land, dessen Wälder und
> Auen mir vertraut sind. Die Sprache lieb' ich, die mein Vater
> sprach. Ist dies Tugend? Doch wie kann ich einen staatlichen
> Komplex lieben, der sich allmählich bildete, durch
> Eroberungslust, durch Heirat der Ahnen meinen Herren; wie
> kann ich diesen Herren lieben, von dem ich nichts weiß, als daß
> er mein Herr ist, nicht mein Leben und Gut zu schützen, son-
> dern neues Land zu erwerben für seine Söhne mit meinem
> Blut.— Nein! nennt ihr das Vaterland, so lieb' ich's nicht und
> keiner liebt's.[121]

In its complexity *Fink* lends itself to numerous interpretations
(such as a critique of the monarchy and aristocracy, and the conflict
of liberalism and conservatism), but the analogy of the duel to war is
especially appealing, given that the work was written mainly during
the First World War and given the similarities established earlier
between the two forms of battle. On 24 September 1914 Schnitzler
records in his diary a dream in which images of the War interweave
with thoughts of his works:

> Träume: ..., stehe dann an einem Restauranttisch wo Franz
> Ferdinand mit Gemahlin und noch zwei Leute (diese 3 ganz
> schattenhaft)—rede mit ihm, er sich nach mir umwendend;
> über politisches—etwa, was mit Bessarabien zu thun;...ich
> erzähle (lese vor) Stoff an O.,—sehr gute insbesondre
> einen—O. sagt ... das ist wie jetzt beim rothen Kreuz.
> Ich:—"Du weißt ja—ich schreibe immer die Dinge vorher, die
> später geschehen.—" (...) O. sagt, ich erzähle von all den
> Stoffen, weil ich mich an den zweiten Theil Medardus nicht
> wage, was ich zugebe.—[122]

On 1 June 1914, twenty-seven days before the assassination at Sarajevo, Schnitzler dreams that he is encouraged by a group of Jesuits to murder Franz Ferdinand; Schnitzler declines, "wortlos."

5.6 Politics and Schnitzler's "Schweigen"

When Karl Kraus praised Schnitzler in 1918 for having remained silent on the War,[123] he was certainly recalling a challenge he had made in his earlier essay on the "Große Zeit" in *Die Fackel*, 5 December 1914: "Wer etwas zu sagen hat, trete vor und schweige!"[124]

On several occasions before, during, and after the War Schnitzler published his opinions on a political matter, or considered doing so. Once he wanted to address the Emperor personally. The first case occurred in 1907 when the newspaper *Morgen* published the responses of numerous prominent figures to a questionnaire on the personal integrity of the controversial publisher of the political weekly *Die Zukunft*, Maximilian Harden.[125]

In his first letter to the *Morgen* Schnitzler states his reluctance to publicize his opinions, but he stresses that given the situation, his silence might be misinterpreted by those who do not wish him well: "Und nur die Erwägung, daß innerhalb unserer, durch Mißtrauen, Übelwollen und Unterschieben persönlicher Motive vergifteten Atmosphäre, mein Schweigen falsch gedeutet werden könnte, veranlaßt mich hier auszusprechen, daß ich an der Ehrenhaftigkeit Hardens so wenig je gezweifelt habe, wie an der Stärke seiner Begabung. Wenn ich mich auch mit seinen Ansichten nach Inhalt und Ton nicht selten in Widerspruch gefühlt habe."[126] The editor censored Schnitzler's letter and stressed his final sentence, making it appear that Schnitzler had serious differences of opinion with Harden. Furious at the misportrayal of his views, Schnitzler wrote to the editor of *Morgen*, condemning his censorship.

This case represents not only a public statement on a political issue by Schnitzler, but more importantly it demonstrates his desire to speak out when he fears that his silence might be misinterpreted, and his realization that by exposing his views to the public through the media, he is exposing himself to misrepresentation by the press. In this way a situation develops over which he has no control. This incident must have made Schnitzler more reluctant than ever to speak out openly on political issues. On 9 January 1917 Schnitzler visits his pacifist friend, Josef Popper-Lynkeus and to the two discuss issuing a statement to the peoples of the enemy nations, to disclaim any sense of animosity and attempt to promote peace: "Vm. bei Popper. Erzählte ihm unsre Schweizer Erfahrungen zu Beginn des Kriegs;—über die augenblickl. Situation; ich sprach von meiner Idee einer Proclamation an die feindlichen Völker; er hatte die selbe gehabt.—"127

In July 1918 an incident occurred that illustrates Schnitzler's readiness to respond to anti-Semitism. He received a letter from Arthur Kaufmann which almost resulted in a letter of protest to Emperor Karl. In his letter Kaufmann tells of a sermon given by a Jesuit minister named Abel, calling for the "Ausrottung" of Jews, the only group that he claimed had not done its duty during the War. Schnitzler's response is immediate. He phones his friend Leo Van-Jung, and they discuss what can be done: "Ich telef. mit Leo, was zu unternehmen;—bin für eine quickliche Klage der jüd. österr. Offiziere gegen Abel; und Zeugenvorladung des Kaisers, des Kriegsministers u.s.w.—...—Dr. Feuchtwang besucht mich; wir besprechen, was in betreff der infamen Hetzreden des Pater Abel und andrer Pfaffen zu thun. Gedanke, einen Brief an den Kaiser zu richten. Schwierigkeiten, wie wir die Auswahl der Unterzeichner bedenken. Laxheit und Renegatentum der Juden."128 Eight days later Schnitzler mentions a plan to bring the Abel affair directly to the Kaiser through acquaintances. After discussing the matter with several friends, Schnitzler apparently decides against writing to the Emperor. His last mention of the Abel affair is on 28 July 1918, when he is shocked by Felix Salten's aloofness to the whole problem of anti-Semitism: "... Nun ja—Pogrom, meint er [Salten];—damit fängt es eben an, dann die Revolution...—War es nicht immer so? Man könne, solle nicht einmal was dagegen unternehmen."129

Barely three months later Schnitzler reports in his diary of rumors of an expected "Pogrom" in the second district of Vienna. With the approaching fall of the monarchy, the end of the war, and the rising tide of anti-Semitism, Schnitzler attempts to define his own position in post-War Austrian society: "Ich setze meine Ansichten auseinander—als österr. Staatsbürger jüdischer Race zur deutschen Kultur mich bekennend."130 When the collapse of the Dual Monarchy finally does come on 10 November 1918 Schnitzler sees no cause for celebration. For him, the form of government is not the decisive factor in real demonstrable change. He notes that it is the very same people who at the beginning of the War supported the Kaiser who are now supporting the Republic. On Armistice Day, 11 November 1918, Schnitzler is overwhelmed by the abdication within three days of the German and Austro-Hungarian monarchs, but also by what he calls the "furchtbar-unsinnigen" cease-fire conditions imposed on Germany by the allies. On 9 February 1919 Schnitzler is approached by Walter Johannes Stein and Ludwig Graf Polzer with a request that he sign an "Aufruf an das 'Deutsche Volk und die Kulturvölker,' für Wilson bestimmt."[131] Schnitzler writes in his diary that because in the introduction of the document "in der für die Kriegskatastrophe nur Deutschlands Mentalität verantwortlich gemacht wird (Verfasser der Theosoph Rudolf Steiner) werde ich nicht unterzeichnen.[!]"[132]

Four months later, on 3 June 1919, Schnitzler once again reels at the conditions of the peace treaty imposed on Germany and Austria. Here he condemns the Allies' talk of "justice" and "peace between peoples" as horrendous "lies":

> Die Friedensbedingungen der Entente für uns.—Worte sind nichtig.— Nicht was hier geschieht, empfind ich als das ungeheuerliche—Triumphe sind dazu da[,] um ausgekostet zu werden. Aber die Phrasen von Gerechtigkeit und Völkerfrieden, die das[,] was wir jetzt erleben, eingeleitet haben und noch begleiten—die sind das Neue an der Sache. Grausamkeit, Machtrausch, Schurkerei, Dummheit—das wiederholt sich in allen "großen Epochen der Geschichte," auch Lüge;...aber Lüge, die sich im Augenblick selbst, auch für den Blindesten als Lüge demaskirt—Lüge ohne Zweck, ohne Witz, ohne Sinn, ohne Größe;—die erleben wir zum ersten Mal.[133]

Schnitzler's pessimism was not unfounded, and his opinions as expressed above had numerous precedents in his condemnation of politics and politicians. On 11 January 1919 he wrote that it is scarcely possible to condemn politics enough: "die Bosheit und Leichtfertigkeit—überall—, in allen großen—und in allen kleinen Momenten ist ungeheuerlich."[134] Five days later, in a conversation with Olga, Schnitzler reaffirms his thesis that any plans to improve the world, based on the assumption that an ethical improvement of human beings is possible, is doomed to failure.[135]

Yet Schnitzler for all his pessimism was practical and optimistic enough to cast his ballot in the elections of 16 February 1919 for what he felt was the least objectionable party—the Social Democrats—lest the rightists should come to power:

> Wir gaben unsre Stimme für die sozialdemokr. Kandidaten—so widerlich mir die Arbeiterzeitung, die ganze Partei mit ihrer einerseits zum Antisemitismus, anderseits zum Bolschewismus schielenden Haltung geworden ist. Aber es handelt sich darum so weit von rechts wegzurücken als möglich—und ferner: der sozialdem. Partei eine ansehnliche Minorität zu verschaffen, da sonst Unruhen sehr wahrscheinlich.—...[136]

And so, despite his dislike of politics, Schnitzler participated actively in the process.

Schnitzler felt isolated in post-War Austria. The Allies were imposing harsh conditions on Germany and Austria, and the anti-Semites were threatening to destroy Austria from within. Schnitzler's only form of release was his literary works, which contain evidence that he did not remain silent on the War but rather chose to express himself in the medium he felt was least likely to distort his antiwar message. He had long ago rejected the option of emigrating from his beloved "Heimat," and so he chose instead to withdraw into his works, disguising his critique of contemporary politics so that few if any of his contemporaries could fathom or decode it.

6

Postwar Reflections and a Look into the Future:
1920-1931

6.1 The Myth of "Die versunkene Welt."
Schnitzler's Analysis of the Causes of the First World War

In *Komödie der Verführung* (1923,[1] hereafter referred to as *Verführung*) Schnitzler again writes of the events that lead to a war. Here, however, he goes beyond analogy and deals directly with the causes of the First World War. The historical setting of the play represents more than a mere backdrop to the action. The three acts are specifically dated in the stage directions as occurring on 1 May 1914, a day in mid-June, 1914, and 1 August 1914. Schnitzler's reasons for choosing the first day of the World War for his final act go beyond those yet suggested by critics. Some assert that Schnitzler wanted to portray the Dual-Monarchy's tragic "Tanz in den Abgrund."[2] Others claim that he was reminiscing sentimentally about the end of a great era.

It is puzzling that anyone familiar with Schnitzler's works could regard the historical settings in such a literal manner so as to ignore their potential contemporary relevance. Schnitzler's opposition to war is all the more poignant because his historical works demonstrate the folly of the First World War through their illustration of the common motivation for all wars, whether in 1520 or 1914.

C. E. Williams in 1974 and Renate Wagner in 1981 echo the old and still widely accepted notion[3] that Schnitzler's works are outdated after the First World War, and that he was an apolitical writer.

Williams argues that Schnitzler's later works (with the exception of *Verführung* did not contain any valuable comment on contemporary history: "In December 1914 Schnitzler anticipated that his work would echo the experience of the war years. Such a task appears to have been beyond his creative compass."[4] Renate Wagner, while noting the frequency of war in Schnitzler's works, does not offer any detailed analysis. She concludes her paragraph on the subject with the not entirely satisfactory explanation of why Schnitzler failed to write about the First World War: "Obwohl...er den Weltkrieg in die einbringt, will Schnitzler doch den Krieg an sich nicht in einem Kunstwerk verewigen."[5] Although Schnitzler tried to free himself from the labels applied to his post-War works, critics like Wagner and Williams still maintain that Schnitzler was preoccupied with the past and was no longer able to analyze the events of the present, let alone anticipate the future. Only Brigitte Schneider-Halvorson realizes the significance of war in *Verführung* both and *Der Gang zum Weiher*: "Foremost in Schnitzler's mind rank the ideas of war and peace because he wrote both dramas under the influence either of war or of its devastating consequences for Germany and Austria."[6]

Schnitzler chose to end his play on 1 August 1914 because the war was the consequence of the story he wanted to tell. Most pacifist novels describe the horrors of war, yet they deal primarily with the effects, not the causes. Perhaps Schnitzler felt the strongest pacifist work, one that might help educate society about war, would be one that exposes war's underlying causes. *Verführung* represents the conversion to a realistic drama of Schnitzler's theoretical arguments in "Und einmal."

As in *Fink*, many of the figures in are modeled on real individuals. Yet as examples of the personality types outlined in "Und einmal" and the later work *Der Geist im Wort und der Geist in der Tat*,[7] they are perhaps the most representative characters in any of Schnitzler's works. Schnitzler is not content to present the stylized character-types too often the standard in books intended solely to proselytize. Even in *Der Ruf* and *Medardus* political action is prompted by personal motives only indirectly related to the political issues. For example, Schnitzler describes how political action results from the love-triangle between Julia, Braunigl, and Westerhaus. The conflict between the two men results in the misuse of their professions (attorney-general and bank president) as weapons. The indirect and unexpected side-effect is war. Just as in *Der Gang*, the erotic and the political themes in *Verführung* are inextricably interwoven.

Verführung, originally titled "Der Verführer," went through numerous changes, even complete rewrites during the First World War, before it became *Komödie der Verführung*.[8] It is clear that Schnitzler gave the choice of a title much thought, changing it several times over the span of twenty years. The original title, "Verführer," implies erotic seduction by a single seducer, in all likelihood Max von Reisenberg. But in the final version the broad term, seduction ("Verführung"), conjures up a nihilistic comedy, not only a portrayal of "die Wiener Vorkriegsgesellschaft in den letzten Phasen ihres Unterganges"[9] but further, the seduction of the masses in all those countries involved in the War, by their governments, greedy bankers and profiteers, careless diplomats, uncaring monarchs, and by their (the masses') own lack of imagination.[10]

Schnitzler apparently alludes to the willing seduction of the European populace by their own governments. The term "Verführung" becomes ironic and the word "Komödie" appears in a bitter-sarcastic light. As the world in *Verführung* slips rapidly toward disaster, some of Schnitzler's characters (like the peoples of Europe) blithely continue their private frivolities. Others heartlessly plan ahead for the War in the hopes of reaping personal profit, while still others attempt to escape. The suicide of Falkenir and Aurelie might be seen as the ultimate recognition of and voluntary submission to the immutability of human nature.

Schnitzler's much cited letter to Jakob Wassermann (11 November 1924) contains an important key to one interpretation of *Verführung* :

> Sind etwa die Typen, um nicht zu sagen die Individuen, vom Erdboden verschwunden, die ich geschildert habe [in *Verführung*] und wie ich hoffe noch einige Zeit hindurch zu schildern mir erlauben werde? Gibt es heute keine Aurelie, keine Judith, keine Seraphine, keinen Ambros Döhl, keinen Falkenir, keinen Eligius Fenz mehr? Der Rittmeister Skodny hat vielleicht seine Uniform in den Kasten gehängt oder verkauft, aber schon der Prinz Arduin existiert nach wie vor, wenn er sich auch vielleicht für eine Weile etwas zurückgezogen in einem seiner Schlösser aufhält.[11]

Even if the world he describes were "abgetan," as Wassermann suggests, Schnitzler maintains it would be no less a subject for an author to write about. If a writer wishes to portray people and events from 1789 or 1520, especially as they might relate to the people and events of the early twentieth century, he asks, should this be held against him? In defending his approach, Schnitzler once again reveals his technique of drawing parallels between contemporary and past events and people. It is not the role of a writer to determine if a world has vanished, Schnitzler says, but rather to preserve the present, conjure up the forgotten past, and on the question of the future he leaves the author's options open: "... aber ich will nicht um des Rhythmus willen eine Beiläufigkeit sagen." Schnitzler implies that the writer who comprehends the past and the present is able to do more than merely speculate about the future.[12]

Not insignificantly, the first act is set at a fancy-dress ball in the gardens of Prince Arduin's estate on 1 May 1914. Despite the obvious signs that a war is looming, everyone seems to be oblivious to the dangers. The Princess von Degenbach, like her counterpart in *Fink*, chooses to remain ignorant of contemporary politics: "Nur mit der Politik will ich nichts zu tun haben."[13] Here Schnitzler attacks members of the aristocracy who ignore the affairs of state over which they ostensibly have control.

The difference between this critique of war and those in Schnitzler's pre-1914 works lies in the more emphatic expression of his pacifism after the First World War. He is now more aware of the specific causes of war, which he criticizes in the context of this sociopolitical "comedy." In an aphorism Schnitzler determines that money is the most crucial factor in starting a war. Indeed, he believes money constitutes the basis for militarism itself.[14] Accordingly, in *Verführung* a conversation between Braunigl (the state attorney-general), Westerhaus (the profiteering banker and Braunigl's rival for Julia), and Skodny (the cavalry captain) reveals the importance of money for each in his own profession. Unfortunately money brings out the worst traits in the first two men whose status permits them to utilize it as a weapon against others. Only the soldier refuses to worship money, but he fails to see its harmful potential. Braunigl and Westerhaus both know that money can buy them power and the objects of their erotic desires.[15]

In another aphorism Schnitzler describes three areas of human endeavor that permit self-serving individuals who engage in them to damage rather than help society.[16] The three areas, namely politics, journalism, and financial speculation, are represented in *Verführung* by the characters Arduin, Ambros, and Westerhaus, respectively. The damage they cause leads indirectly to the First World War. Since Schnitzler's critique of irresponsible journalism has been discussed in the section on *Fink*, my analysis of *Verführung* will focus primarily on Westerhaus and Arduin.

Although he betrays his ignorance of politics, Prince Arduin nevertheless knows whom to ask if a war is impending. He turns to the bank president Westerhaus. Schnitzler's critique acquires an international dimension when Arduin in a conversation with Westerhaus blames him and big business in all industrialized nations for war: "Wenn es Ihnen so beliebt und Ihren Herren-Berufskollegen in Frankreich, England, Amerika, Japan, dann werden wir eben Krieg haben."[17]

After the two Balkan wars, it had become public knowledge that monetary speculation on wars could lead to big profits (or losses) in the stock market. The banker, Westerhaus, is obviously based on the father of Schnitzler's close friend Stephi Bachrach. Julius Bachrach, banker and stock market dilettante, literally lost millions in the speculation that Austria would involve itself in the first Balkan war. Austria did not, and on 24 November 1912 Bachrach committed suicide, leaving his family in poverty and debt. In June 1914 there were many more like Bachrach, and not just in Vienna. By this time, however, the public had grown callous to the threat of war and regarded such talk as mere stock market tactics. Schnitzler nevertheless was not content merely to transfer Bachrach's death to *Verführung* without historical context. He therefore sought an actual event in June 1914 with which to combine the Balkan war and the demise of Bachrach.[18] Schneider-Halvorson supplies the missing critical link when she writes of the historical significance of Schnitzler's choice of mid-June 1914 for his second act in *Verführung* :

> The telephone in Westerhaus' office rings almost constantly, as he receives reports of the newest political developments. One such development, known under the cover word "Kameltreiber," refers to the Berlin-Baghdad-Railway project between Germany

and Turkey. England had a key interest in this issue because of her shipping activities on the Euphrates river. On June 15, 1914, the exact day on which Act II takes place in this drama, an Anglo-German agreement was initiated, which "settled the Baghdad-Railway problem, the Germans promising not to construct the line south of Basra and recognizing England's preponderant interest in the shipping on the Euphrates. The agreement reflected a real desire on both sides to remove many outstanding colonial difficulties." It caused Westerhaus' financial ruin, for his speculations were based on the outbreak of war.[19]

In citing an event in mid-June 1914 that almost brought about a war between England and Germany, Schnitzler is perhaps reminding his audience that political tensions were at the breaking point even before the assassination of Franz Ferdinand at the end of that same month, but that reconciliation is often possible through competent diplomacy.

The audience viewing *Verführung* in 1924 was naturally afforded an historical perspective on the work. The theatergoers had lived through the War and the period leading up to it. Their knowledge of the disastrous outcome of the political events during the summer of 1914, not shared by the characters in the work, gives added significance to details that to the modern reader may appear trivial. This is especially evident, for example, when Braunigl professes the belief popular in Austria in August 1914, that "Ein Krieg (...) zweifellos reinigend wirken würde, nicht nur in politischer Hinsicht, auch ethisch und moralisch..."[20] By 1924 the failure of the new Republic had shattered any illusions about a political rebirth after the War. Anyone who had lived through the War, hearing Braunigl's words in 1924, would have to consider them tragically naive. Schnitzler discovered that the most powerful pacifist statement after the War would simply be to show people as they had been a mere ten years before.

When the character Elisabeth dismisses the rumors of war as mere "Börsenmanöver," Schnitzler indicts stockmarket speculators and big business for contributing to the War. Just as Bachrach had done in real life, Schnitzler's Westerhaus speculates on the outbreak of war, and, losing his money, commits suicide. The difference between the fictional and the real characters lies in the complex personal relationships that also figure in Westerhaus' demise (he is tricked and falsely imprisoned). In a conversation between Westerhaus and Judith, several facts emerge bearing on capitalism as a cause of war. Westerhaus is the epitome of the egotistical banker, only too ready to admit that he has no fear of the impending war because he has no son who might be called up to fight. He prides himself on his ability to anticipate future events and feels that it is his right to profit from this "gift." In his shortsightedness, which prevents him from seeing that big business determines to a large extent the direction of international politics, he denies any responsibility for the War: "Und nicht ich bin es, der die Politik—oder gar die Weltgeschichte macht, wie manche Leute glauben."[21]

Westerhaus admits that he gambles on war, not as much for profit, as for the thrill of risking everything. He is the classic example of Schnitzler's character-type [in *Der Geist im Wort und der Geist in der Tat* (1927)], the adventurer—one who desires excitement or danger and engages in activities that can bring disaster to many. Judith correctly defines one of his motives as erotic (though she is incorrect in discounting the factors of greed, an absence of morality, and a naive desire for adventure) when she asserts that Westerhaus's self-destructive behavior is the result of his unrequited love for Julia: "Und dir liegt an Unschuldigen so wenig wie an Schuldigen. Auch nicht an deinem Gewinn—und nicht an der Gefahr;—der Sinn deines Lebens heißt Julia."[22]

Prince Arduin, another character important to the war theme, plays at least four roles in the drama, each connected to the impending war. First, he is a general in the Austro-Hungarian hussars, his rank befitting his high social standing. As we have already seen, however, he is ignorant of military affairs. The token nature of his military rank is symbolized in the stage directions in Act I when his general's uniform is barely visible beneath a black fancy-dress costume.[23]

Second, Arduin is the epitome of Schnitzler's cosmopolitan of the future. Since the demise of the "Großherzogtum von Perosa" (symbolic of both the demise of the Austrian Empire and the utopian elimination of all international boundaries), he can no longer afford himself the "luxury" of a patriotism confined to any single country. Arduin is truly a citizen of all Europe. As the direct descendant of some of the important bloodlines of Italy, Austria, England, Russia, his allegiance cannot be limited to any single nation. When war finally breaks out on August 1, 1914, Arduin will not forego his planned boat trip from the Danish port of Gilleleije (the fairy-tale-like setting of Act III). In words which might also be interpreted as referring to the demise of the Monarchy and the aristocracy, Arduin implies that the world is not yet ready for eternal peace: "Dieser Krieg bricht nicht nur gegen meine Voraussicht, sondern gegen alle menschliche Vernunft aus. Ich tue da nicht mit, weder auf der einen noch auf der anderen Seite. Daß man meinen Entschluß als Mangel an Courage auffassen könnte, habe ich nicht zu befürchten. Aber—das ist gewiß, in dieser Nachwelt habe ich nichts mehr zu suchen."[24] The patriotic writer Ambros and the adventurer Max von Reisenberg react differently to the news of the War. While their primary motives are different, both of them will eventually enlist in the Austrian army because of a romantic disappointment.

In yet another capacity, Arduin plays the role of diplomat when the Austrian government recognizes his international familial ties, and hopes to utilize them to its advantage. Unfortunately, the governments of Europe cannot match the Prince's cosmopolitanism, and his missions fail. The declining role of the Monarchy in political decision-making adds to the farcical impression of the secret diplomatic missions. An irony lies in the fact that familial connections between the monarchs of Germany and England actually led to the War rather than prevented it. Arduin's fourth role is an anxious suitor whose amorous preoccupation with Aurelie[25] leaves little psychic energy for his peace mission. In a conversation with Aurelie, Arduin's obsession with the romantic/erotic is evident in his refusal to even hear her questions about his diplomatic missions. He responds only with jealous inquiries about her relationship with the artist, Gysar. Aurelie, rejecting Arduin's romantic overtures, condemns him for his false sense of honor and knightly bravado when, in a fit of jealousy he speaks of killing his rival, Falkenir: "Was du nicht sagst! Und wenn das Begräbnis stattfindet, sprengst du wohl mit dem Pferd über den Sarg.— Ich denke, du könntest die Torheiten sein lassen. Es ist nicht mehr Zeit dazu."[26]

Schnitzler demonstrably achieves a heightened sense of realism in *Verführung* through his allusions to the Baltic wars and the First World War. The Prince's fairy-tale yacht ("Märchenyacht") is a curious anomaly of this realism however, a point deserving special mention here. I believe that the yacht symbolizes the dream of lasting peace. For Arduin it is the only escape from a world not yet ready for cosmopolitanism and peace. On board his fairy-tale yacht, Arduin is released from the confines of the second decade of the twentieth century. Time is suspended; the distinctions between past, present and future cease to exist. This represents the opposite state of Schnitzler's concept of "Phantasielosigkeit." Perhaps someday eternal peace might be achieved, but for Schnitzler in 1924, such a day could only be envisioned in terms of a mythical, dreamlike yacht, sailing off into the unknown, leaving a seething, self-destructive world behind it. Gilda, the young Danish girl wistfully bids farewell to Arduin's yacht—and to peace: "Nun ist es ganz verschwunden—das Zauberschiff. Nun sieht man gar nichts mehr davon."[27]

To achieve a lasting peace, Schnitzler believed the order of political institutions needed to be drastically altered. Because such changes did not occur in the decade following the First World War, Schnitzler was justifiably pessimistic about the immediate future. Yet as is reflected in his essay on Romain Rolland (see appendix 4), he had no idea as to the magnitude of the "next war," which he nevertheless predicted would take place. *Verführung* represents a transition from the theoretical essays against war to the practical realm of a drama that criticizes the psychological, social, and political causes of the First World War. Although his plan for an organization resembling the United Nations, (*AuB*, 209-210) never became the subject of a literary work, most other features of his essays and aphorisms against war, "Und einmal," found expression in his late dramatic and narrative works and fragments.

6.2 A Return to the Historical Drama: Diplomacy, Absolutism, and "Phantasielosigkeit"

In his later work *Der Gang zum Weiher* Schnitzler returned to the historical drama. Drawing parallels between 1750 and 1914, he portrayed history as a cyclical phenomenon. Schnitzler's diaries offer documentation for the theory that he criticized contemporary political figures and events by veiling them in the cloak of history. His diary also supports the view that the human psyche is basically unchanging. On 5 February 1916 Schnitzler writes that the duke in his short story, *Die Frau des Richters* (1924), will represent the late Archduke Franz Ferdinand transposed to the eighteenth century: "—Vm dictirt ich Verf.

[*Komödie der Verführung*] Skizze 2. A. zu Ende. Dann andres; u.a. kurzes Scen. einer Komödie, wo es mir passirte, daß die ursprünglich moderne Figur (etwa der Erzherzog F.F.) —allmälig [sic], mit Handlung und Sprache sich gegen 1750 hin stilisirte."[28]   Indicating that he is employing the same technique as in other post-War works, Schnitzler adds: "Charakteristisch für meine ganze Production jetzt.—"[29]

Europeans continued to be deluded by their governments and press even eight years after World War One. Perhaps because of people's inability to view the underlying causes objectively, Schnitzler chose to write about an earlier fictional war as a parallel. This becomes all the more likely when one reflects that Schnitzler believed the underlying causes of all wars to be the same.[30]

Although *Der Gang zum Weiher* (hereafter referred to as *Der Gang*) was completed in first version form in 1921 and not published until 1926, much of the play was written during the First World War. This, combined with the fact that the action of the drama (set in 1750) plays against a background of impending war—indeed leads up to the war—invites a comparison between the two wars, the fictional one and the real one. Schnitzler chose to write about a fictional war; it is likely that he was using the pseudo historical setting of *Der Gang* as an analogy for his own time. In his diary on 24 May 1915 Schnitzler writes of thoughts he had had during a walk: "... —plötzlich Einfälle zum Weiher, —mit Beziehung auf den Krieg— ..."[31]

Critics from Josef Körner (1927) to Brigitte Schneider-Halvorson (1983) have pondered the thematic complexity of *Der Gang*, yet none has been able to find a unifying thread for the numerous plots. When Körner criticized the apparent lack of unity, Schnitzler responded:

> Ihr Verhältnis zum "Gang zum Weiher" ist mir ganz unbegreiflich; unbegreiflich vor allem, daß Sie die tiefwurzelnde Beziehung zwischen dem erotischen und dem politischen Teil des Dramas nicht gelten lassen. Niemals ist ein Einfall in mir mit solch zwingender Einheitlichkeit aufgetaucht, vom ersten Augenblick an (die Grundidee stammt aus dem Jahr 1907) waren die erotischen Vorgänge in diese politische Atmosphäre gestellt, das Verhältnis des Dichters zum Krieger, des Kriegers zum Politiker, der Leonilda einerseits zum Dichter, andererseits zum

> Soldaten war mir von Anbeginn an das Wesentliche, unter einem anderen Himmel als dem, den ich über sie gespannt habe, konnten die seelischen Vorgänge, auf die es mir ankam, sich überhaupt nicht entwickeln;...—die Notwendigkeit der Verknüpfungen und die Verknüpfung der Notwendigkeiten hätten Ihnen aufgehen müssen.[32]

Körner virtually ignores the political theme of *Der Gang* and accuses Schnitzler of contributing nothing new to the question of war and peace: "Nicht [sic] was über Krieg und Frieden geredet wird, verdient näheres Eingehen; dies ist zwar von achtungswürdigster Gesinnung, jedoch von recht dürftiger Gemeinplätzigkeit."[33] In his defense Schnitzler argues that there is nothing new to be said on the subject of pacifism. He implies, however, that it is nevertheless useful to reiterate the value of peace, using a dramatic work as his forum for the pacifist views expressed in "Und einmal":

> Wenn Sie finden, daß ich über den Pazifismus als solchen nichts Neues sage, so haben Sie gewiß recht, aber als Vorwurf (wie es von Ihnen doch gemeint ist) werde ich das erst empfinden, wenn Sie mir einen Menschen nennen, der seit einigen hundert Jahren über den Pazifismus überhaupt etwas Neues gesagt hat. Und selbst wenn man die Stellen über Krieg und Frieden, wenn man die Bedeutung der Szene zwischen dem Kanzler und dem Sohn des Marschalls nicht nach Gebühr einzuschätzen weiß, so erscheint es mir doch wenig angemessen einer Mißbilligung oder einen Mangel an Einverständnis durch geradezu herabsetzende Beziehungen, wie z. B. die von einer "recht dürftigen Gemeinpläztigkeit" Ausdruck zu geben.[34]

Speaking in broad terms, Harold Dickerson attempts to show that the mystical pond is "the one symbol in the drama that gives coherence to its disparate and seemingly unrelated parts,"[35] yet he fails to account for the theme of war and peace. According to Dickerson, Schnitzler "attempted to exploit the possibilities of water symbolism to establish a bond between the insensate but life-giving forces of nature and the human experience of love, death and fate."[36]

Brigitte Schneider-Halvorson is the first critic to emphasize the relative importance of the war and peace theme in the play: "In addition to the war issue pushed by Konrad and his father, the remaining part of the play deals with peace efforts on the part of the Chancellor, as well as with the problem of friendship between himself and the emperor."[37]

War looms like a dark cloud over the action in this play. Interconnecting themes form a chain of causality that leads to war, yet each character employs some measure of free will in contributing to or resisting the next link in the chain. For example, the Chancellor is dismayed and temporarily forgets his role as diplomat in the prevention of the impending war when the aging poet Sylvester Thorn asks for his daughter's hand in marriage. This delay is one of the factors contributing to the eventual outbreak of the war.

Ostensibly fearing that the return of the young soldier, Konrad von Ursenbeck, to the border might lead to an unauthorized attack, the Chancellor later orders him to wait at the Mayenau palace until he (the Chancellor) returns from his peace mission to the capital. The Chancellor's real reason is his desire to foster the relationship between Konrad and his daughter, Leonilda, so that the latter will not marry Sylvester Thorn. Because of his involvement with Leonilda, Konrad agrees to the "request." Each knows that it is the personal motive rather than the political one that leads to action. Political motivation, while also significant, is primarily a handy excuse for selfish personal actions.

Leonilda develops over the course of the drama from a childish girl, adoring the image she has maintained for years of the poet, Sylvester Thorn, to a mature, independent woman. Yet despite this development, her naive attitude about war remains unchanged. Leonilda reflects the traditional desire to celebrate the defeat of the enemy when in response to her father's wish for a future "Friedensfest," she adds: "Ein Siegesfest!"[38] Only her aunt, Anselma, is concerned about her loved ones when her brother the Chancellor departs to fight in the war.

Several primary factors that lead to war in *Der Gang* reflect the similarities between that work and "Und einmal." It is certainly no coincidence that these same factors helped bring about the First World War. First, there is a long standing hostility between the people of the two nations (here Austria and Italy, but compare also France and Germany), based on past territorial wars and national rivalry. An inability to overcome the past and make constructive changes is, according to "Und einmal," one of the problems that has to be overcome to prevent future wars.

The question of territorial claims is raised in the dialogue between Konrad and the Chancellor, the Freiherr von Mayenau (Act I). The debate here reveals the senselessness of territorial wars. As Schnitzler indicates in "Und einmal" (*AuB*, 221), ownership can only be substantiated so far back in history. Beyond a certain point all arguments on the subject degenerate into the assertion by both sides that the territory is theirs by "divine right":

> **KONRAD:** (...) Raub sagt Ihr? Raub, Herr Ohm, an einem Land, / Das doch das uns're war vor dreißig Jahren—?
> **FREIHERR:** Vor achtzig ihr's.
> **KONRAD:** Und wessen vor dreihundert? / Vor tausend? / Und wem war's bestimmt von Gott?
> **FREIHERR:** So bist du rasch am Ende aller Fragen.[39]

"Divine right," Schnitzler says, was an attempt to apply a facade of ethics to the eternal rule of "might makes right." By remembering that the land had once been Austrian (perhaps Schnitzler alludes in *Der Gang* to the Südtirol region, but one is also reminded of the struggle between Germany and France for Alsace-Lorraine), the people recall that it had previously been taken away by Italy. Thus the old enmities are perpetuated and the next war is ensured.

Schnitzler's condemnation of the the dogma of the necessity of war, explicit in "Und einmal" (*AuB*, 202), is clearly implied in *Der Gang*. In Act I, for example, Leonilda reports that a court courier has brought word to Marschall von Ursenbeck to attack the enemy. When the Chancellor questions her about her source of information, she admits that it is a rumor heard the day before at the royal court. The rumor is shown to be pure invention, based simply on the notion of the inevitability of war. Such rumors and misinformation were similarly widespread during the First World War when the press did its best with propaganda to add to the hatred between the opposing nations.

Schnitzler also criticizes the excessive political power wielded by high-ranking military officers (as in Germany and Austria-Hungary just before the First World War).[40] The military leaders including the Marschall are power-mad and eager for a conflict whereby they can wrest control of the country from the indecisive monarch. This internal conflict invites attack from neighboring states aware of the weakened government.

It appears that Schnitzler found a basis in the Balkan Wars of 1912 and 1913 for the fictional events and characters in *Der Gang*. The conflict between the bellicose Marschall von Ursenbeck (and his son Konrad!) and the ineffective diplomat, Chancellor Graf von Mayenau parallels the conflict between Austrian Chief of General Staff, Baron Franz Conrad von Hötzendorf and Minister of Foreign Affairs, Graf Leopold von Berchtold, over the possible intervention of Austria-Hungary in the Scutari Crisis (Turkey against Montenegro) of April-May, 1913. Ernst C. Helmreich writes of the characteristic reactions of both men to the peaceful resolution of the crisis in which Conrad had advocated an Austro-Hungarian attack on Montenegro and Serbia: "The crisis was broken, and the bourse took an upward turn. In Vienna Berchtold breathed a sigh of relief, and rejoiced that events had taken a peaceful turn. Conrad was not so happy. He regarded it as another lost opportunity for assuring the future of the monarchy."[41]

Although the term "militarism" did not gain broad currency until the end of the nineteenth century, it could certainly be applied to the politics of the aristocracy in *Der Gang*. Konrad is a naive young patriot (reminiscent of Fritz von Unruh in 1914) whose bellicose attitude is the result of his rigid military upbringing. He is aware that the desire for war stems largely from his craving for danger and adventure (a characteristic Schnitzler describes in "Und einmal"). The Marschall's reasons are even less admirable than Konrad's desire for adventure, for they are based on a learned fallacy rather than on misdirected instincts. The Marschall is driven by the dogma of the necessity of war. The scene between Konrad and the Chancellor raises as well the question of pacifism versus militarism. The polemical dialogue is reminiscent of passages from "Und einmal" and constitutes a statement of Schnitzler's pacifism. The two men discuss such problems as territorial disputes, allegiance to Emperor and nation, authoritarianism, militarism, and the opposition of the innocence of youth and the brutality of war. Schnitzler not only argues for peace but refutes the best arguments of war's proponents.

Like his counterparts in the First World War, Konrad is fully aware that the Emperor issued the order to mobilize. But the behind-the-scenes intrigue of power-seeking generals and politicians totally eludes him. When he is confronted with the fact that their selfish desire for glory could cause the death of thousands of innocent, nameless and fameless soldiers—himself included, Konrad correctly points out that he is a mere pawn in the game of war. He adds that even if the decision to mobilize had been premature or even wrong, in the eyes of the enemy the present delay in action makes a "heroic gesture" appear as a foolish child's game. Konrad is a victim of his society's false sense of honor. Konrad recounts an experience that reveals that the natural bonds between human beings transcend national boundaries. Because of his traditional militarist upbringing, however, he does not see the experience in this light. Rather, he recalls it as "dreamlike" or like "poison" in his veins. The real danger in further delaying the attack lies in the fact that the soldiers' gusto for war, so carefully nurtured by their superiors, is gradually replaced by a sense of camaraderie and humanity that knows no national boundaries. Konrad's monologue (though he himself does not understand the message, nor would he believe it if he did comprehend it), presents a strong case for pacifism:

> Wir lebten nicht— / Wir dämmerten dahin. Der Waffen Blitzen, / Sonst ahnungsvoller Gruß ersehnter Schlacht, / War leeres Spiel des Lichts; ihr Klirren—sonst / Uns köstlichste Musik—sinnloser Lärm. / Und unser Haß, glutroser Brand geboren, / Zu Aschenfunken matten Spotts versprüht, / Bläst vor der Feinde Zelte ihn der Wind. / Von drüben kommt ein derber Spaß zurück. / Beifallsgelächter schallt in unsern Reih'n— / Bei jenen hebt ein helles Singen an— / Die unsern lauschen—summen—trällern mit— / Und endlich tönt—als lägen nicht Todfeinde / Gerüstet bis zur Stirn—: als lägen sich / Verschiedenfarb'ge Söldner eines Heeres, / Gewärtig frohen Kampfspiels, gegenüber—, / Tönt—ein gemeinsam Lied zum Himmel auf.[42]

It is ironic that the reality of common humanity appears to Konrad as a weird dream. The imagery of a virtual musical interlude is also significant inasmuch as music is the "international language"—one that knows no linguistic borders. It exemplifies the brotherhood of all men.

While on watch at the border, Konrad stumbles upon a young

enemy soldier. The mutuality of his feeling of kinship is exemplified in Konrad's inability to recall who was first to greet the other. The conversation was as one between friends or brothers rather than enemies:

> **FREIHERR:** Und was für Dinge sind's, die ihr beredet?
> **KONRAD:** Wie junge Leute tun—von Jagd, von Frauen.—
> **FREIHERR:** (lächelnd) Nicht eben Staatsgeheimnisse.
> **KONRAD:** Von Knabenspielen.[43]

The Chancellor, attempting to show Konrad the insanity of war, emphasizes the fact that the two young men had every reason to be friends. He pointedly adds to Konrad's statement that the two had discussed the games they played as children: "Sie liegen euch nicht allzu weit zurück" (*DdW.* Vol. 8, p. 31). The "game of war" appears all the more grotesque when viewed in contrast to the games of children. Like a school child obediently learning his lessons, Konrad had been educated in militarism. At this juncture, feeling more at ease with the Chancellor, Konrad supplies the details of his conversation with the enemy soldier. They talked, he says, of "Heimat, Eltern—seine Mutter lebt." (*DdW.* Vol. 8, p. 31).

The Chancellor's words here reflect Schnitzler's condemnation of politicians and diplomats who cause wars and do not fight in them themselves.[44]   Instead they treat each other cordially and send their children off to fight the wars they cause: "... So wie ihr beide / Freundnachbarlich euch unterhieltet—wärs / Den Kanzlern, den Gesandten beider Länder / Auch nicht verwehrt."[45]

In *Der Gang* as in "Und einmal" Schnitzler indicts diplomats for failing to prevent war.[46] The retired Chancellor, bored with inactivity, accepts the role of diplomat as much from boredom as from a genuine desire to preserve peace. He is more concerned with the intrigues surrounding his daughter than he is in his political mission. Because he misorders his priorities, war results. It is only by chance that personal affairs do not prevent him from reaching the Marchese before he leaves the city. Even so, their agreement to reconcile their countries' differences comes too late to prevent the war. Significantly, the accord is achieved only because the two men are friends, not because of the ideal of peace. Nevertheless, apart from his desire for action (not unlike Konrad's desire for adventure) and his compromising of truth through political rhetoric, the Chancellor has a seemingly genuine understanding of war. It is clear that diplomats can afford to behave as civil human beings; they are not required to perform actions dependent on the sustenance of hatred, an emotion that is undermined by brotherly love.[47]

The Chancellor does not wish to compromise his stance for peace. Even when Konrad reasons that any further delay in attacking the enemy would result in ever more serious consequences, the Chancellor refuses to support war as an alternative. He diplomatically but decisively sidesteps the call to lead his country into battle:

> FREIHERR: Ich las—und zweif'le nicht, daß klarer noch / Als in dem Brief an mich—in jenem andern, / Den für den Kaiser du im Gürtel trägst, / Des Marschalls Gründe aufgezeichnet steh'n. / Auch wenn sie alle mir unfehlbar schienen— / ich könnte nur ihr mattes Echo sein.[48]

This reluctance to speak up in support of the letter, even if the arguments were irrefutable, makes tempting a similar explanation for Schnitzler's refusal to publish "Und einmal" on the grounds that nothing new has been said on the subject for centuries. Perhaps he felt that his purely theoretical writings (as opposed to his veiled critique of war in his literary works) would only represent a "mattes Echo" of earlier pacifist treatises.

Konrad attacks the Chancellor for being a naively idealistic pacifist. The Chancellor counters by defining his terms of peaceful coexistence between nations. This attitude closely resembles Schnitzler's own pragmatic pacifism as expressed in "Und einmal":

> KONRAD: Und glaubt—nun wäre wirklich, was Ihr Dunst / Der Hölle nennt, für ewig fortgeblasen? / Und Ihr wärt auserwählt, in dieser Welt / Ein Reich der Lieb' und Güte aufzurichten?!—
> FREIHERR: Der Liebe—kaum. Doch der Verträglichkeit, / Darin der Nachbar seinen Nachbar—wenn / Nicht gelten—doch womöglich leben ließe. / Der Güte?—Nein. Doch eins, darin die Bosheit / Nicht wie ein toll geword'ner Kreisel rast. / Zu and'rer Schaden, kaum zu eig'nem Heil. / Und gar für ewig?—Gestern, heut und morgen / Hab' ich als uns gegönnte Frist erkannt. / Und klüger als in Zukunftsfernen sich / Ein Wahnbild hohen

Menschentums zu träumen, / Scheint's mir, auf sicher'm, eng
umzirktem Grund / Der Gegenwart bescheid'nes Haus zu bauen.
/ Viel Arbeit steht bevor.[49]

Like the Chancellor, Schnitzler did not believe in some higher
form of humanity emerging in the future. Human beings he felt, would
remain basically unchanged and the best any individual can do is to
strive within one's personal sphere of influence for peace today and
tomorrow. The Chancellor strays, however, from the path of a dedicated peace-seeker. He displays here the traits of the inept diplomat
criticized in "Und einmal." Indeed at first he assumes the role of
peacemaker only to escape the boredom of retirement, and possibly to
again wield political power.[50]

Because of ill feelings from an earlier difference of opinion, the
Chancellor temporarily withholds his service from the Emperor (and
the pursuit of peace). In a clear parallel to Franz Josef and the Dual
Monarchy he criticizes the Emperor for his inability to rule well
enough to elicit from his subjects a sense of unity of empire and
nation:

LEONILDA: Ist's nicht das gleiche: Reich und Vaterland? /
FREIHERR: Es könnte sein. Es sollte sein. Das ist's, / Woran
sich eines Fürsten Größe kündet: / Wenn sich in seiner
Untertanen Herzen / Von beiden das Gefühl,—in ihren Köpfen/
Von beiden der Begriff zur Einheit bildet. / ...[51]

Furthermore, instead of devoting himself entirely to the pursuit
of peace the Chancellor involves himself in his daughter's love-life.
These delays almost cost him the crucial meeting with the Italian
diplomat. They do cost the peace. Despite the signing of a peace
treaty, news of the agreement reaches the border too late to prevent the
war.

6.3 War and the Later Fragments: "Boxeraufstand," "Abenteurernovelle," and "Der Landsknecht"

Among Schnitzler's unfinished works are three late fragments
involving war. The first of these, "Boxeraufstand," is written from the
perspective of a British army officer, whose task is to help suppress the

Boxer Rebellion of 1900.[52] Schnitzler tersely recounts the political events leading up to the story. The narrator avers: "Doch wir wollen nicht von Politik reden,"[53] but in reality he does just the opposite. The disclaimer actually emphasizes the story's political significance. Through his study of the psychology of a man about to be executed, Schnitzler exemplifies all politically motivated executions.[54]

The soldier/narrator in "Boxeraufstand" is moved to seek a reprieve for one particular Chinese, because he is calmly reading a novel as he awaits his execution. This gesture strikes a chord in the soldier's heart: "Ich fand es ungeheuerlich, daß man diesen Menschen erschießen sollte, am Ende gar ehe er den Roman zu Ende gelesen."[55] Although he detects the fear of death in the eyes of others awaiting execution, the soldier feels nothing for them—only for the one man who shows no fear at all. The common cultural—and cultured—experience of reading a novel causes the soldier to feel kinship with the convicted man whose language he does not speak. The narrator, who believes that the man is destined to die, admires his stoic resignation. The Chinese does not believe in predestination and therefore it cannot be said that he is going to die until the moment of his death. This rejection of the notion of predestination is the very fact that alters what some might have accepted as fate. The soldier feels compelled to seek the man's reprieve, despite an explicit order from the Emperor that no pardons be granted.[56]

The narrator rides to his Colonel in order to plead for the man's life. Although the Colonel believes that the Chinese has employed a clever trick to win over the narrator, he grants the pardon. After releasing his Chinese, the narrator gives the command to execute the remaining condemned Chinese. He reveals his lack of imagination when he ironically shows no remorse for the killing of the others, but only for the pardon of the one. Once the affair is over, the momentary feeling of affinity, of common humanity with the doomed man, is replaced by alienation: "Von nun an hätte jede von ihnen seinen Roman in der Tasche haben können, es hätte keinem geholfen... Im übrigen hatte mir der Chinese keineswegs imponiert, ich hatte ihn auch nicht bewundert, ich weiß nur eins, von allen Menschen, denen ich auf der Welt begegnet, war er derjenige, der mir am fremdesten war."[57] The novel, the very symbol of humanity, has lost its significance to the narrator, who now lapses into his military role, doing his duty oblivious of human values. In light of Schnitzler's response to the intended execution of

Ernst Toller, his critique in "Boxeraufstand" of the British domination of the Chinese represents a broader attack on all imperialism.

The "Abenteuernovelle" is set in 1520 in Italy during an outbreak of the plague.[58] The hero, Anselmo, is his family's only survivor, so he sets out to seek adventure. In one of his most significant encounters, Anselmo stumbles upon a regional war, complicated by a factional split. Although an outsider, Anselmo is obliged by an old man to choose sides. Like Arduin in *Komödie der Verführung*, Anselmo is unable to make such a choice, but not because he feels an affinity with both sides—rather because he cannot identify with either. As a stranger it is impossible for him to determine which is in the right. When Anselmo confronts the old man with his dilemma, he is merely told that circumstances demand that he choose: "'Unser Land hat ja hundert Provinzen, die miteinander oft in Fehde liegen und in bittereren als sie sie gemeinsam gegen ein fremdes Land führen. Aber die Dinge stehen nun so, daß Ihr Euch als ein junger Mensch, um nicht von beiden Seiten allerlei Unangenehmes zu erleben, wohl werdet entscheiden müssen.'"[59] This situation parallels social pressure to enlist and later to submit to universal conscription during the First World War. A young man who has no desire to fight and no interest in the war is compelled by governments (here the old man) to enlist or suffer the consequences. Either way, he sacrifices his liberty.

The mystical element in the story, involving the prophetic visions of Geronte, who is able to predict for people the exact moment of their deaths, takes on a new dimension when viewed in the context of Schnitzler's concept of the lack of imagination. Here, Schnitzler postulates that the ability to conceive of one's own death constitutes the opposite extreme of "Phantasielosigkeit" (an aspect of which is the inability to truly perceive anything but the immediate present).

Indeed, many of those who learn about their own future deaths from Geronte spend their lives in misery and madness, just as Schnitzler postulates in "Und einmal." Also at play in Geronte's prophetic ability is the question of fate versus free will. In the projected conclusion, Anselmo commits suicide by poison because he cannot bear to wait for the moment prophesied by Geronte. Geronte's prophetic abilities, however, had been temporarily blocked by anger when he found Anselmo with his daughter, Lucrezia. Unable to correctly predict the day of Anselmo's death, Geronte merely fabricated one. Ironically, Anselmo dies on the "preordained" day, but only after he learns that Geronte had falsified the prediction. Here Schnitzler illustrates his belief that man determines his own "destiny."

In his diary on 12 June 1917, Schnitzler writes of the interrelatedness of his future works involving war, politics, the Monarchy, and history:

> Mit O. Windischgrätzhöhe. Über meine nächsten und fernern Pläne.—Der Einaktercyclus (Casanova, Frau des Richters, Landsknecht) von dem das erste annähernd fertig, das zweite begonnen und verhaut, das dritte im Scenarium da—als Vorarbeit empfunden zum "Weiher"—der Weiher als eine Art Prolog zum Josef—den ich wohl nie schreiben werde.[60]

The "Landsknecht" fragment mentioned above was intended to be a type of morality play between the sensible spirit (the preacher) and the wild adventurer (the mercenary).[61] The prowar arguments of the mercenary, Dietrich von Friesen, are refuted at every turn by the preacher. Finally, when Dietrich sees himself beaten, he resorts to empty rhetoric. The two characters are, however, a much closer match for one another than is revealed at first glance.[62] The effect is that the two forces virtually cancel each other out. Only in the moral sense is the superiority of one over the other evident. The preacher is a preserver of positive cultural values that shall remain long after the war is over. The preacher's position here reflects Schnitzler's perception of the role of the writer during the First World War: "Es werden andere Zeiten kommen, da wird man denen danken, die durch all dies Grauen und all diese Wirrsal bewahrt haben, was göttlich ist und Euresgleichen fluchen."[63] The final part of Dietrich's response reflects Schnitzler's realistic view of the world in 1930, a world still as full of hatred as it had been in 1914. For this reason Schnitzler remained skeptical about prospects for even short-term peace in Europe. Echoing Schnitzler's pessimitic view of human nature, Dietrich von Friesen says: "...Wahr ist Lust und Haß, Abenteuer und Rausch und Tod. Auch Liebe ist Lüge...."[64]

In "Und einmal" Schnitzler rejects the notion that any wars are truly fought over religious differences: "... es hat sich nie um etwas anderes als um Machtkämpfe gehandelt, doch waren die Ideen als Vorwände, geglaubte oder ungeglaubte, niemals zu entbehren. Es ist eine historische Fälschung, daß der 30 jährige Krieg ein Religionskrieg war. Beweis dagegen, daß schon wenige Jahre nach Beginn Protestanten im Heere des Kaisers und Katholiken bei seinen Gegnern kämpften."[65] On several occasions in "Landsknecht" as well, Schnitzler attacks the notion that the Thirty Years War was a religious war. First, when the Lieutenant asks (*EuV.* p. 451) if all in the town are not Protestants, Weibel replies: "Sie wechseln jetzt, je nachdem wer kommt." Later, the Colonel tells the preacher (p. 467): "Es geht längst um den Glauben nicht mehr. Das wißt Ihr, Pfarrer, so gut wie ich. Wir fragen längst nicht mehr darnach, wer von unseren Leuten evangelisch und wer katholisch ist. Der Krieg ist ein Gewerbe oder ein Abenteuer, wie es sich eben fügt."

An illustration of religion as a mere pretext for war is the parallel case of a duel between the Protestant preacher's "son," Erasmus (neither the preacher nor Erasmus knows that Dietrich is the real father), and the Catholic captain, Dietrich von Friesen (significantly, a most un-Catholic name). The two fight when Dietrich threatens to tell the preacher that he is Erasmus's real father. Out of love for his son, Dietrich allows himself to be killed in the ensuing struggle, and Erasmus, still protecting the preacher's honor, lies to his superiors (he has just enlisted in the Catholic army), saying that the duel ensued when Dietrich insulted his (Erasmus's Protestant) religion. Before Dietrich dies, a Catholic soldier overhears him tell Erasmus to greet his father (the preacher). Quite clearly, the lie that religion is the cause of the duel parallels the misperception that religion was a cause of the Thirty Years' War. If religion were the primary factor in the war, Erasmus would have been hanged by his Catholic superiors for his defense of the preacher's Protestant beliefs.

Instead, the Colonel gives Erasmus the choice of dying for the murder of Dietrich or taking up the flag of the Protestant army and fulfilling his duties as a mercenary. In a scene reminiscent of Schnitzler's poem, "Ballade von den drei Brüdern," Erasmus decides to follow the flag rather than go to the gallows. The Colonel tells Erasmus: "Es geht immer nur ums eigene Leben. Wähle, Erasmus! Tod auf der Stelle oder mit uns."[66] After being seduced into enlisting by Dietrich, Erasmus is compelled to serve or die. His choice between two evils might be compared to universal conscription during the First World War—which Schnitzler referred to cynically as "die allgemeine Sklaverei,"[67] and which he strongly believed should be abolished.[68]

In the first paragraph of his final work on the duel theme, "Der Sekundant" (1927-1931)—apparently set in pre-War Vienna, Schnitzler makes a cynical statement that seems to have eluded critics. Ostensibly the narrator is writing about the pre-War period, but his perspective is clearly that of post-1918. Here, by stating preference even for the motives that led to duels, Schnitzler demonstrates the futility of the First World War and attacks the false code of honor (read also conscription) that helped bring about the death of millions of soldiers:

> ... das Leben war schöner, bot jedenfalls einen edleren Anblick damals—unter anderem gewiß auch darum, weil man es manchmal aufs Spiel setzen mußte für irgend etwas, das in einem höheren oder wenigstens anderen Sinn möglicherweise gar nicht vorhanden oder das wenigstens den Einsatz, nach heutigem Maß gemessen, eigentlich nicht wert war, für die Ehre zum Beispiel oder für die Tugend einer geliebten Frau oder den guten Ruf einer Schwester, und was dergleichen Nichtigkeiten mehr sind. Immerhin bleibt es zu bedenken, daß man im Laufe der letzten Jahrzehnte auch für viel Geringeres völlig nutzlos und auf Befehl oder Wunsch anderer Leute sein Leben zu opfern genötigt war.[69]

7

Conclusion

After the early polemical argument in "Über den Patriotismus" (1880), Schnitzler's condemnation of militarism and national chauvinism emerged as an important theme in his oeuvre, culminating in a critique of war and its causes and a defense of what Robert O. Weiss calls "humanistic pacifism."[1]

In both the duel and war, Schnitzler believed that the rights of the individual were being usurped by the state, and it is not unlikely that he intended the duel as an analogy for war, especially in later works. At the heart of his argument in both cases was the exposure of the false code of honor—an integral facet of militarist ideology.

Schnitzler criticized the peculiarities and faults of the archaic Austro-Hungarian military and the militarism of the declining Monarchy. Finally, he returned to the question of war and peace, this time demonstrating the connections between the social and political factors that contribute to war and the perennial problems of personal relationships.

It is not likely that Schnitzler consciously engaged in any systematic study of war in his works; his diary entries show surprise at the frequency of the war theme when this point is brought to his attention by others. Yet Schnitzler's own words as a young man, to the effect that an in-depth study of all previous wars would merit the effort, combined with the revelation of many of his works as such an effort, indicates that Schnitzler approached the topic of war in his works in a critical manner. The range of wars in his works include religious war (the

Thirty Years' War in "Der Landsknecht"), revolutionary war (the French Revolution in *Der grüne Kakadu*), feudal war *(Der Schleier)*, imperialist war ("Boxeraufstand" and *Der Gang*), and the First World War *(Verführung)*. The diversity of war alone indicates Schnitzler uses war not merely as background, but rather in an effort to make his works case studies of the different types of war.

Through the medium of the historical drama, a genre he uses before and after 1914, Schnitzler demonstrated the senselessness of war and anticipated the First World War.[2] Schnitzler employs various veiling techniques in his critique of war and militarism. Among them are the historical drama as a parallel to contemporary society, the duel as an analogy for war, and the ambiguity of dialectical arguments. Schnitzler's fear of retribution and loss of income, his wariness of critics, and his skepticism about the immediate possibilities for positive social change only partially answer the question as to why he avoided the direct approach. Another significant possibility is Schnitzler's determination to write literary works that appear objective. In an aphorism he writes: "Es ist dem Dichter unbenommen, die Freiheit heißer zu lieben, als der Held, den er gestaltet. Aber wehe ihm, wenn von diesem Überfluß eigener Liebe auch nur ein Tropfen in seines Helden Worte überströmt."[3]

Before 1914 Schnitzler's critique of war was confined to the traditional mode of presenting its evils in an almost naturalistic manner. The First World War, however, had a profound effect on Schnitzler's works, although this has not yet been recognized by scholars. Through the opposition of an historical drama *(Der Gang)* to a contemporary piece about the period leading up to the First World War *(Verführung)*, Schnitzler illustrates the similarities between the underlying psychological causes for war (drawing upon his own personal experiences and those of his friends and acquaintances for examples). In each case he also demonstrates the political factors that made war possible. Schnitzler's unequivocal condemnation of war and universal conscription in his aphoristic and essayistic writings as well as in his late literary works illustrate his pacifistic tendencies.

Schnitzler's pacifism is further documented by his association with prominent European pacifists and their works. Yet his was a solitary, humanistic pacifism, tinged with the pessimistic belief that millennia might pass before a lasting peace would be realized. He believed that only through the radical restructuring of political institutions could any progess toward Kant's ideal of "perpetual peace" be achieved. As a physician, Schnitzler realized that disease cannot be prevented merely by treating the symptoms. He came to view militarism as a social disease and war as the symptom of the illness. For this reason he chose (especially in later works) to write not about war itself, but about its causes, perhaps in the hope that through recognition of those causes, preventive (immunological, if you will) measures might be taken to prevent the recurrence of war.

The purpose of this work has been to examine Schnitzler's critique of war and militarism throughout his literary career, and to demonstrate that because this critique has as its basis the continuing misuse of the human instinct of aggression by absolutist governments, Schnitzler's works are neither outdated nor merely representative of a "versunkene Welt."[4]

Schnitzler's expansive "Nachlaß" contains information about other planned works involving war and politics. For example, Schnitzler planned in his fragment, "Die Sängerin" (*EuV*, pp. 404-410), to have as a possible setting one of the Napoleonic wars of the early nineteenth century. Also, in a five-line sketch written in 1916, Schnitzler discusses a work of decidedly contemporary political nature: "Ein sozialdemokratisches Blatt will für die Aufhebung eines bestimmten Sittlichkeitsparagraphen eintreten. Ein Mitglied der Partei, die von ihnen bekämpft wird, vergeht sich nun gegen diesen Paragraphen, und so schieben sie den Kampf wieder auf. (Politische Komödie!)"[5]

Finally, as I have demonstrated with "Und einmal," Schnitzler's aphoristic writings contain a wealth of as-yet only scantily dealt-with material relevant to the interpretation of his literary works. Schnitzler's interest in psychology is well documented, yet little research has been done to examine the possibility of a connection between his literary works and such theoretical essays as *Der Geist im Wort und der Geist in der Tat* (1927) or the more recently published "Psychologisches" in *Aphorismen und Betrachtungen* (1967). Such connections could ultimately lead to a revalutation of Schnitzler's entire oeuvre.

Notes to Chapter 1

1. Alfred Vagts, *A History of Militarism, Civilian and Military* (New York: Collier-Macmillan, 1959), p. 14.
2. Volker Berghahn, *Militarism 1861-1979* (Leamington Spa: Berg Publishers, 1981), p. 11.
3. Peter Brock, *Pacifism in Europe to 1914* (Princeton, New Jersey: Princeton University Press, 1972).
4. Gordon N. Bergquist, *The Pen and the Sword: War and Peace in the Prose and Plays of Bernard Shaw* (Salzburg: Institut für englische Sprache und Literatur, Universität Salzburg, 1977), pp. 4-5.
5. Friedrich Vollhardt, "Wer etwas zu sagen hat, trete vor und schweige!: Anmerkungen zu einer unbekannten Erklärung Dr. Arthur Schnitzlers (zum Fall Ernst Toller) aus dem Jahr 1919, *"Literatur und Kritik*, 157/158 (August/September 1981), 462-473.
6. Robert Kann, "Die historische Situation und die entscheidenden politischen Ereignisse zur Zeit und im Leben Arthur Schnitzlers," *Literatur und Kritik*, 161/162 (February/March 1982), 19-25.
7. Robert Kann, "Das Österreich Arthur Schnitzlers," *Forum. Österreichische Monatsblätter für kulturelle Freiheit*, 6, No. 1, (1959), 421-423..
8. Letter dated Dec. 22, 1914 from Arthur Schnitzler to his sister-in-law, Elisabeth Steinrück. In: Reinhard Urbach, ed. "Briefe zur Politik." *Neues Forum*, 15, no. 178 (1968), 678. (See also Appendix 1.)
9. Schnitzler's aphorisms on politics were edited by Robert O. Weiss in *Aphorismen und Betrachtungen*, Gesammelte Werke, (Frankfurt am Main: S. Fischer Verlag, 1967), in the chapter "Politik, Gesellschaft," pp. 231-240. Jeffrey B. Berlin reviews Schnitzler's political aphorisms in: Jeffrey B. Berlin. "Political Criticism in Arthur Schnitzler's *Aphorismen und Betrachtungen, Neophilologus,* 57, no. 2 (April 1973), 173-178.
10. Brigitte Lina Schneider-Halvorson, *The Late Dramatic Works of Arthur Schnitzler* (Bern: Peter Lang, 1983).

Notes to Chapter 2

In the notes to this and succeeding chapters, the following abbreviations are used:

AuB = *Aphorismen und Betrachtungen*
DdW = *Das dramatische Werk*
DeW = *Das erzählerische Werk*
EuV = *Entworfenes und Verworfenes*

1. Theodor Reik, "Zerstörung des ritterlichen Heldenbegriffes," *Pan*, 2, no. 1-45 (1911-1912), 590.
2. Arthur Schnitzler, *Tagebuch 1913-1916*. Ed. Werner Welzig. (Wien: Verlag der Österreichischen Akademie der Wissenschaften,1983), p. 278.
3. Arthur Schnitzler, "Über den Patriotismus." *Der freie Landesbote*, München, 15 November 1880.
4. Arthur Schnitzler, *Tagebuch 1879-1892*. Ed. Werner Welzig. (Wien: Verlag der Österreichischen Akademie der Wissenschaften,1987), p. 45. Diary entry of 28 April 1880. Compare also Aldous Huxley's definition of patriotism in his 1937 *Encyclopaedia of Pacifism*. For him patriotism is idolatry of a small part rather than a love of the Whole (he capitalizes the word "Whole," comparing it in the religious sense to God): "The worship of a part as though it were the Whole provokes strife with the worshippers of other isolated parts. Each system of idolatry encourages its adherents to hate the adherents of all other systems. In the case of patriotism we see that an idolatrous love of one's country is always accompanied by dislike and contempt of other people's countries." In: Aldous Huxley, ed. *Encyclopaedia of Pacifism*. 1937 (rpt. New York: Garland, 1972), p. 87.
5. Arthur Schnitzler, *Jugend in Wien. Eine Autobiographie* (Wien: Fritz Molden, 1968), p. 107.
6. Even Otto Schinnerer in "The Early Works of Arthur Schnitzler," *Germanic Review,* 4 (1929), 153-197, offers only a summary of the essay.

140   Adrian Clive Roberts

7.   Arthur Schnitzler, "Über den Patriotismus."
8.   Ibid.
9.   Ibid.
10. Allan Mitchell writes: "If there was a blotch on this exemplary
     record of moderation, in the German view, it was an unfortunate
     tendency to rhetorical excess like that displayed at Cherbourg in
     August 1880: Gambetta's unabashed justification of French mili-
     tary rearmament, in order that the nation might 'regain its place
     in the world,' caused a stir of hostility in Berlin that reminded
     Saint-Vallier of 1875 [the hoax in 1875 of an impending war
     between France and Germany]. Paris was advised that Bismarck
     denounced the speech as a 'challenge and a provocation to
     Germany' and that 'manifestly he has modified his policy, his
     language, the orientation of his newspapers.' ... As for the inter-
     nal circumstances, it is important to recall that Gambetta's visit
     to Cherbourg was made with Grévy [the French president] and
     that his oration was a deliberate exercise in hyperbole. Whereas
     the president carefully maintained an unruffled dignity befitting
     his office, Gambetta sought to make a display of his own pas-
     sionate dedication to the French people and 'patrie.'" Allan
     Mitchell, *The German Influence in France after 1870: The
     Formation of the French Republic* (Chapel Hill: University of
     North Carolina Press, 1979), p. 204.
11. Arthur Schnitzler, *Buch der Sprüche und Bedenken.
     Aphorismen und Fragmente* (Wien: Im Phaidon Verlag, 1927),
     p. 10. Most recently in *AuB*, p. 8.
12. Heinrich Schnitzler, ed., *Arthur Schnitzler: Briefe 1875-1912*
     (Frankfurt am Main: S. Fischer, 1981), p. viii.
13. Arthur Schnitzler, *AuB*, p. 125.
14. Quoted in Christine R. Barker, *Erich Maria Remarque*
     (London: Oswald Wolff, 1979), p. 15. Remarque's final sentence
     quoted above could as easily apply to Schnitzler.
15. According to Rolf-Peter Janz and Klaus Laermann, the Austrian
     policy of the "Einjährig-Freiwillige," introduced on 5 December
     1868, was based on the Prussian law already in effect since 9
     November 1867. Rolf-Peter Janz and Klaus Laermann, *Arthur
     Schnitzler: Zur Diagnose des Wiener Bürgertums im Fin de siè-
     cle* (Stuttgart: J.B. Metzlersche Verlagsbuchhandlung, 1977), p.
     190.

16. William M. Johnston, *The Austrian Mind* (Berkeley: The University of California Press, 1972), p. 51.
17. Alfred Vagts, *A History of Militarism—Civilian and Military*, 1937 (rev. United States of America: Meridian Books), p. 253.
18. For the nationalities problem in the army, see William M. Johnston, *The Austrian Mind*, p. 51.
19. Arthur Schnitzler, *Tagebuch 1879-1892*, p. 144. Diary entry of 16 December 1882.
20. Arthur Schnitzler, *Tagebuch 1879-1892*, p. 160. Diary entry of 3 October 1883.
21. See Irwin Abrams, Introduction to the English translation of *Die Waffen nieder, Lay Down Your Arms. The Autobiography of Martha von Tilling*. Trans. T. Holmes (New York: Garland, 1972), pp. 6-13.
22. Abrams, p. 11. Abrams explains the paradoxical nature of the success of Suttner's novel as follows: "Bertha von Suttner liked to think that the popularity of her book was due to its timeliness. Twenty years earlier the postwar spirit in Germany and France would have prevented an antiwar book from having any success whatsoever. Furthermore the burden of armaments had to become heavier to be felt by the masses."
23. Abrams, p. 7.
24. Bertha von Suttner, *Die Waffen nieder* (1889; rpt. Wien: H. Javorsky, 1967), p. 298. This currently popular notion of the assurance of peace through military escalation was also espoused by Alfred Nobel himself during a visit to Suttner following a Peace Congress held in Bern in 1892: "My factories may end war sooner than your Congresses. The day when two army corps will be able to destroy each other in one second, all civilised nations will recoil from war in horror and disband their armies." In: Fritz Henriksson, *The Nobel Prizes and Their Founder Alfred Nobel* (Stockholm: Alb. Bonniers Boktryckeri, 1938), p. 47.
25. Bertha von Suttner, *Die Waffen nieder*, p. 299.
26. Ibid., pp. 291-292. Here she predicts the First World War with the understated expression "über unseren Häuptern schwebende europäischen Riesenkrieg."
27. Arthur Schnitzler, *Jugend in Wien*, p. 100.

28.   Demonstrating Schnitzler's view that war is not a natural phe-
       nomenon but rather something artificial—hence is potentially
       avoidable—the quotation conntinues as follows: "Streit zwischen
       zwei Menschen ist etwas natürliches; Streit zwischen zwei
       Völkern künstlich— Von einem angeborenen Hasse zweier
       Nationen zu sprechen, ist widersinnig. 'Es wäre eine Aufgabe
       der Durchführung werth, an den einzelnen Kriegen, die bis auf
       den heutigen Tag geführt wurden, das Gemachte nachzuweisen.'
       Es is unlogisch aus dem Gefühl der Vaterlandsliebe das des
       Nationalitätenhasses zu entwickeln. Ich gestehe aufrichtig, daß
       es einzelne Nationen gibt, die mir höchst unsympatisch sind
       —aber ich hasse keine.-" Arthur Schnitzler, *Tagebuch 1879-
       1892*, p. 61.

Notes to Chapter 3

1.   Arthur Schnitzler, *Jugend in Wien. Eine Autobiographie* (Wien:
      Fritz Molden, 1968), p. 155.
2.   Klaus Laermann quotes the Waidhofener Decree issued on
      March 11, 1896 as follows: "'In vollster Würdigung der
      Tatsache, daß zwischen Ariern und Juden ein so tiefer morali-
      scher und physischer Unterschied besteht und daß durch jüdi-
      sches Unwesen unsere Eigenart schon so viel gelitten, in
      Anbetracht der vielen Beweise, die auch der jüdische Student
      von seiner Ehrlosigkeit und Charakterlosigkeit gegeben und da
      er der Ehre nach unseren deutschen Begriffen völlig bar ist, faßt
      die   heutige   Versammlung   deutscher   wehrhafter
      Studentenverbindungen den Beschluß *Dem Juden auf keine
      Waffe mehr Genugtuung zu geben, da er deren unwürdig ist!*'"
      Rolf-Peter Janz and Klaus Laermann. *Zur Diagnose des Wiener
      Bürgertums im Fin de siècle* (Stuttgart: J.B. Metzlersche
      Verlagsbuchhandlung, 1977), pp. 133-134.
3.   In *Jugend in Wien*, Schnitzler quotes the Waidhofener Decree as
      follows: "'Jeder Sohn einer jüdischen Mutter, jeder Mensch, in
      dessen Adern jüdisches Blut rollt, ist von Geburt aus ehrlos,
      jeder feineren Regung bar. Er kann nicht unterscheiden zwi-
      schen Schmutzigem und Reinem. Er ist ein etisch tiefstehendes

Subjekt. Der Verkehr mit einem Juden ist daher entehrend; man
muß jede Gemeinschaft mit Juden vermeiden. Einen Juden kann
man nicht beleidigen, ein Jude kann daher keine Genugtuung für
erlittene Beleidigungen verlangen.'" Arthur Schnitzler, *Jugend
in Wien* (Wien: Verlag Fritz Molden, 1968), p. 156.

4.   Arthur Schnitzler, *Aphorismen und Betrachtungen*. Ed. Robert
O. Weiss (Frankfurt am Main: S. Fischer, 1967), p. 322.

5.   Arthur Schnitzler, *Arthur Schnitzler. Tagebuch 1917-1919*. Ed.
Werner Welzig (Wien: Verlag der Österreichischen Akademie
der Wissenschaften, 1985), p. 266. Diary entry of June 25, 1919.
See also, as to the "Duellzwang" and the "falscher Ehrenbegriff,"
Bertha von Suttner's *Die Waffen nieder*, pp. 88-89. Here one
finds a precedent for Schnitzler's opinions on the "Duellzwang"
through the viewpoint of the officer, Friedrich Tilling, who
argues against the traditional military stand of his father-in-law, a
retired general. Tilling rejects the false concept of honor and the
"Duellzwang" that results from it. He attributes both the duel
and war to this misrepresented sense of honor, just as Schnitzler
would later do: "... der Begriff der Ehre [wird] auch eine
Wandlung erfahren: einmal wird eine erhaltene Injurie, wenn sie
unverdient ist, nicht auf den Empfänger, sondern auf den rohen
Geber als Schmach zurückfallen;...'" (*Die Waffen nieder*, pp. 88-
89).

6.   Rolf-Peter Janz and Klaus Laermann, *Zur Diagnose des Wiener
Bürgertums im Fin de siècle*, p. 143. Laermann explains why the
duel was outlawed by feudal rulers: "Die Duellverbote wendeten
sich also einmal gegen die anarchische Tendenz des Feudaladels,
seinen politischen Machtverlust durch gesellschaftliche
Demonstration von Gewalt zu kompensieren, und zum anderen
gegen die Aufsäßigkeit von (zumeist adeligen) Offizieren, die
ihre privaten Ehrenhändel ohne Billigung der staatlichen
Zentralgewalt meinten austragen zu können" (p. 144).

7.   Roman historians in the first century B.C. and the first century
A.D. documented the "Kampfordal" practiced by numerous
Germanic tribes. See Martin Wierschin: *Meister Liechtenauers
Kunst des Fechtens* (München: C.H. Beck, 1965), pp. 45-46.
Wierschin writes: "Die erste sichere Nachricht über gerichtliche
Zweikämpfe bei den germanischen Völkern findet sich bei
Veleius Paterculus. Von den germanischen Volksrechten enthält

zuerst die 'Lex Gundobada' des Burgundenherzogs Gundobald
Bestimmungen über das Kampfordal."

8.   Egon Eis, *Duell: Geschichte und Geschichten des Zweikampfes*
(München: Kurt Desch, 1971), p. 252.

9.   Judicial duels, though less and less frequent, continued to be
fought up until the early nineteenth century. See Egon Eis, p.
252.

10. Egon Eis, *Duell*, p. 266.

11. Alan Sked describes as follows the character of the code of
honor and the "council of honor" responsible for its enforcement:
"The 'Ehrenrath'...promoted regimental self-consciousness and
its rules, if unwritten, were adhered to scrupulously, even by
army officialdom. Regimental commanders were never known
to oppose its decisions and very often invoked it themselves if
they wished to avoid protracted legal proceedings. A form of
'Ehrenrath,' in fact, was legalized after 1866.
The 'Ehrenrath,' however, was not a regimental institution; each
officer's regiment had one of its own and each was strictly sepa-
rated from the next." Alan Sked. *The Survival of the Habsburg
Empire* (London: Longman Group, 1979), pp. 27-28.

12. The importance of the code of honor in Austria is emphasized by
William M. Johnston: "The code of honor ('Ehrenkodex'), which
Schopenhauer called a code for fools, dogged officers. It acted
as a superego requiring them to settle disputes by dueling.
Although the duel had died out in England before 1850, in
Austria-Hungary until 1911 a challenge by one officer to another
posed a sacred obligation. An officer who declined a challenge
would lose his commission, besides being cut dead in good society. Up to 1900 civilian courts in Austria-Hungary refrained
from enforcing against officers laws that made dueling punishable by imprisonment." (In: William M. Johnston, *The Austrian
Mind*, pp. 53-54).

13. Georg Brandes, *The World at War*. (New York: Macmillan,
1917), pp. 179-180. It is significant that Brandes writes of the
duel as being "still ineradicable in Germany and France" (p.
179).

14. In the introduction to her edition of Schnitzler's dramatic fragment, "Ritterlichkeit" (Bonn: Bouvier, 1975), Rena Schlein
writes that Schnitzler sent Goldmann a telegram on the day fol-

lowing his duel, saying, "Also dazu schreibe ich extra Stücke gegens Duell (...) Arthur" (p. 6). Schlein adds the footnote: "'Stücke gegens Duell': gemeint sind die beiden Dramen *Liebelei* und *Freiwild*" (p. 6).

15. Rena R. Schlein, "Das Duellmotiv in Schnitzlers Dramen 'Ritterlichkeit', *Das weite Land*, und *Das Wort*," *Modern Austrian Literature*, 8, no. 3/4 (1975),

16. Rena R. Schlein, "Das Duellmotiv," p. 225.

17. Arthur Schnitzler, *AuB*, p. 321.

18. Bertrand Russell, *Why Men Fight. A Method of Abolishing the International Duel* (New York: Garland, 1971).

19. Bertrand Russell, *Why Men Fight*, p. 114.

20. Arthur Schnitzler, *AuB*, pp. 214-215.

21. Rolf Allerdissen, *Arthur Schnitzler: Impressionistisches Rollenspiel und skeptischer Moralismus in seinen Erzählungen* (Bonn: Bouvier, 1985), p. 55.

22. Arthur Schnitzler, *Freiwild*. In: *Das dramatische Werk*. Vol. 2 (Frankfurt am Main: S. Fischer, 1968), p. 36. In his 1914 article "Der Krieg bei Arthur Schnitzler," Theodor Reik (praising Schnitzler) interprets this quotation in a strictly literal sense, as an endorsement of Karinski's pursuit of the military profession.

23. Arthur Schnitzler. *AuB*, p. 205: "Es gab keine Möglichkeit, sich gegen das Schrapnell zu verteidigen. Auch davonlaufen durften sie nicht, dann wären sie mit Recht wegen Feigheit erschossen worden. Die Wehrpflicht hatte sie wehrlos gemacht. 1915." [By "mit Recht" Schnitzler means "according to the law," not "with justification" (= "mit recht").]

24. Arthur Schnitzler, *Der grüne Kakadu*. In: *Das dramatische Werk*, vol. 3 (Frankfurt am Main: S. Fischer, 1969), p. 10.

25. Schnitzler writes in "Und einmal": "Der beste Patriot wird immer der sein, der sein Vaterland am meisten genützt hat, nicht der, der es am heißesten geliebt hat.... Daher ist ein namenloser Fabrikarbeiter ein besserer Patriot als ein General, der nie im Feld gestanden ist, manchmal auch einer, der viele Schlachten mitgemacht hat." (*AuB*, p. 236).

26. Arthur Schnitzler, *DdW*, Vol. 3, p. 11.

27. Although it passed Berlin censors in 1896 with only minor changes being required, Viennese censors banned *Freiwild* on the grounds that an officer of the Austro-Hungarian army "durfte

ehedem nicht auf der Bühne geohrfeigt werden, auch nicht als verdiente Züchtigung." Theodor Kappstein. *Artur* (sic) *Schnitzler und seine besten Bühnenwerke* (Berlin and Leipzig: Franz Schneider, 1925), p. 49.

28. Arthur Schnitzler, *DdW*, Vol. 3, p. 13.

29. Hartmut Scheible, *Arthur Schnitzler in Selbstzeugnissen und Bilddokumenten.* (Reinbek bei Hamburg: Rowohlt Taschenbuch, 1976), p. 74. Scheible continues, elaborating upon Schnitzler's veiling of historical fact in a fictional work in an attempt to avoid possible censorship: "Daß die Zensur das Stück ohne weiteres freigab—nur der Herzog von Chartres mußte den Phantasienamen Cadignan erhalten—, ist nur dadurch erklärbar, daß im Zeitalter des Historismus jedes historische Dekor (wie etwa in *Der Schleier der Beatrice*) als zufällig gelten mußte."

30. Arthur Schnitzler, *AuB*, pp. 233-234: "Die Revolution des Proletariats... war eine Notwendigkeit, wenn auch, oder obwohl sie oder weil sie nicht gelang. Aber schlimmer ist, daß diese Revolution des Proletariats sich selber proletarisiert hat, in einer kläglicheren Weise als es die französische 1789 tat. Jene begann doch immerhin als eine Revolution des Geistes.... Unsere Revolution aber ist aus dem Ressentiment geboren: nicht der Wunsch, die eigenen Verhältnisse zu bessern war das Primäre, sondern der Drang, Rache zu nehmen an denen, die es so lange besser gehabt hatten. In Rußland kam diese unreinste Idee sozusagen am reinsten heraus. 1918."

31. Arthur Schnitzler, *Tagebuch 1879-1892*, p. 46. Diary entry of 28 April 1880.

32. Arthur Schnitzler, *AuB*, p. 85. See also Jeffrey B. Berlin's "Political Criticism in Arthur Schnitzler's *Aphorismen und Betrachtungen*," *Neophilologus,* 57, no. 2, (April 1973), 173-178.

33. Arthur Schnitzler. "Ballade von den drei Brüdern," *Neues Forum* XV. Jahr, Heft 178 (October 1968), 676. Once again there is an astounding similarity between the words of Arthur Schnitzler and Bertha von Suttner. The two met several times before Suttner's death in 1914, and Schnitzler's eulogy to her is to be found among his essays on war in "Und einmal." Suttner's character, Tilling, attacks the double standards whereby militarist governments condemn murder on one hand and applaud it on the

other during wartime. His words are almost identical to those used by Schnitzler in "Ballade von den drei Brüdern": "Und im Kriegsspiel herrschen... unausgesprochene Übereinkommen: Totschlag gilt nicht mehr als Totschlag, Raub ist nicht Raub—sondern Requisition, brennende Dörfer stellen keine Brandsunglücke, sondern genommene Positionen vor." Bertha von Suttner, *Die Waffen nieder*, p. 70.

34. There has been little agreement as to Schnitzler's reason for his choice of the setting. Reinhard Urbach feels that Schnitzler was following the "Zug der Zeit" of the Renaissance, as had Hofmannsthal before him in *Gestern*, into a realm "die in der Nachfolge Burckhardts und Nietzsches als eine Welt des Rausches und des Ruhms, des Trunks und der Kunst empfunden wurde, eine Welt des gesteigerten Lebens und gegenwärtigen Todes." Reinhard Urbach, *Arthur Schnitzler*, p. 76. Schnitzler's chosen form—an emulation of the Shakespearean drama with its five-acts, blank verse, and the concluding heroic couplet—makes it appropriate for a work on the Renaissance. Françoise Derré is of the opinion that the Renaissance setting was chosen primarily for its aesthetic possibilities, and further, that the psychological study of two young people was more important to Schnitzler than the accurate historical portrayal of Italian society in the sixteenth century. (Françoise Derré, *L'Oeuvre d'Arthur Schnitzler. Imagerie viennoise et problémes humains* [Paris: Marcel Didier, 1966, p. 290]).

35. Reinhard Urbach points out the significance of each action in the play, given that the figures are aware that this could likely be their last night on earth: "Vor der Katastrophe wurde jede Handlung bedeutsam, jede Geste ein Symbol für menschliches Verhalten." In: Reinhard Urbach, *Arthur Schnitzler*, p. 77.

36. Arthur Schnitzler, *Der Schleier der Beatrice*. In: *Das dramatische Werk*, vol. 3. (Frankfurt am Main: S. Fischer, 1969), pp. 52-53.

37. Ibid., p. 51.

38. Ibid., pp. 88-89.

39. Ibid., p. 89.

40. Arthur Schnitzler, *AuB*, p. 201.

41. Arthur Schnitzler, *DdW*, Vol. 3, p. 101.

42. Ibid., p. 153.

43. Arthur Schnitzler, *AuB*, p. 209.

44. Reinhard Urbach, *Arthur Schnitzler*, p. 80. Urbach writes: "Wenn er [der Herzog] die Schönheit postuliert, heißt das zwar, daß Moral und Gesetz aufgehoben sind im Angesicht des Todes, aber es bedeutet nicht Anarchie, sondern Umkehrung des Gesetzes. ... Durch die Fülle des Lebens überwindet er den Tod."

45. Arthur Schnitzler, *Tagebuch 1913-1916*. Ed. Werner Welzig. (Wien: Verlag der Österreichischen Akademie der Wissenschaften, 1983), p. 136. Later diary entries show that Schnitzler did in fact engage in several readings of sections from *Der Schleier der Beatrice* to numerous wartime audiences.

46. Letter from Hermann Bahr to Arthur Schnitzler dated 1904. In: Heinrich Schnitzler, et al. *Arthur Schnitzler: Sein Leben, Sein Werk, Seine Zeit*, p. 78.

Notes to Chapter 4

1. Such works include *Leutnant Gustl* (1900), *Der einsame Weg* (1903), *Das Tagebuch der Redegonda* (1909), and *Das weite Land* (1910). My discussion here is limited to the first two works; they contain the most extensive critique of militarism.

2. Arthur Schnitzler, *Jugend in Wien*. p. 158. To emphasize the level of anti-Semitism in the army, Schnitzler precedes his understated analysis quoted above with a description of violent attacks on Jews by anti-Semitic students in the "medizinischen Unterstützungsverein" at the University of Vienna: "Bei späteren Versammlungen kam es zu Prügeleien, und als einmal oder öfters antisemitische Studenten mit Knüppeln und Stöcken über jüdische Mitglieder herfielen, die nach Abhaltung einer Besprechung den Hörsaal verließen, wurde der Verein behördlich aufgelöst" (*Jugend in Wien*, p. 158).

3. Arthur Schnitzler, *Leutnant Gustl*. In: *Das erzählerische Werk*, Vol. 2 (Frankfurt am Main: S. Fischer, 1961), p. 212.

4. Arthur Schnitzler, *DeW*, Vol. 2, pp. 208-209.

5. Ibid., p. 215.

6. Occasionally, as in the following example of the stage directions to *Freiwild*, Schnitzler makes a brief allusion to the social inter-action between German-Austrians and Hungarians in the Imperial army: "LEUTNANT VOGEL, ... Leicht ungarischer etwas affektierter Akzent, wie ihn geborene Österreicher bekommen, die in ungarischen Regimentern dienen; ..." (*Das dramatische Werk*, Vol. 2, p. 8.)

7. Klaus Laermann cites the Austrian law, "paragraphs 158-165, R.G.Bl. Nr. 117" of May 27, 1852 banning duels. Rolf-Peter Janz and Klaus Laermann, *Arthur Schnitzler: Zur Diagnose des Wiener Bürgertums im Fin de siècle* (Stuttgart: Metzler, 1977), pp. 145 and 191).

8. Ibid., p. 144.

9. Alfred Fritsche, *Dekadenz im Werk Arthur Schnitzlers* (Frankfurt am Main: Peter Lang, 1974), p. 141.

10. In Schnitzler's *Das Tagebuch der Redegonda* (1908), the narrator (a civil servant) describes the condescending attitude of the officer caste toward civilians, and the resulting lack of social contact: "Die Offiziere (pflegten) mit der Zivilbevölkerung beinahe gar keinen Verkehr und (hielten) an dieser Exklusivität selbst gegenüber uns Herren von der politischen Behörde in fast verletzender Weise fest." Schnitzler later jabs at the boredom of military life when the narrator, in love with an officer's wife, daydreams of her confessing to him the "Minderwertigkeit ihres Verkehrs." In: Arthur Schnitzler, *Das erzählerische Werk*, Vol. 3 (Frankfurt am Main: S. Fischer, 1962), pp. 153-154.

11. Arthur Schnitzler, *Leutnant Gustl*, DeW, Vol 2, p. 217.

12. Ibid., p. 236.

13. Ibid., p. 211.

14. The patriotic festival mentioned above and Gustl's motivation perhaps find their roots in a diary entry Schnitzler makes on August 23, 1880: "Montag früh.—Mit Jacques war ich beim Volksfest.—Der Koth und die Loyalität machten die Passage schwer... Was ich dieser Tage in einem kurzen Aufsatz über den Patriotismus ["Über den Patriotismus"] niedergelegt habe, kommt mir von Herzen.—... Ich möchte eine Schilderung der Volksbegeisterung bei so einem Fest entwerfen, die in ein Drama paßte, in dem Regierung und Volk nicht gut weg kämen. Mein ästhetisches Gefühl wird ganz besonders durch gewisse Dinge

150 Adrian Clive Roberts

beleidigt. Wenn z.B. ein Besoffener, der vorüberrennt oder wankt, stößt, aus dem Mund nach Wein, nach achttägigem Schmutze duftend—einem seinem Athem übers Gesicht wehen läßt, während er ruft: Hoch der Kaiser!..." Arthur Schnitzler, *Tagebuch 1879-1892*, pp. 89-90. Gustl is representative of just such a "Volk," and the Austro-Hungarian monarchy is such a government.

15. Gustav Davis, *Lieutenant Gustl*, Feuilleton. In: *Die Reichswehr*, December 28, 1900, pp. 1-2.

16. Otto P. Schinnerer quotes the letter dated January 3, 1901 from army headquarters to Schnitzler as follows: "Sie haben bekannt zu geben, ob Sie der Verfasser des am 25. Dezember 1900 in der *Neuen Freien Presse* erschienenen Feuilletons 'Leutnant Gustl' sind. Diese Meldung hat bis 6.d.M. eingesendet zu werden.-" Otto P. Schinnerer. "Schnitzler and the Military Censorship. Unpublished Correspondence." *Germanic Review*, 5 (1930), p. 239.

17. Ibid., p. 240.

18. Ibid., pp. 241-242.

19. Joseph Roth, *Radetzkymarsch* (1932, rpt. Köln: Kiepenheuer und Witsch, 1963).

20. Perhaps the most significant parallel is between Roth's character, Lieutenant Trotta and Schnitzler himself. Schnitzler's sense of justice causes him to point out (through the medium of literature) the wrongs inflicted on society in the name of political and military necessity. Like Trotta, whose heroic deed is magnified and distorted for political purposes, Schnitzler is abused by critics in order to protect the interests of the state and the military. Like Trotta, Schnitzler loses his commission over the refusal of the state to accept and deal with its own injustices.

21. Arthur Schnitzler, *Der einsame Weg*. In: *Das dramatische Werk*, Vol. 4 (Frankfurt am Main: S. Fischer, 1970), p. 8.

22. Ibid., pp. 8-9.

23. Ibid., p. 9.

24. Ibid., p. 16.

25. Ibid., pp. 30-31.

26. Ibid., p. 48.

27. Ibid., p. 48.

28. Ibid., pp. 83-84. Theodor Reik cites the same words in his 1914

essay on Schnitzler and war but he incorrectly attributes this view to Schnitzler himself, rather than merely to his character, Sala.

29. Arthur Schnitzler, *Der Ruf des Lebens*. In: *Das dramatische Werk*. Vol. 4. (Frankfurt am Main: S. Fischer, 1970), p. 246.

30. The Colonel's point of view is adapted by some artists and writers who felt useless during the First World War: "Lächerlich, ja unwürdig, erscheint mir der Kleinmut mancher Künstler, die sich plötzlich überflüssig erscheinen, weil nun nach ihren Erzeugnissen keine Nachfrage ist. Das Militär ist sich durch ein halbes Jahrhundert, währenddessen wir es scheinbar nicht gebraucht haben, gewiß nicht überflüssig erschienen und hat mit dieser Empfindung völlig recht gehabt. Aber ebensowenig sind die Künstler nun überflüssig geworden. Sie sollen im stillen weiter manövrieren und stets in Bereitschaft sein. Jeden Moment kann der Friede ausbrechen..." Arthur Schnitzler, *AuB*, p. 195.

31. Arthur Schnitzler, *DdW*, Vol. 4, p. 247.

32. Ibid., p. 241.

33. Arthur Schnitzler, *Tagebuch 1879-1892*, p. 46

34. Letter from Arthur Schnitzler to Leo Fromm (January 24, 1915). In: Henry Schnitzler, "Patriotismus und Schauspielkunst." In: *Kleine Schriften der Gesellschaft für Theatergeschichte*, 11 (Berlin: Selbstverlag der Gesellschaft für Theatergeschichte, 1953), p. 23. Compare here Schnitzler's condemnation in his essays on war (*AuB*, p. 225) of the term "Große Zeit" in reference to the First World War: "Sobald ich einen im Feld Erblindeten kennengelernt haben werde, der auch um den Preis seines Augenlichtes nicht darauf verzichten würde, diese große Zeit tätig und leidend mitgemacht zu haben, erst dann werde ich glauben, daß es wirklich eine große Zeit gewesen ist." Compare also the remarks of Suttner's heroine Martha (*Die Waffen nieder*) in response to her father's assertion that every soldier would gladly die for the "Vaterland": "Wenn einer nach verlorener Schlacht mit zerschmetterten Gliedern auf dem Felde liegen bleibt...und da aufgefunden durch vier oder fünf Tage an Durst, Hunger, unter unsäglichen Schmerzen, lebend verfaulend ...—ich möchte wissen, ob er die ganze Zeit über mit jenem Rufe gern stirbt." Bertha von Suttner. *Die Waffen nieder*, p. 159.

152   Adrian Clive Roberts

35.   Henry Schnitzler, "Patriotismus und Schauspielkunst," p. 24.
Arthur Schnitzler writes of patriotism: "Für mich ist in Friedens-
wie in Kriegszeiten nur der ein Patriot, der die Sache seines
Vaterlandes fördert, indem er an seinem, ihm zugewiesenen Platz
nach dem Maß seiner Begabung redlich seine Pflicht erfüllt,
ohne seine Nachbarn in ihrem gleichen Bemühen durch schein-
patriotische Wichtigtürei zu behindern;..."

36.   Arthur Schnitzler, *AuB*, p. 228. Schnitzler writes: "Das
Individuum als solches will nie den Krieg. Es will die Tat (im
guten oder üblen Sinne), die Gefahr, das Abenteuer, den Ruhm,
die Ehre und benützt den Krieg als Mittel und zwar als das
unverantwortlichste Mittel zu seinem Zweck. Denn all dies, Tat
und Abenteuer, Gefahr und Ehre ist auch auf andere Weise zu
bekommen, nur bedarf es dazu eines größeren geistigen
Aufwands und vor allem einer gewissen Selbständigkeit des
Denkens. Vor allem des Entschlusses."

37.   Arthur Schnitzler, *DdW*, Vol. 4, p. 249.

38.   Arthur Schnitzler, *AuB*, p. 207. Schnitzler's first prerequisite
for peace discussions stipulates that "1. Die Schuldfrage hinsichtlich aller vorhergegangenen und insbesondere hinsichtlich
des letzten Krieges (wäre auszuschalten). Man nehme als
entschieden an, daß alle Staaten an diesem Krieg schuld sind,
daß ihn aber kein einziger Staat als solcher, insbesondere kein
Volk gewollt hat, sondern überall nur eine verschwindende Zahl
von einzelnen."

39.   Immanuel Kant, *Immanuel Kants Werke: Schriften von 1790-
1796* (Berlin: Bruno Cassirer, 1923), p. 427.

40.   Despite the similarity between Schnitzler's and Kant's notions on
the prevention of war, Schnitzler was apparently not very familiar with Kant's works. He records a conversation with Arthur
Kaufmann on Kant in his diary on May 10, 1917: "Mit Arth.
Kfm....'Wenn ich diese Schönheit sehe' [the two had been on a
nature hike together] sagte K., so ist mir fast, als müßt ich mich
religiös nennen—'Sie sinds—da Sie diese Schönheit empfinden.
Es wäre eine gute Beschäftigung für Sie, diese geschändeten
Worte—wie Freiheit, Religion, wieder ehrlich zu machen—' Wir
kommen auf Kant;—ob ich ihn nicht doch lesen sollte. 'Nein er
würde Sie ungeduldig machen;—das meiste haben Sie doch
schon anticipirt....'" In: Arthur Schnitzler. *Tagebuch 1917-1919*.

Ed. Werner Welzig. (Wien: Österreichische Akademie der Wissenschaften, 1985), p. 42. Diary entry of May 10, 1917.

41. Bertha von Suttner, *Die Waffen nieder*, p. 221.

42. Schnitzler himself is present in *Der Ruf* in his capacity as a doctor and psychologist. The family doctor, Schindler, alone perceives the truth behind Albrecht's death and calls him a fool.

43. Arthur Schnitzler, *Tagebuch 1879-1892*, p. 50.

44. Arthur Schnitzler, *Der junge Medardus*. In: Das dramatische Werk, vol. 5. (Frankfurt am Main: S. Fischer, 1971), p. 81. See also Mark Twain's (Samuel Clemens's) *The War Prayer* (written before 1912) for similar thoughts on the hypocrisy of battle prayer (1923; rpt. New York: Harper and Row, 1971).

45. Arthur Schnitzler, *DdW*, Vol.5, p. 82.

46. Eschenbacher is a genuine hero because he is willing to die for his belief in freedom, and to protect his family and the country of his birth.

47. Arthur Schnitzler, *DdW*, Vol. 5, p. 85.

48. In a story similar to Frau Klähr's, Bertrand Russell tells of a British taxi driver who is hounded to suicide by the jeers and taunts of his fellow citizens when he is determined physically unfit to join the British army. Bertrand Russell. *Why Men Fight: A Method of Abolishing the International Duel* (New York: Garland, 1971), pp. 48-49. The social pressure to enlist (compare also the "Duellzwang") equates here with universal conscription.

49. Arthur Schnitzler, *DdW*, Vol. 5, p. 85. Compare also Schnitzler's letter to Dr. Fromm with regard to *Der Ruf*. The "Treiben in den Straßen" anticipates the war fervor throughout Europe in September, 1914.

50. Arthur Schnitzler, *DdW*, Vol. 5, p. 103.

51. A later aphorism by Schnitzler condemning conscription develops the same direct approach to pacifism: "Kriegsgreuel: Ein wehrloser Verwundeter wurde auf dem Schlachtfeld geblendet, verstümmelt, von einem Feind natürlich. Ich weiß noch Ärgeres zu erzählen: ein Dutzend Soldaten saßen in einem Schützengraben, ein Schrapnell kam, der eine wurde blind, dem anderen wurde der Bauch aufgeschlitzt, dem dritten den Kehlkopf zerfetzt, dem vierten das ganze Gesicht weggerissen,... Die Wehrpflicht hatte sie wehrlos gemacht. 1915" In: Arthur

154   Adrian Clive Roberts

Schnitzler, *AuB*, p. 205. Though Schnitzler recognized that the character of war had been modified by the horrendous technological changes of the modern industrial age, he credited universal conscription with the major role in its transformation.

52.   Arthur Schnitzler, *DdW*, Vol. 5, p. 107.

53.   Ibid., p. 265.

54.   Medardus's lack of direction is reflected in Agathe's words: "Für den Medardus aber hätte nichts besseres kommen können als der Krieg. Zu den Soldaten gehört er hin" (Ibid., pp. 81-82). One is reminded here of Karinski in *Freiwild*, and also of the decadent boredom prevailing in Europe at the turn of the century.

55.   Arthur Schnitzler. *Arthur Schnitzler: Briefe 1913-1931*. Ed. Peter Michael Braunwarth, Richard Miklin, Susanne Pertlik and Heinrich Schnitzler (Frankfurt am Main: S. Fischer, 1984), pp. 64-65.

56.   Arthur Schnitzler, B*riefe 1913-1931*, pp. 66-67.

57.   Maja D. Reid, "Die Hirtenflöte." *Modern Austrian Literature* 4, no. 2, (Summer 1971), 19.

58.   Schnitzler also illustrates the inverted priorities of modern society when technological artifacts are glorified in a great museum. Here, machines from the past, present, and future reveal society's preoccupation with science at the expense of its humanity. The squire's ruthless business dealings with foreign inventors, builders, diplomats, and politicians might be seen as a critique of modern commerce and diplomacy.

59.   Arthur Schnitzler, "Die Hirtenflöte." In: *Das erzählerische Werk*, vol. 3 (Frankfurt am Main: S. Fischer, 1962), p. 127.

60.   Already in his early diary entry of 28 April 1880 on war and revolution, Schnitzler concludes that: "Alles ist schlecht! und jede Veränderung, die, nach der Organisation der Species Mensch, möglich ist, würde zu noch schlechterem führen— ..." Arthur Schnitzler, *Tagebuch 1879-1892*, p. 46. Schnitzler rejected any ideology based on the belief that a lasting improvement in world order is possible: "Jeder denkende Mensch, wenn er nicht an einem höhern oder geringern Grade der Monomanie leidet, muß ja, in den Fußstapfen des gesunden Menschenverstands gehend zu der Überzeugung kommen, daß eine bleibende Verbesserung unsrer in der Verschiedenheit der Individualitäten und im Zufall beruhenden Weltordnung ein Traum optimistisch angelegter

Köpfe bleiben wird und muß. Zu diesem 'Princip'—ein sehr negatives Princip!—bin ich gekommen." Ibid., p. 50. Diary entry of May 9, 1880. Thirty years later, in "Die Hirtenflöte," Schnitzler seems to reaffirm this pessimistic view.

61. Arthur Schnitzler, *DeW*, Vol. 3, p. 128.
62. Arthur Schnitzler, *DeW*, Vol. 3, p. 129.
63. This admiration of military symbols is reminiscent of a similar incident in *Medardus*.
64. In Erich Maria Remarque's pacifist novel, *Im Westen nichts Neues* (1929), the protagonist, Paul Bäumer, suffers a similarly tragic death.

Notes to Chapter 5

1. Arthur Schnitzler, *Tagebuch 1913-1916*, pp. 128-129.
2. In a letter to Theodor Tagger dated 11 December 1916, Schnitzler writes: "Sie wissen ja, daß ich nichts Dummes habe drucken lassen, aber wer sagt Ihnen, daß ich dergleichen nicht geschrieben oder zum mindesten gedacht habe?" In: Arthur Schnitzler, B*riefe 1913-1931*. p. 117.
3. Arthur Schnitzler, *Tagebuch 1913-1916*, p. 242.
4. Arthur Schnitzler, *Tagebuch 1913-1916*, p. 134. Schnitzler probably refers here to a letter (now in the Arthur Schnitzler Institute in Vienna) dated 20 August 1914 from his friend Eugen Deimel, who had emigrated to America quite some time before.
5. These essays were first published posthumously by Heinrich Schnitzler in 1939 in Stockholm under the title "Über Krieg und Frieden."
    Arthur Schnitzler writes: "Deutschland und Österreich hatten sich natürlich auch für den Krieg gerüstet, aber niemals für etwas anderes als für einen Verteidigungskrieg. Frankreich, Rußland, England haben den Angriff vorbereitet, das kann niemals geleugnet werden, hierfür liegen Dokumente vor, sowohl diplomatischer als journalistischer und solche weltgeschichtlicher Natur." Arthur Schnitzler, *AuB*, p. 191.
6. Arthur Schnitzler, *AuB*, p. 192. The fact that he addresses the essay to his fellow countrymen indicates the likelihood that he

intended to publish the text at some future time.

7.   Theodor Reik, "Der Krieg bei Arthur Schnitzler." *Berliner Tageblatt*, 36, (7 September 1914), Beiblatt "Zeitgeist." Reik's article is reprinted in Hans-Ulrich Lindken's *Arthur Schnitzler: Aspekte und Akzente. Materialien zu Leben und Werk*, Chapter 8 ("Politisches"), (Frankfurt am Main: Peter Lang, 1984), pp. 393-398.

8.   Theodor Reik, "Der Krieg." Compare also Karl Kraus on Arthur Schnitzler's "Schweigen" during and after the First World War. Karl Kraus, *Werke*, Vol. 7, Ed. Heinrich Fischer (München: Kösel, 1967), p. 134.

9.   Arthur Schnitzler, *Tagebuch 1913-1916*, Ed. Werner Welzig (Wien: Verlag der Österreichischen Akademie der Wissenschaften 1983), p. 135.

10. Elisabeth Heresch, *Schnitzler und Russland*, (Wien: Braumüller, 1982), p. 117.

11. Arthur Schnitzler, *Tagebuch 1913-1916*, pp. 152-153.

12. Stefan Zweig, unpublished letter to Arthur Schnitzler, 3 December 1914, cited here with permission. ("Arthur Schnitzler, Nachlaß." University of California, Los Angeles. Special Collection no. 511, reel 27, file FF.)

13. Arthur Schnitzler, "Arthur Schnitzlers Protest." In: *Zürcher Zeitung*, 22 December 1914.

14. Cited in Reinhard Urbach, *Arthur Schnitzler* (Velber bei Hannover: Friedrich, 1972), p. 69.

15. Martin Swales, *Arthur Schnitzler: A Critical Study* (Oxford: At the Clarendon Press, 1971), p. 168.

16. Ibid., p. 169.

17. Renate Wagner, *Arthur Schnitzler: Eine Biographie* (Wien: Molden, 1981), p. 290.

18. Letter dated December 9, 1915 from Arthur Schnitzler to Georg Brandes. Kurt Bergel. *Georg Brandes und Arthur Schnitzler: Ein Briefwechsel* (Bern: Francke, 1956), p. 117.

19. In his diary, Schnitzler rejects what would be empty rhetoric in the face of the insurmountable political realities of Europe in 1915: "Nm Heinrich Mendel; über seinen Actionsplan: Schriftsteller (u.a. prominente Leute) der kriegsführenden Staaten sollen in der Schweiz sich versammeln, einen Aufruf erlassen gegen die Verhetzung der Völker, darauf hinweisen, daß

die Völker einander nicht hassen, nur die Regierungen etc. Wer
ev. dazu zu gewinnen sei, wen ich in Österreich vorschlage.—
Ich verhalte mich, den jetzigen Weltzustand betrachtend zu der
Idee sehr skeptisch. Was gesagt werden könnte ist Phrase,
Selbstverständlichkeiten;—kommt man aufs concrete, so ist das
politische nicht zu umgehen, wofür heute, aus innern und äußern
Gründen Discussionsmöglichkeit zwischen Angehörigen
feindlicher Mächte nicht vorhanden.—" In: *Arthur Schnitzler:
Tagebuch 1913-1916*, pp. 172-173.
20.   Arthur Schnitzler, *AuB*, p. 187. "Suttner," October 1914.
21.   In fact Schnitzler first mentions the Suttners in his diary on 12
May 1891. Arthur Schnitzler. *Tagebuch 1879-1892*, p. 330. It
is therefore highly likely that Schnitzler had read and been influenced by Suttner's pacifist novel, *Die Waffen nieder* (1889),
though his diary makes no mention of the work.
22.   Arthur Schnitzler, *Tagebuch 1913-1916*, p. 71.
23.   Ibid., p. 85.
24.   Ibid., p. 103.
25.   Rolland won the Nobel Prize for Literature in 1915 (awarded in
1916).
See the letters of Arthur Schnitzler to Romain Rolland in *Arthur
Schnitzler: Briefe 1913-1931* (Frankfurt am Main: S. Fischer,
1984), pp. 63-64 and pp. 69-70.
27.   Stefan Zweig. Unpublished letter dated 3 December 1914 to
Arthur Schnitzler, cited with permission. "Arthur Schnitzler.
Nachlaß." UCLA.
28.   Romain Rolland, *Je commence à devenir dangereux. Choix de
lettres de R. R. à sa mère 1914-1919* (Paris: Albin Michel,
1971), p. 72.
29.   Stefan Zweig, published letter dated 16 January 1915 to Arthur
Schnitzler, cited with permission. "Arthur Schnitzler. Nachlaß."
UCLA.
30.   Romain Rolland, *Au-dessus de la mêlée* (Paris: Paul Ollendorff,
1915), 163 pp.
In a letter to Hermann Hesse dated 20 January 1932, Rolland
indicates that during the first months of the War he [like
Schnitzler!] had difficulty freeing himself "from the thick clouds
of ignorance massed together for us by the governments and by
their press ..." In: Hermann Hesse, *Hermann Hesse and*

Romain Rolland. Correspondence, Diary Entries and Reflections, 1915 to 1940. Trans. M. G. Hesse (London: Oswald Wolff, 1978), p. 119.

31. Arthur Schnitzler, *Tagebuch 1913-1916*, p. 272.
32. See Robert O. Weiss's comments as to why he did not include this essay in his edition of "Und einmal." In: Arthur Schnitzler, *AuB*, p. 507, note 7.
33. Arthur Schnitzler, "Und einmal wird der Friede wiederkommen" (University of California, Los Angeles. Special Collection no. 511, reel 23, file 230), p. 35.
    Fourteen years after the war, in a letter to Hesse, Rolland recognizes and even regrets the chauvinism inherent in *Au-dessus*, but he is not willing to retract his words for he believes them to be a document of the past, written honestly in the passion of the moment. See Hermann Hesse, *Hermann Hesse and Romain Rolland.* In his letter to Hesse dated 20 January 1932 Rolland writes: "...there can be no doubt as to how I personally judge my first articles on the war. I myself denounce today their exaggerations and errors.—*But I do not have the right to change them.* They are historical texts. I have written them. *I must take responsibility for them*" (p. 119).
34. Schnitzler describes Rolland as appearing "müd,...krank und hypochondrisch..., ganz schwarz gekleidet (ohne in Trauer zu sein); mit schönen blauen Augen, die mehr Herz als Geist ausstrahlen." In: Arthur Schnitzler, "Unveröffentlichte Tagebücher" (Wien: Österreichische Akademie der Wissenschaften. Diplomatische Abschrift).
35. Arthur Schnitzler, "Unveröffentlichte Tagebücher."
36. Arthur Schnitzler, *AuB*, "Politik, Gesellschaft," pp. 231-240.
37. Arthur Schnitzler, "Unveröffentlichte Tagebücher."
38. Ibid.
39. Ibid.
40. D. A. Prater, *European of Yesterday. A Biography of Stefan Zweig* (Oxford: At the Clarendon Press, 1972).
41. Cedric Ellis Williams, *The Broken Eagle: The Politics of Austrian Literature from Empire to Anschluß* (London: Paul Elek, 1974).
42. Arthur Schnitzler, *Tagebuch 1913-1916*, p. 133.
43. Ibid., p. 260.

44. Karl Kraus, *Die Fackel*, (Vol. 20, No. 484-498), p. 127.
45. Arthur Schnitzler, *Tagebuch 1913-1916*, p. 268.
46. Ibid., p. 317.
47. Arthur Schnitzler, *Tagebuch 1917-1919* (Wien: Österreichische Akademie der Wissenschaften, 1985), p. 247.
48. Arthur Schnitzler, *Tagebuch 1913-1916*, p. 92.
49. Ulrich K. Goldsmith, ed. "Der Briefwechsel Fritz von Unruhs mit Arthur Schnitzler." *Modern Austrian Literature* 10, No. 3/4 (1977), pp. 69-127.
50. Ibid., p. 109.
51. Fritz von Unruh. *Ein Geschlecht. Tragödie* (Leipzig: Kurt Wolff, 1918), p. 63.
52. Arthur Schnitzler, "Unveröffentlichte Tagebücher."
53. Arthur Schnitzler, "Unveröffentlichte Tagebücher." Diary entry of 20 March 1924: "*Unruh* kam; was er sagte, war viel klarer und echter als was er vorgelesen.... *Unruh* erzählte von seinen Kriegserlebnissen;...die anonymen Drohbriefe gegen ihn (Unruh); die ununterbrochene Lebensgefahr in der er durch die Hakenkreuzler schwebt;—Alles einfach, lebendig bewegt;—könnte er durch das geschriebene Wort eben so wirken, dann wär' er der große Dichter, der er bei allen genialen Zügen heute *nicht* ist. Als ganzes und ganzer aber war er heute und ist er wunderbar;—ich liebte ihn sehr...."
54. Arthur Schnitzler, *Tagebuch 1917-1919* (Wien: Österreichische Akademie der Wissenschaften, 1985), pp. 84-85.
55. Latzko's cynical words "Der hatte auch sein Bein hingeopfert 'für's Vaterland,'" Andreas Latzko, *Menschen im Krieg* (Zürich: Max Rascher, 1917), p. 181 are echoed in Schnitzler's undated aphorism: "Man sagt, er ist den schönen Heldentod gestorben. Warum sagt man nie, er hat eine herrliche Heldentod erlitten? Man sagt, er ist für das Vaterland gefallen. Warum sagt man nie, er hat sich für das Vaterland beide Beine amputieren lassen? "Die Etymologie der Machthaber," *AuB*, p. 220. Schnitzler illustrates the numbing effect of conventional war rhetoric when he replaces the almost mystical term "Heldentod" with the gruesome notion of "Helden-verstümmelung." The result is the demystification of death and those who cause it.
56. Arthur Schnitzler, "Unveröffentlichte Tagebücher."
57. Ibid.

58. Nicolai quotes the manifesto as follows: "Es ist nicht wahr, daß Deutschland diesen Krieg verschuldet hat. Weder das Volk hat ihn gewollt, noch die Regierung, noch der Kaiser." In: Georg Friedrich Nicolai, *Die Biologie des Krieges. Betrachtungen eines Naturforschers den Deutschen zur Besinnung.* (Zürich: Art. Institut Orell Füssli, 1919), p. 7.
59. Ibid., pp. 287-288. This quotation is from the section "Kulturpatriotismus." Nicolai's use of the term "Vaterland" here implies simply one's "country." Elsewhere Nicolai, like Schnitzler, attributes political character to the term.
60. Ibid., p. 259.
61. Arthur Schnitzler, "Unveröffentlichte Tagebücher." On 30 July 1922 Schnitzler writes in his diary: "... Die Satire glänzend, bis zum großartigen;—man gesteht ihm unwillkürlich bezwungen durch seine Kraft, das Recht auf Übertreibungen und Ungerechtigkeiten (durch Verschweigen von mancherlei) zu—ohne die ja Satire nie auszukommen vermag."
62. Karl Kraus, *The Last Days of Mankind*, p. 258.
63. Arthur Schnitzler. "Unveröffentlichte Tagebücher." Diary entry of 29 May 1927. Friedrich Gustav Piffl (1864-1932), to whom Schnitzler refers here was Archbishop of Vienna during the final years of the First World War. He was responsible for the appointment on 9 April 1917 of the anti-Semitic Max von Millenkovich as director of the Burgtheater.
64. Letter dated 7 November 1929 from Arthur Schnitzler to Richard Nickolaus Graf Coudenhove-Kalergi. In: *Arthur Schnitzler: Briefe 1913-1931* (Frankfurt am Main: S. Fischer, 1984), p. 628.
65. Arthur Schnitzler, "Unveröffentlichte Tagebücher."
66. Arthur Schnitzler, *AuB*, p. 225. Undated aphorism. Schnitzler echoes Karl Kraus's identical use of the terms "Große Zeit" and "Kleine Zeit" in his essay, "In dieser großen Zeit." In: *Die Fackel*, Vol. 16, No. 404 (5 December 1914), pp. 1-2. Kraus writes: "In dieser großen Zeit die ich noch gekannt habe, wie sie so klein war; die wieder klein werden wird, wenn ihr dazu noch Zeit bleibt..., mögen Sie von mir kein eigenes Wort erwarten...."
67. Arthur Schnitzler. "Unveröffentlichte Tagebücher" (Wien: Österreichische Akademie der Wissenschaften. Diplomatische Abschrift). The essays on war remained unpublished until 1939 when Schnitzler's son Heinrich published *Über Krieg und*

Frieden, an abridged version of the loosely organized material
from a folder among his father's posthumous documents, labeled
"Und einmal wird der Friede wiederkommen..." Many of the
essays and aphorisms remained unpublished until their inclusion
in the volume of Schnitzler's collected works entitled
Aphorismen und Betrachtungen (1967), edited by Robert O.
Weiss. Because I shall limit my discussion here to the material
contained in the chapter "Und einmal..." (pp. 187-230) of the
volume *Aphorismen und Betrachtungen,* my designation "Und
einmal" will refer only to the material in that work.

68.   Arthur Schnitzler, *AuB,* p. 220. On 21 September 1908, just six
years before the War, Schnitzler writes in his diary the keen
insights of his then six-year-old son, Heinrich, on war and military service: "....Heini neulich: 'Warum bin ich nicht lieber ein
Mädel geworden ... Plötzlich wird ein Plakat erscheinen darauf
wird stehn "Krieg" und ich werde leider dabei sein..' Später im
Bett: 'Ja .. jetzt kommt die Schule, dann kommt das Militär ..
und dann kommt das Sterben.'" Arthur Schnitzler.
"Unveröffentlichte Tagebücher."

69.   Arthur Schnitzler, "Unveröffentlichte Tagebücher." The above
quotation represents details recalled from a conversation with his
pacifist friend, Josef Popper-Lynkeus. During the War,
Schnitzler became close friends with Popper-Lynkeus, author of
Die allgemeine Nährpflicht als Lösung der sozialen Frage
(1912), and *Krieg, Wehrpflicht und Staatsverfassung* (1921).
The two men shared many views on war, including an unequivocal condemnation of universal conscription.

70.   See such works as Ernst Jünger's *In Stahlgewittern* (1920) and
Ludwig Renn's *Krieg* (1929).

71.   Ironically, the airplane supplied the warring governments with a
way in which to bring back the positive notion of "ritterliches
Heldentum" to further the cause of the War. In Germany for
example, the outdated cavalry simply changed its mounts from
horses to airplanes and the "knights of the air" were born.
In the early years of the War the primitive state of aero technology (i.e., slow, inefficient planes and weapon systems) actually
allowed a favorable comparison between aerial combat and the
sport of knightly jousting. Germany's leading ace, Cavalry
Captain ("Rittmeister") Manfred Albrecht Freiherr von

Richthofen (appropriately known as the "Red Knight of Germany" or the "Red Baron" because of his blood-red plane), writes in his autobiography: "Der Luftkampf ist in diesem Weltkrieg der Rest des ritterlichen Zweikampfes.... Ein ritterlicher Kampf mit gleichen Waffen, jeder mit einem Maschinengewehr und einem Flugzeug, ein wenig sportliches Können und: im übrigen wird nur das Herz gewogen." In: Manfred von Richthofen, *Ein Heldenleben* (Berlin: Ullstein, 1920), pp. 162-163.

72. Arthur Schnitzler, *AuB*, p. 215.
73. Ibid., p. 201.
74. Ibid., p. 207.
75. Ibid., p. 224.
76. Ibid., p. 224.
77. Arthur Schnitzler, *AuB*, p. 211. Compare Bertha von Suttner on the education of the young toward a positive attitude on war in *Die Waffen nieder,* pp. 3-4.
78. Cited in Friedrich Heer's introduction to Bertha von Suttner, *Die Waffen nieder* (Wien: H. Javorsky, 1967), p. i.
79. Theodor Reik, "Zerstörung des ritterlichen Heldenbegriffes." *Pan,* 2, no. 1-45 (1911-1912), p. 591.
80. Arthur Schnitzler, *AuB*, p. 201. Schnitzler's ideas seem to overlap once again with Suttner's. Suttner writes in *Die Waffen nieder* (p. 118): [in a conversation between Martha and Friedrich von Tilling] Friedrich: "'...Man sollte glauben, wenn man beim Anblick eines vereinzelten Leidens von Mitgefühl ergriffen ist, daß vertausendfachtes Leid auch tausendmal stärkeres Mitgefühl wecken müßte. Aber das Gegenteil tritt ein: die Massenhaftigkeit stumpfte ab....'" Tilling is one of but a few individuals who is able, in the absence of compassion, to nevertheless rationalize the greater suffering of a thousand as opposed to that of one person.
81. Arthur Schnitzler, *AuB*, p. 223.
82. Arthur Schnitzler, *AuB*, pp. 222-223.
83. Reinhart Müller-Freienfels, "Das Lebensgefühl in Arthur Schnitzler's Dramen." Dissertation. Frankfurt am Main, 1954, p. 66.
84. Arthur Schnitzler, *AuB*, p. 222.
85. Arthur Schnitzler, "Schicksal und Wille," in: *Buch der Sprüche*

und Bedenken. Aphorismen und Fragmente (Wien: Phaidon, 1927), pp. 56-57.

86.   Arthur Schnitzler, *AuB*, p. 230   In *Die Waffen nieder*, Bertha von Suttner also points out the illogical conection between prayer and predestination: "(Tante Marie:) '...für einen Soldaten gibt's auch nichts besseres als den Krieg. So müßt auch du die Sache betrachten, liebes Kind—Beruferfüllung geht doch allem voran. Was sein muß.—' 'Ja, du hast recht, Tante, was sein muß—das Unabänderliche.—' 'Das von Gott gewollte' schaltete Tante Marie bekräftigend ein. 'Man muß mit Fassung und Ergebung ertragen.' 'Bravo, Martha. Es kommt ja doch alles so wie von der weisen und allgütigen Vorsehung in unabänderlichem Ratschluß vorher bestimmt ist. Die Sterbestunde eines jedem, die steht schon in der Stunde seiner Geburt an geschrieben. Und wir wollen für unsere lieben Krieger so viel und insbrünstig beten.—'" In: Bertha von Suttner, *Die Waffen nieder*, p. 14.

87.   Of all the wisdom and prophecy in "Und einmal," one paragraph appears to stand out in its contemporary relevance to the nuclear threat, though Schnitzler could never have anticipated the magnitude of present day dangers: "Irgendwo in der Welt steht eine verkorkte Flasche. Darin wirbelt, zuckt, brodelt es in steter Bewegung. Und überall ist große Angst, daß die Flasche zerspringen und der glühend flüssige Inhalt sowie die fliegenden Splitter viel Unheil anrichten könnten. Nach einem merkwürdigen Gesetz aber ist das Recht, diese Flasche zu entkorken, nur einer bestimmten Gruppe von Leuten anheimgegeben, und die Gefahr des Verletzt- und Getötetwerdens durch den ausströmenden Inhalt der Flasche steigt um so höher, je entfernter von der Flasche man sich aufhält..." Arthur Schnitzler, *AuB*, pp. 224-225.) The proximity to the bottle, is figurative; those closest to it would be the politicians who have the power to unleash its contents.

88.   Because of the relative inaccesibility of the documents, both remained unknown, the first, entitled "Kriegsgeschichte," until 1967, the second, "Der Oberstabsarzt," until 1977. In both cases the fragments, edited by Reinhard Urbach, appeared without any commentary, and no criticism has since been written. See: Arthur Schnitzler. "Kriegsgeschichte," *Literatur und Kritik*, 13,

no. 101 (May 1967), pp. 133-134.

89. Arthur Schnitzler, "Unveröffentlichte Tagebücher."

90. Arthur Schnitzler, *Tagebuch 1913-1916*, p. 191. Schnitzler writes: "Notizen zu einer 'Kriegsnovelle.'"

91. Renate Wagner, *Arthur Schnitzler: Eine Biographie*, p. 279.

92. Arthur Schnitzler, *AuB*, p. 413. Compare Schnitzler's letter to Georg Brandes, dated 9 December 1915, in: Kurt Bergel, *Georg Brandes und Arthur Schnitzler: Ein Briefwechsel* (Bern: Francke, 1956), pp. 117-118. Compare also Schnitzler's letter to Thomas Mann, dated November 6, 1924, in: Hertha Krotkoff, ed. "Arthur Schnitzler—Thomas Mann: Briefe," *Modern Austrian Literature*, 7, no. 1/2 (1974), 22-23.

93. Arthur Schnitzler, *Entworfenes und Verworfenes*, p. 410.

94. Arthur Schnitzler, *EuV*, p. 411.

95. Ibid., p. 411.

96. If Schnitzler were using Stephi Bachrach as a model for the female lead in his story, then the death of the former might explain that of the latter.

97. Plans for the work were made in 1915 and the fragment was written in 1927. Arthur Schnitzler, *EuV*, p. 522.

98. Ibid., p. 438.

99. On 13 October 1914, for example, Schnitzler visited the Rothschild-Spital and observed his friend Otto Zuckerkandl operating on wounded soldiers. See A. S., *Tagebuch 1913-1916*, p. 143.

100. Arthur Schnitzler, *EuV*, p. 435.

101. Ibid., p. 438.

102. Arthur Schnitzler's profound affection for Stephi Bachrach made her a model for numerous other figures in his later works. Fräulein Else's apparent suicide with veronal and morphine is certainly traceable to Stephi's own suicide in 1917 using the same drugs.

103. Arthur Schnitzler, *EuV*, p. 438. The tired pessimism with which Schnitzler observed, but could not prevent, Stephi's demise is reflected in the conclusion of "Der Oberstabsarzt." Rudi is killed in battle (unlike Rudi Olden who lived until 1940), the Austrian army is forced into a retreat, and Gerty falls seriously ill. A strange sense of indifference towards everything that has happened overcomes Robert. An unwitting victim of the

War, he meekly reproaches himself for his inability to feel genuine emotions any longer, and Gerty ironically falls victim not to the War, but to influenza.

104. Dating Schnitzler's works is thus a difficult task. His diaries serve, however, as a source for the chronological development of each work.

105. Arthur Schnitzler, *Tagebuch 1909-1912*, pp. 191-192. Diary entry of 12 November 1910: "-Nm. notirte ich etliches zu dem Stoff des Journalisten, der sich mit sich selber schlagen muss.—"

106. Arthur Schnitzler, *DdW*, Vol. 7, p. 102.

107. Ibid., p. 115.

108. Ibid., p. 125.

109. Arthur Schnitzler, *AuB*, p. 215.

110. Arthur Schnitzler, *DdW*, Vol. 7, pp. 147-148.

111. Ibid., p. 182.

112. Arthur Schnitzler, *AuB*, pp. 362-449. Schnitzler agonized over publishing "Materialien" because he feared that it might merely lend fuel to the fires of anti-Semitism.

113. Arthur Schnitzler, *DdW*, Vol. 7, p. 157.

114. Arthur Schnitzler, *Tagebuch 1913-1916*, p. 294.

115. Offermanns writes: "Vermutlich zielt die Figur des Leuchters satirisch auf den autokratischen Chefredakteur der Neuen Freien Presse Moritz Benedikt, gegen den auch die Pressekritik von Karl Kraus beharrlich gerichtet ist." Offermanns. "Arthur Schnitzlers Komödie 'Fink und Fliederbusch,'" *Modern Austrian Literature*, 3, no. 2 (1970), p.22.

116. Arthur Schnitzler, *Arthur Schnitzler: Briefe 1913-1931*. Ed. Peter Michael Braunwarth, Richard Miklin, Susanne Pertlik, and Heinrich Schnitzler (Frankfurt am Main: S. Fischer, 1984), p. 853.

117. Arthur Schnitzler, *Tagebuch 1913-1916*, p. 140. Schnitzler again mentions Fischer in connection with the underestimation of Austria by Germany: "Abend Hptm. Matras, der meinen Beistand in allerlei lit. und geschäftl. Angelegenheiten erbat. Wir sprachen Politik—und insbesondre über die Unterschätzung österreichischen Geistes im Reich (Verlag Fischer u.a.)." Arthur Schnitzler, *Tagebuch 1917-1919*, p. 225.

118. See the full text of Schnitzler's letter to Fischer in: Arthur Schnitzler, *Arthur Schnitzler: Briefe 1913-1931*, pp. 45-47.

119. Arthur Schnitzler, *Tagebuch 1913-1916*, p. 149.
120. Arthur Schnitzler, *DeW*, Vol. 4. 1963, p. 93.
121. Arthur Schnitzler, *AuB*, "Politik, Gesellschaft," pp. 231-232.
122. Arthur Schnitzler, *Tagebuch 1913-1916*, p. 138.
123. Karl Kraus, *Werke*, Vol. 7, Ed. Heinrich Fischer (München: Kösel, 1967), p. 134. Kraus writes: "Artur [sic] Schnitzler / Sein Wort vom Sterben wog nicht schwer. / Doch wo viel Feinde, ist viel Ehr: / er hat in Schlachten und Siegen / geschwiegen."
124. Karl Kraus. "In dieser großen Zeit." In: *Die Fackel*, Vol. 16, no. 404 (December 1914), 2.

    See also Friedrich Vollhardt. "Wer etwas zu sagen hat, trete vor und schweige! Anmerkungen zu einer unbekannten Erklärung Dr. Arthur Schnitzlers (zum Fall Ernst Tollers) aus dem Jahr 1919." In: *Literatur und Kritik*, 157/158 (August/ September 1981), 462-473. Vollhardt concludes that Schnitzler's response to a forged document opposing the intended execution of Ernst Toller does not constitute enough evidence to refute the contention that Schnitzler remained silent on political issues. Schnitzler's diary entry of 25 June 1919 reveals the forger to be the actor Alexander Moissi, at that time a professed communist. Vollhardt appears to have been unaware of the forger's identity for makes no mention of Moissi in his essay.
125. Heinrich Schnitzler and Therese Nickl explain the situation leading to Schnitzler's letter of 5 December 1907 to the editor of the *Morgen*: "Harden [the pseudonym of Maximilian Felix Ernst Witkowski] hatte den engsten Kreis um Wilhelm II. und die 'Hofkamarilla' übler Machenschaften (u.a. Spiritismus, Homosexualität) beschuldigt. Der Freund des Kaisers, Philipp Fürst zu Eulenburg-Hertefeld (1847-1921), verklagte ihn wegen Verleumdung, und Harden wurde Ende Dezember 1907 verurteilt. ... Die in einer Rundfrage um Stellungsnahme gebetenen Schriftsteller sollten die Frage beantworten, ob man es bei Harden 'mit einem Manne zu tun habe, der seine zweifellos hervorragenden Gaben zum Zwecke des allgemeinen Wohls verwendet, oder ob er sich ihrer lediglich in seinem Privatinteresse bedient.'" In: Arthur Schnitzler. *Arthur Schnitzler: Briefe 1875-1912*, Ed. Heinrich Schnitzler (Frankfurt am Main: S. Fischer, 1981), p. 935, note 2.
126. Schnitzler's letter to the editor of the *Morgen*, dated 5 December

1907. Ibid., p. 569.

127. Arthur Schnitzler, *Tagebuch 1917-1919*, p. 11.

128. Ibid., p. 162.

129. Ibid., p. 166.

130. Ibid., p. 196.

131. Ibid., p. 229.

132. Ibid., p. 229.

133. Ibid., p. 257. Compare also the following diary entry (same source, p. 266) dated 25 June 1919. Here Schnitzler again rejects the idea of making public declarations about war and peace, preferring instead to work pragmatically on the revision of the misunderstood concept of "honor": "Hugo Ganz regt zu einem öffentlichen Aufruf an Barbusse u.a. an, gegen die ehrenrührigen Forderungen des deutschen Friedensvertrags, die den nächsten Krieg hervorrufen werden. Halte das für aussichtslos. Wichtiger wäre es, den falschen Begriff 'Ehre' zu revidieren—und das Gefühl allgemein zu machen, daß die eigne Ehre niemals durch einen andern verletzt werden kann.—" Cf. *AuB*, p. 224.

134. Arthur Schnitzler, *Tagebuch 1917-1919*, p. 218.

135. Schnitzler writes: "Leute die in Weltverbesserungsplänen eine Möglichkeit ethischer Besserung der Menschheitsmasse in Rechnung stellen, erscheinen mir wie Mathematiker, die ein Problem auf der Basis von 2 X 2 = 5 weiterzuentwickeln suchen. Güte so selten wie Genie,—da Güte Genie des Herzens. Von allen Menschen, denen ich begegnet bin, hat es nur (vielleicht) Popper Lynkeus." Arthur Schnitzler, *Tagebuch 1917-1919*, p. 221.

136. Arthur Schnitzler, *Tagebuch 1917-1919*, pp. 231-232.

Notes to Chapter 6

1.   Schnitzler began the work in earnest in 1915 and continued revising it even after its publication.

2.   Ernst L. Offermanns, *Arthur Schnitzler: Das Komödienwerk als Kritik des Impressionismus* (München: Wilhelm Fink, 1973), p. 169.

3.   Stefan Zweig is credited with being the first to have called

168   Adrian Clive Roberts

Schnitzler's post-War works literature of a "versunkene Welt." The label stuck, and Jakob Wassermann wrote to Schnitzler, accusing him of writing about an "abgetane, zum Tod verurteilte Welt" (26 October 1924).

4.   Cedric Ellis Williams, *The Broken Eagle: The Politics of Austrian Literature from Empire to Anschluß* (London: Paul Elek, 1974), p. 59. Williams treats Arthur Schnitzler under the chapter heading "Arthur Schnitzler: The Astigmatic Vision" (pp. 45-59).

5.   Renate Wagner, *Arthur Schnitzler: Eine Biographie* (Wien: Fritz Molden, 1981), pp. 278-279.

6.   Brigitte Lina Schneider-Halvorson, *The Late Dramatic Works of Arthur Schnitzler* (Bern: Peter Lang, 1983), p. 107.

7.   Arthur Schnitzler, *Der Geist im Wort und der Geist in der Tat* (Berlin: S. Fischer, 1927). This work was most recently published as a chapter by the same name in *AuB.*, pp. 135-166.

8.   Arthur Schnitzler, "Unveröffentlichte Tagebücher" (Wien: Österreichische Akademie der Wissenschaften. Diplomatische Abschrift). Diary entry of 4 April 1924. Schnitzler writes: "—Mit Heini u Hans Jakob Pohl gen[.];—über den Titel meines Stücks (das Jakob noch nicht kennt); statt Verführ[er] vielleicht 'Die Komödie vom Verführer'.—" This title is one step short of the final version.

9.   William H. Rey, "Judith—Aurelie—Seraphine. Zu Schnitzler's 'Komödie der Verführung'." In: Leland R. Phelps, ed. *Creative Encounter. Festschrift for Herman Salinger*. (Chapel Hill: University of North Carolina Press, 1978), p. 134.

10. In her chapter on *Verführung* Schneider-Halvorson makes a fleeting allusion to the personification in the characters Westerhaus and Arduin of the three causes of war discussed by Schnitzler in *Über Krieg und Frieden* (the posthumously published version of some of the materials in "Und einmal..."): "In his estimation, wars are only possible under three conditions, namely: '1. durch die Schurkerei der Mächtigen, 2. die Dummheit der Diplomatie, und 3. die Phantasielosigkeit der Völker.' The first two points are demonstrated by Westerhaus and Arduin, the third one was hinted at in different places." Schneider-Halvorson, *The Late Dramatic Works*, pp. 79-80. Schneider-Halvorson's interpretation of this play supports my hypothesis that there is a strong

connection between Schnitzler's essays on war and his post-War literary works. Although war is only an aspect of her interpretation, Schneider-Halvorson goes beyond all previous critics in her discussion of war in *Verführung*.

11.   Letter from Arthur Schnitzler to Jakob Wassermann, in: Heinrich Schnitzler, ed., "Arthur Schnitzler—Briefe." *Neue Rundschau*, 68, no. 1 (1957), 99.

12.   A conversation in *Verführung* between Ambros and Arduin implies that a true "Dichter" (not a "Literat" like Ambros) is able through an understanding of human nature and political tides to anticipate future events. Schnitzler also attacks journalists who are interested only in furthering their careers. Arduin is surprised that Ambros appears to have information on the status of the impending war, which has eluded him in his diplomatic missions:

ARDUIN: Seit wann haben Dichter Informationen?
AMBROS: Dichter nicht, aber Journalisten.

DdW. Vol. 8, p. 209

The irony lies in the circumstances that although the journalist has more information than the diplomat (whose job it is to know what is happening in political circles), his knowledge is useless because it is gained too late in order to prevent the war. It can only sensationalize the conflict.

13.   Arthur Schnitzler, *DdW*, Vol. 8, pp. 116-117.

14.   In "Und einmal" (*AuB*, p. 229) Schnitzler writes: "Epoche Karl V. Er kann nicht Krieg führen, weil er kein Geld hat. Einzig reelle und erlaubte Basis des Militarismus."

15.   Arthur Schnitzler, *DdW*, Vol. 8, p. 117.

16.   Schnitzler writes: "Das unnützeste und zugleich gefährlichste Element der menschlichen Gesellschaft bilden Individuen, deren zielgerichtete Begabung zu ihrer geistigen Beweglichkeit in einem auffälligen Mißverhältnis steht...Auf drei Lebensgebieten aber ist eine... Kontrolle praktisch nicht durchführbar, auf den Gebieten der *Politik*, des *Journalismus* und der *Spekulation*. ... Ihrem unwiderstehlichen angeborenen Drange folgend, sind sie nur darauf bedacht, ohne einen inneren oder auch nur äußeren

Anlaß abzuwarten, das Räderwerk ihres Wesens in Gang zu setzen, das dann wie eine kunstvoll-nutzlose Maschine hungrig im Leeren läuft, zu nichts anderem gut als Lärm zu verbreiten und oft genug im näheren und auch ferneren Umkreis Unheil anzurichten." Arthur Schnitzler, B*uch der Sprüche und Bedenken. Aphorismen und Fragmente* (Wien: Phaidon, 1927), pp. 144-145.

17. Arthur Schnitzler, *DdW*, Vol. 8, p. 120. Schneider-Halvorson's interpretation of Lieutenant Leindorf's ensuing statement that the rumors of war are unfounded, is correct in as far as she says it reflects irony. The irony, however, lies not in the fact that "those closest to the source know the least," (Schneider-Halvorson, *The Late Dramatic Works*, p. 67.) but in the axiom that those who will be first affected by the war (the soldiers) are generally the last ones to find out about it.

18. Schnitzler used real political events as underlying catalysts for action in his works as early as 1880 in the case of the Gambetta speech in "Über den Patriotismus," mentioned earlier.

19. Schneider-Halvorson, *The Late Dramatic Works*, p. 63.

20. Arthur Schnitzler, *DdW*, Vol. 8, p. 170.

21. Ibid., p. 167.

22. Ibid., p. 167.

23. Ibid., p. 119.

24. Ibid., p. 222.

25. Aurelie is Schnitzler's version of the modern liberated woman who, like Leonilda in *Der Gang*, belongs to no man but who ultimately chooses to die alongside Falkenir rather than face a world bent on self-destruction.

26. Arthur Schnitzler, *DdW*, Vol. 8, p. 163.

27. Ibid., p. 242.

28. Arthur Schnitzler, *Tagebuch 1913-1916*, p. 264. Schnitzler's portrait of the Duke is a critical one, as is reflected in the words of Josef Körner: "Der neue Herzog, von Pariser Enzyklopädisten mit den Idealen der Aufklärung erfüllt, tritt besten Willens sein hohes Amt an. Aber schon am ersten Tage seines Waltens begegnet ihm so viel Niedrigkeit und Bosheit, daß er der Ansteckung erliegt und 'in kurzer Frist ein Fürst wird von ganz ähnlicher Art wie seine Ahnen es gewesen: Kein geradezu schlimmer Herr..., aber auch keiner von den besten.'" In: Josef

Körner, "Arthur Schnitzlers Spätwerk," *Preußische Jahrbücher*, Vol. 208, no. 2 (1927), 155.

29. Arthur Schnitzler, *Tagebuch 1913-1916*, p. 264.

30. Similarly, in Suttner's *Die Waffen nieder*, Martha responds to her militaristic father's suggestion that she keep for posterity all the the newspaper articles about the current war: "Und ich habe sie aufgehoben. Das sollte man immer tun; und wenn ein neuer Völkerzwist heranzieht, dann lese man nicht die neuesten Zeitungen, sondern die, welche von vorigem Krieg datieren, und man wird sehen, was alle den Prophezeiungen und Prahlereien und auch den Berichten und Nachrichten für Wahrheitswert beizumessen ist. Das ist lehrreich." Bertha von Suttner, *Die Waffen nieder*, pp. 156-157.

31. Arthur Schnitzler, *Tagebuch 1913-1916*, p. 200.

32. Arthur Schnitzler, Draft of a letter to Josef Körner, dated 11 July 1927. Arthur Schnitzler. "Nachlaß." Microfilm collection 511, reel A, file 20, page 106. Special Collections, Research Library, University of California, Los Angeles.
     Schnitzler encountered a similar problem with his friend, Felix Salten: "*Dieses nicht sehen WOLLEN:*—dieser nur auf das erotische Problem gebannte Blick,—dieses geflissentliche Nicht ahnen [sic] von der politischen Hälfte;—dieses Nichtmerken der Kanzlergestalt;—das Überhören der Verse, von denen manche doch wirklich schön, und dramatisch schön sind...." In: Arthur Schnitzler, "Unveröffentlichte Tagebücher." (Wien: Österreichische Akademie der Wissenschaften. Diplomatische Abschrift.)

33. Josef Körner, "Arthur Schnitzlers Spätwerk," p. 81.

34. Arthur Schnitzler. Letter to Josef Körner, 11 July 1927. ("Nachlaß," UCLA). The scene between the Chancellor and the Marschall's son will be discussed at a later point in this section; it merits special attention.

35. Harold Dickerson, "Water and Vision as Mystical Elements in Schnitzler's *Der Gang zum Weiher*," *Modern Austrian Literature*, 4, no. 3 (Fall 1971), 25.

36. Dickerson, p. 28.

37. Schneider-Halvorson. *The Late Dramatic Works, p. 98.*

38. Arthur Schnitzler, *Der Gang zum Weiher*, *DdW*, Vol. 8 (Frankfurt am Main: S. Fischer, 1974), p. 110. A parallel figure

to Leonilda may be seen in Marcolina (Schnitzler's *Casanovas Heimfahrt*, [1918]). She also represents Schnitzler's modern, liberated woman, yet she too remains naive about war. As in *Der Gang*, there is a war in the offing. A double meaning emerges when Marcolina innocently asks, upon hearing that several regiments have marched off in the direction of Milan, "Gibt's Krieg?" (Arthur Schnitzler. *Casanovas Heimfahrt.* In: *Das erzählerische Werk*, Vol. 5 (Frankfurt am Main: S. Fischer, 1964), p. 46. The senselessness of war is reflected in the wording of Olivo's sarcastic rhetorical question: "Weiß man den überhaupt auf welche Seite wir uns schlagen werden, auf die spanische oder auf die französische?" (Arthur Schnitzler, *DeW*, Vol. 5, p. 46.)

39.   Arthur Schnitzler, *DdW*, Vol. 8, p. 26.

40.   An inconsistency is brought up by Hugo von Hofmannsthal concerning the concepts "Heimatsliebe" and "Vaterlandsgefühl" during the time in question: "*Hugo* warf die Frage auf, ob zu der von mir supponirten Zeit 1750 der Begriff 'Heimatsliebe' (im Gegensatz zu Vaterlandsgefühl schon vorhanden gewesen);—" Arthur Schnitzler, "Unveröffentlichte Tagebücher." In May 1915, with Italy about to enter the War against Austria and Germany, Schnitzler reveals as his own, the sentiments he attributes to Sylvester: "Nach Tisch bei Richard....Wir empfinden die Demütigung, die Österreichs abgewiesene Anerbieten bedeuten;—empfinden das Schicksal dieses Landes so tief wie andre, tiefer vielleicht. Wie verwurzelt ist man doch mit dem Land, das einen geboren! Was gehn uns am Ende die Mitbürger, die Diplomaten, die Monarchen an? Das Land! Die Heimat!—" Arthur Schnitzler, *Tagebuch 1913-1916*, p. 199. Cf.: Sylvester: "Denn Heimat war es nun—nicht Vaterland, / Nicht eines Fürsten Zufallsreich, das morgen / Vielleicht zerfallen wird, wie's gestern ward. / Jetzt war's die Heimat erst, die mich umgab— / Der Erdenfleck, der mir gehört, so wie / Ich ihm, wer immer ihn als Fürst beherrsche." *DdW*., Vol. 8, p. 39.

41.   Ernst Christian Helmreich, *The Diplomacy of the Balkan Wars 1912-1913* (Cambridge: Harvard University Press, 1938), p. 324. Schnitzler's diary entry of May 24, 1913 refers to both Conrad and Berchtold: "...Conrad v. Hötzendorf, der Patriot.— Graf Berchtold, unser Minister des Äußern,—beim Rennen, am

Tag von Skutari,—..." (Arthur Schnitzler. *Tagebuch 1913-1916*, p. 40.)

42. Arthur Schnitzler, *DdW*, Vol. 8, p. 30. Compare "Und einmal": Es wiederholen sich die Anekdoten von den Feinden, die einander in den Schützengräben gegenüberliegen, einander in den Schießpausen Zeichen geben, sich in der neutralen Mitte begegnen, Zigaretten und Nahrungsmittel austauschen, einander die Hände drücken (einmal sollen sich zwei weinend um den Hals gefallen sein) und dann in ihre Gräben zurückkehren, um sich gegenseitig totzuschießen, ohne Haß. Sie haben sich kennengelernt." *AuB*, p. 219

43. Arthur Schnitzler, *DdW*, Vol. 8, p. 31.

44. This point of view appears in numerous places in "Und einmal" and is expressed very clearly in the following quotation from Schnitzler's diary (December 10, 1915). Schnitzler, representing the perspective of the (pacifist) individualist, argues against Dr. Simon, who speaks for the (militarist) state: "Mit O. zu Wassermanns, wo Dr. Simon aus Frankfurt a.M., ein sehr kluger Mann, der wohl politisch-handelspolitisch hier weilt und mit dem es eine erregte Discussion gab. Er als Vertreter des 'Staatsgedankens' gegen mich als 'Individualisten etc.' 'Tod fürs Vaterland etc...' Ich mußte ihm erwidern: 'Die Probe aufs Exempel steht aus.' Er: Es wär ein harter Kampf gewesen; aber er sei schließlich zur Überzeugung gekommen—er nützte dem Vaterland mehr, wenn er nicht ins Feld, sondern zu Hause etc. Ich: 'Geb ich Ihnen ohne weiters zu— Sie aber hatten selbst die Entscheidung—hunderttausende der gleichen Ansicht werden nicht gefragt, *müssen* in den Schützengräben, auch wenn sie daheim...' Hier flüchtete er ins 'innre Gefühl'—die heilige Freistatt, wo der Verfolger vor dem Thron stehen bleiben muß." Arthur Schnitzler, *Tagebuch 1913-1916*, p. 245.

45. Arthur Schnitzler, *DdW*, Vol. 8, p. 32.

46. Inept diplomacy is the second of Schnitzler's three causes for war as listed in "Und einmal," *AuB*, p. 201. In "Und einmal" he writes of diplomats: "Hier werden Geschäfte gemacht mit Geld, Macht, Ruhm, Fragen der Karriere. Selten unter ihnen ein Staatsmann, der ins Weite blick te." (*AuB*, p. 219.)

47. Schnitzler's attack on diplomats appears again in his fragment "Zug der Schatten" (1930); his character Karl Benn says: "Ich

bin kein Diplomat, Herr Doktor. Darf ich aufrichtig mit Ihnen sprechen?" Arthur Schnitzler, *Zug der Schatten* Ed. Françoise Derrè. (Frankfurt am Main: S. Fischer, 1970), p. 53.

48. Arthur Schnitzler, *DdW*, Vol. 8, pp. 32-33.

49. Ibid., p. 81. The Chancellor's words: "...wenn nicht gelten—doch womöglich leben (lassen)" might be seen as a rebuttal to Theodor Reik's interpretation of Schnitzler's works on war in his article "Der Krieg bei Arthur Schnitzler" (1914), cited earlier, when Reik writes: "Dieser Krieg, der heute geführt wird, ist für Österreich und Deutschland eine erlösende Tat: denn sie stehen Mächten gegenüber, deren ungeheurer Haß nicht zum Schweigen gebracht werden könnte. Es handelte sich nicht um Macht- und Rechtsfragen, sondern um das Recht da zu sein und zu wirken." (*Berliner Tageblatt*, 30 December 1914). The Chancellor's words also echo the actions of Friedrich von Tilling in Suttner's *Die Waffen nieder*. Tilling starts with great aspirations of preventing war through entlightening the King of France about war, but ends his life content with having made a modest contribution to peace.

50. Schneider-Halvorson concedes a sense of "moral adversity" within the Chancellor, but adds: "All indications in the drama, nevertheless, point out that Schnitzler's idea of pacifism was not intended to be merely an intellectual exercise." In: Schneider-Halvorson, *The Late Dramatic Works*, p. 107. Schneider Halvorson, however, neither explains nor pursues her reference to Schnitzler's "idea of pacifism."

51. Arthur Schnitzler, *DdW*, Vol. 8, p. 21.

52. "Boxeraufstand," although not dated, was most likely written in 1926. This curious story differs from Schnitzler's other works in that it is not set in Europe. He demonstrates an understanding of the Boxers—a group of Chinese who in 1900 sought to expel all foreigners from China and abolish Christianity there. On 14 September 1915, Schnitzler visited Josef Popper-Lynkeus who at the time was an avid reader of Chinese short stories. Schnitzler records in his diary Popper's insistence that he borrow several of these works. Perhaps Schnitzler acquired an interest in the Boxer Rebellion as a result of reading the stories.

53. Arthur Schnitzler, "Boxeraufstand," in: Arthur Schnitzler, *Das erzählerische Werk*, Vol. 6 (Frankfurt am Main: S. Fischer,

1965), p. 207.

The story begins as follows: "Er war damals Oberleutnant. Boxeraufstand in China, gefährlich, unnachsichtig. Seine Majestät hatte befohlen, daß kein Pardon gegeben werde. Es nützte nicht viel. Nationalistische Bewegung. Freiheitsbewegung. Doch wir [the British!?] wollen nicht von Politik reden. Überall in Städten, in Dörfern, auf dem Land Aufruhr, da und dort wurde er niedergeschlagen, Hunderte, Tausende wurden gehängt, füsiliert." Presumably the first sentence, "Er war damals Oberleutnant" was intended to later be changed to "ich" to be consistent with the first-person narrative of the rest of the story.

54.   Indeed in a statement condemning the prepared execution of the then self-professed communist, Ernst Toller, Schnitzler had expressed his abhorrence of such violence: "Denn ich für meinen Theil schließe mich dem an den bayrischen Ministerpräsidenten gerichteten Protest nicht nur mit aller Entschiedenheit an, sondern ich dehne ihn hiemit aus auf sämtliche übrigen politischen und pseudo-politischen Gewaltakte und Bübereien, in welchem Lande, in welcher Partei, durch welche Instanz immer,— und, ob sie nun an Proletariern, Bürgern, Literaten oder selbst an Fürsten verübt worden wären und weiterhin verübt werden sollten." (Arthur Schnitzler. "Unveröffentlichte Erklärung" [zum Fall Ernst Toller]. Handwritten draft of a letter dated 11 June 1919. Deutsches Literaturarchiv, Marbach am Neckar.) A substantial portion of this letter was edited by Friedrich Vollhardt in "Wer etwas zu sagen hat, trete vor und schweige!— Anmerkungen zu einer unbekannten Erklärung Dr. Arthur Schnitzlers (zum Fall Ernst Toller) aus dem Jahre 1919." *Literatur und Kritik*, 157/158 (August/September 1981), p. 470.

55.   Arthur Schnitzler, *DeW*, Vol. 6, p. 208.

56.   Ibid., p. 209.

57.   Ibid., p. 210.

58.   The work, first conceived in 1902, was intended as a five- act drama in verse. After modifications in 1909, 1911, and 1913, the play became a narrative work in 1925. The version published by S. Fischer was written in the first months of 1928. Arthur Schnitzler, *DeW*, Vol. 6, p. 276. Nachwort und bibliographisches Verzeichnis.

59.   Arthur Schnitzler, "Abenteurernovelle," *DeW*, Vol. 6, pp. 211-

253, pp. 237-238.

60. Arthur Schnitzler, *Tagebuch 1917-1919*, p. 54. Schnitzler's diaries during the First World War reveal that he engaged in substantial background research for a work ("Landsknecht") on the Thirty Years' War. Among other works, Schnitzler read Gustav Freytag's *Bilder aus der deutschen Vergangenheit aus dem Jahrhundert des großen Krieges* (1876), Eduard Vehse's *Geschichte der deutschen Höfe seit der Reformation* (1851-1860), and Ricarda Huch's novel, *Der große Krieg in Deutschland*, (1912-1914). The "Landsknecht" occupied Schnitzler over several decades from 1904 to 1930. He produced two additional sketches in 1917 and 1927.

61. Arthur Schnitzler, *Tagebuch 1917-1919*, p. 99. Diary entry of 22 December 1917. Schnitzler writes of "Landsknecht": "Die Idee im dreißigjährigen Krieg (ich dachte meines Einakterstoffes:) Kampf zwischen Pfarrer und Landsknecht—zwischen Sinn (Geist) und Abenteuer—zwischen Himmel und Hölle.—"

62. The opposition of "Pfaffe" and "Abenteurer" in the diagram to *Der Geist im Wort und der Geist in der Tat* (published in 1927, but begun at the latest in 1916—see *AuB*, pp. 346-362) might have evolved from this early polemic between the preacher and the mercenary, or concurrently with it.

63. Arthur Schnitzler, *EuV*, p. 459. Compare also *AuB*, pp. 204-205.

64. Ibid., p. 459.

65. Arthur Schnitzler, *AuB*, p. 216. Essay dated 1919.

66. Arthur Schnitzler, *EuV*, p. 467.

67. Arthur Schnitzler, *Tagebuch 1913-1916*, p. 297.

68. "Was muß nach dem Krieg im Angriff genommen werden: Abschaffung der Sklaverei!—" Arthur Schnitzler, *Tagebuch 1913-1916*, p. 208.

69. Arthur Schnitzler, "Der Sekundant," *DeW*, Vol. 6, pp. 254-273, p. 254.

Notes to Chapter 7

1. In the Introduction to his translation of Schnitzler's essays on war, Weiss defines two types of pacifism:

First, there is the one we may call didactic pacifism. Often based on religious, moral, or quasi-moral grounds, its proponents advocate refusal to participate in any military activity, even in self-defense against unprovoked attack. The second type may be termed humanistic pacifism. Dedicated to the proposition that human life is sacred,... humanistic pacifism seeks to eliminate the causes of war, as a long-term goal.

(Arthur Schnitzler. *Some Day Peace Will Return.* Edited, translated and with an introduction by Robert O. Weiss. [New York: Frederick Ungar, 1972], p. 28.) Weiss's "humanistic pacifism" is roughly equivalent to Brock's "absolute pacifism" discussed earlier in this work.

2. Reinhard Urbach stresses the importance to Schnitzler of the historical approach: "... Noch im Alter blieb er einer Blickrichtung treu, die ihm in der Jugend eingeprägt worden war, und die nicht unterschätzt werden darf: dem Historismus. Die Zukunft is dunkel. In der Vergangenheit ist es hell, sie ist aber abgeschlossen und einsehbar. Die Zukunft ist der Tod. Die Vergangenheit ist das ewige Leben. ..." (Reinhard Urbach. Introduction in: Heinrich Schnitzler, Christian Brandstätter and Reinhard Urbach, eds. *Arthur Schnitzler: Sein Leben, Sein Werk, Seine Zeit* [Frankfurt am Main: S. Fischer, 1981], p. 8.)

3. Arthur Schnitzler. *Buch der Sprüche,* p. 195.

4. See: Stefan Zweig. "Arthur Schnitzler zu seinem sechzigsten Geburtstag" (15. Mai, 1922). (*Neue Rundschau,* 33, no. 5, 1922), pp. 498-513. In his diary on June 2, 1922, Schnitzler rejects Zweig's interpretation of his post-War works: "*Stefan Zweig* (der hu[e]bsch in d N R [der Neuen Rundschau] u[e]ber mich geschrieben)—ich versuche ihm dem Irrtum von der 'versunkne Welt', dem auch er—feu[i]ll[e]tonistisch unterliegt aufzuklären.—" (Arthur Schnitzler. "Unveröffentlichte Tagebücher.") In the play fragment, "Zug der Schatten" (1930) set in post-War Vienna, Schnitzler attacks the concept of the "versunkene Welt." Apart from a further decline in morality after the War, "Zug der Schatten" illustrates Schnitzler's belief that people were the same after the War as they had been before

it. The work has as yet received very little attention from scholars.

5.   Arthur Schnitzler. *EuV*, p. 427.

Appendix 1

Concerning the quotation on page 10, compare also Schnitzler's letters to: 1) Kurt Sonnenfeld (December 18, 1916): "Daß ich mich zu dem Kriege, wie es die Zeitungen gelegentlich wünschten, irgendwie 'äußern' würde, haben Sie wohl selbst nicht erwartet, aber schließlich gibt es überhaupt kein Erlebnis, das auf ein beliebiges menschliches Wesen völlig ohne Wirkung bliebe;—sollten nicht später einmal die Spuren dieses Krieges sich in den Werken der Dichter nachweisen lassen, die das Schicksal in dieser Epoche verschlagen hat? Es wäre verwunderlich", and 2) Elisabeth Steinrück (December 25, 1916): "Wenn die Leute mein 'Schweigen' für 'Schwäche' halten, kann ich begreiflicher Weise nur ebenso lächeln, als ich Benedikt angelächelt habe, der mich im vorigen Jahre (zufallsweis auf einem Spaziergang begegnete) aufforderte, mich in der N. Fr. Pr. zum Weltkrieg zu 'äußern.'—Ich kann warten—und wenn nicht alles trügt, der Weltkrieg auch. Sonderbar ist ja, daß fast in alle meine Stoffe die vor Juli 1914 bereit lagen, Krieg hineingespielt hat,—Atmosphäre, ja zum Theil Bedingung war;—und so wird man vielleicht in manchem, was später kommen wird, Beeinflussung durch Ereignisse sehen—die ich möglicherweise nur 'vorgeahnt' habe.—" In: Arthur Schnitzler, Arthur Schnitzler: *Briefe 1913-1931*, ed. Peter Michael Braunwarth et al. (Frankfurt am Main: S. Fischer, 1984.) 1) pp. 117-118. 2) pp. 118-122.

On 16 February 1919 a telegram addressed to the French pacifist Henri Barbusse was published in the *Neues Wiener Journal* and signed by Richard Beer-Hofmann, Hugo von Hofmannsthal, Arthur Schnitzler, Karl Schönherr, Professor Josef Strzygowski, Professor Julius Tandler, and Anton Wildgans. The telegram thanks Barbusse and his comrades for their friendly gesture of reconcilliation between former enemies, (letter in the Parisian journal *Populaire* from Barbusse and other French writers) and assures them that none of the occurrences of the last four years will hinder efforts to reconstruct friendships. In a letter to the Nobel Prizewinning pacifist, Alfred Hermann Fried (March 19,1919), Schnitzler cites the Barbusse telegram as a rare exception to his decision not to speak out publicly on political issues. Schnitzler explains that he does not feel suited to "journalistic escapades," and because his interests lie in other areas (literature), he can be most effective by engaging his talents there. Schnitzler admits that he has political views, but refrains from making them public since such a publication will inevitably lead to an endless (and inconsequential) struggle between opposing opinions and oblige him to spend more time than it is worth defending his point of view. The implication here is that Schnitzler intends to use his works as a forum for his views on the War: "Barbusse ausführlicher zu antworten, als es in jenem flüchtigen Telegramm geschehen ist, fühle ich kein Bedürfnis, wie ich es ja in dieser ganzen Zeit und übrigens auch schon vor dem Krieg vermieden habe politisch-publizistisch hervorzutreten. Nicht etwa, weil ich glaube, daß ich überhaupt in diesen Dingen nichts zu sagen hätte, oder nicht mitreden dürfte, der Grund ist vielmehr der, daß ich genötigt wäre, wenn ich nur einmal anfinge 'mich zu äußern' mich auch weiterhin im Streit der Meinungen zu beteiligen;—und da nicht nur meine eigentlichen Interessen, sondern vor allem die Art meine Begabung und daher auch die Möglichkeit meines Wirkens doch auf einem andern Gebiete liegen, so finde ich es ebenso überflüssig für mich als für Andere mich auf journalistische Eskapaden einzulassen."

In: Arthur Schnitzler *Briefe 1913-1931,* pp. 178-179, 894.

Appendix 2

Arthur Schnitzler
2. Schularbeit
"Kann uns zum Vaterland die Fremde werden?"

Coelum, non animum mutant, qui trans mare currunt.
Horaz

Wer vermag es wohl, die Gefühle des Menschen zu erklären? Unbegreiflich sind sie in ihren Ursachen, unwiderstehlich in ihrer Macht. Warum ist uns der ein unserer Nebenmann, schon liebenswerth, der ander hassenswürdig erscheint, wer kann's begreifen? Wer ergründet den seltsamen Reiz, mit dem der Frühling, die emporkeimende Natur unser Herz befängt? Wer vermag es, den eigentümlichen Zauber, der in der Liebe zur Mutter, den süßen Schmerz, der in der Sehnsucht nach der Heimat liegt, in den tiefsten Quellen zu verstehen? Niemand vermag es, und wie sehr sich auch der menschliche Geist dagegen sträubt, eine Macht anzuerkennen, deren tiefinnerste Gründe er zu begreifen nicht im Stande ist, er muß sich beugen, er kann dem unwiderstehlichen (sic) nicht widerstehen. Oder sollte es dennoch menschliche Wesen geben, die auch aus solchen Banden sich befreien können? Nein, es lebt keiner, der so frei wäre, und diejenigen Menschen, die wir kalt und gefühllos nennen, auch sie empfinden, wenn auch nicht so warm innig wie die anderen.—
Tief in dem Herzen der Sterblichen wurzelt das Heimatsgefühl. Und so wie jemand, der seine Mutter nie gekannt, dennoch Sehnsucht empfindet [sic] nach der Mutterliebe empfindet, die er als unvergleichbar an Wahrheit und Innigkeit rühmen hört, so befängt auch den, den wir heimatlos nennen, seltsame Sehnsucht nach einem Vaterland, wer eine Heimat nie besessen!

Ob wohl die, welche so glücklich sind, ein Vaterland zu besitzen, eine zweite Heimat finden können, die ihnen all das bietet, was sie in ihrer ersten zurückgelassen haben? Ich erinnere mich hier eines Satzes der Rahel, der sich in einem ihrer Briefe findet, und in welchem sie ungefähr folgendes ausspricht: "Die Menschen, die in ihrem Vaterland unglücklich waren, die hassen es nicht, sondern gedenken stets in Sehnsucht der verlassenen Heimat; wohl aber hassen die ihr Vaterland, welche dort gerechten Tadel sich zugezogen haben, und diese kehren nicht gern zurück."

Es liegt eine tiefe Wahrheit in diesem Satz doch möchte ich außer den Unglücklichen auch den Frevlern noch eine Klasse von Menschen unterscheiden, die ihre Heimat für lange Zeit lassen; es sind die Abenteurer, Leute die viel sehen, die viel neues erfahren wollen, denen die Alltäglichkeit zur oberst ist, und die nur in der steten Abwechslung den wahren Lebensgenuß finden. Solchen Menschen wird die Fremde wahrlich zum Vaterland, die Fremde im weitesten Sinne des Wortes. Sie fühlen sich überall wohl, nur nicht in der Ruhe; das Wandern ist ihr eigentliches Element, die Rastlosigkeit ihre zweite Natur.

Und die Unglücklichen? Ihnen ist dort wohl, wo sie der Heimat nicht gedenken müssen, und doch sehnen sie sich stets nach dem Ort zurück, wo sie ihre Jugendtage verlebt. Ein scheinbarer Widerspruch; und in des Menschen innerstem Wesen begründet. Diese Unglücklichen sind die wirklich bedauernswerten unter den Heimatlosen;—bedauernwerter als die Frevler, die mit Recht aus dem Vaterland verbannt werden. Und nicht allein darum sind jene bedauernswerter, weil sie ein unverschuldetes Unglück verdienen; nein, auch darum müssen wir jenen mehr Mitleid schenken, weil ihnen die Fremde nicht zum Vaterlande werden kann, die Missethäter dagegen auch auf fremdem Boden gar bald sich wohl und heimisch fühlen.

Doch gibt es nicht auch Menschen, die gewissermaßen aus Überzeugung das Vaterland der Fremde nicht vorziehen, die das Weltbürgertum, den Kosmopolitismus nicht nur als Princip anerkennen, sondern auch von der unumstößlichen Wahrheit dieses Princips so völlig durchdrungen sind, daß sie sich ihres Heimatgefühls gänzlich entäußern können? Wie Friedrich Rückert von einem Weisen erzählt, der auf die Frage, ob er sich denn niemals das Vaterland erinnere, dadurch antwortet, daß er auf den Himmel weist—nennt der Dichter diesen Mann mit Recht weise? Das ist eine Frage, die zu beantworten viel Überlegung kostete und deren Beantwortung eben doch nur auf innerer Überzeugung, nicht auf unwiderleglicher Objektivität beruhen konnte.—

Ergreifend schön hat die Volkssage die Qualen der Heimatlosigkeit in der Sage vom ewigen Juden geschildert. Der Tod allein ist's, der jetzt noch des Ahasverus Heimat werden kann, und den Tod kann der ewige Jude nicht finden. Und so muß er wandern, ruhelos wandern.—

From the "Nachlaß" of Arthur Schnitzler. UCLA Special Collections, Main Research Library. Microfilm collection 511, reel 2, File 47—"School Essays."

Appendix 3

"Über den Patriotismus"

von Arthur Schnitzler

Ich stieg die Treppen zum Dachstübchen meines Freundes Balduin hinan. Alle armen Philosophen wohnen in Dachstübchen, weniger weil sie Philosophen, als weil sie arm sind. Als ich ins Zimmer trat, saß Balduin auf seinem Bette und las die Zeitung. Ein Lächeln lag auf seinen Lippen, und wie ich sein Antlitz näher betrachtete, merkte ich, daß seine Augen gedankenvoll auf ein und derselben Stelle ruhen blieben.

"Guten Morgen, Balduin."

"Ah—ich bemerkte Sie nicht—"

"Sie lesen den Leitartikel und lächeln dabei so harmlos! Man sieht doch gleich, daß Sie sich bisher nicht mit Politik beschäftigt haben."

"Auch jetzt nicht," erwiderte Balduin. "Was mich lächeln machte, ist ein Gedanke—ein Wort eigentlich— Warum verziehen Sie den Mund so spöttisch?— Meinen Sie etwa, es wäre besser, wenn den Leuten, welche die Leitartikel schreiben, die Gedanken kommen möchten als denen, die sie lesen—Nicht? doch seh'n Sie nur hieher, mein Lieber!" Er wies mit dem Finger auf eine Stelle. Der Artikel handelte von den letzten Vorgängen in Frankreich (Paris und Cherburg.)

"Nun?" fragte ich gespannt.

"Nicht der politische Gehalt des Aufsatzes ist es, der mich interessirt," entgegnete Balduin; "sondern mein Blick blieb auf diesem Worte haften. Haben Sie schon jemals darüber nachgedacht, was

Patriotismus ist? Ich frage Sie nicht ohne Grund; denn es ist uns zur Gewohnheit geworden, gewisse Ausdrücke einfach zur Kenntnis zu nehmen, sie mit dem Begriffe von irgend etwas Edlen oder Unedlen zu verbinden; damit glauben wir sie abgethan zu haben und sind mit unserer geistigen Arbeit zufrieden. Was ist dann eigentlich der Patriotismus?" fuhr Balduin fort, sich von seinem Sitze erhebend und die Zeitung auf den Tisch werfend. Er sah zu Boden und rasch wieder auf. "Egoismus" erwiderte er sich selbst. "Hören Sie mich an, mein Freund, und Sie werden mir Recht geben. Wenn ich sage, daß ich patriotisch fühle, so heißt das so viel wie: Ich liebe mein Vaterland, das Land, in dem ich geboren bin. Ich liebe es, denn es ist mein Vaterland; ich liebe es, denn ich bin in diesem Land geboren. Das ist anmassend, das ist selbstsüchtig, das ist egoistisch."

"So wäre also Patriotismus geradezu ein Fehler?"

"Wenn wir folgerichtig denken, gewiß. Warum liebt denn Jeder das Land am meisten, das ihn erzeugt hat? Es gibt gewiß angeborne Fähigkeiten, aber keine angeborenen Ideen. Der Patriotismus ist ein Vorurtheil."

"Das ist pessimistisch gesprochen."

"Nein, mein Lieber nur wahr."

"Ich, Balduin, möchte den Patriotismus auf etwas Anderes zurückführen, und ich fürchte, daß sich unsere Anschauungen nicht gut vertragen werden."

"Ich bin begierig."

"Der Patriotismus ist meiner Ansicht nach nichts als eine wohlgerechtfertigte Bescheidenheit."

"Wie das?"

"Denken Sie sich einen Idealisten, Balduin, und diesen Idealisten mitten unter das Getriebe unserer Zeit treten mit großen Gefühlen, gewaltigen Ideen von Menschenliebe, Weltbürgerthum. Er möchte gern alle Völker gleichedel, gleich groß, gleich glücklich sehen. Ich will den günstigsten Fall setzen, und den begeisterten Jüngling, Genossen, Gleichgesinnte Freunde finden lassen. Sie gehen an's Werk, bereit, ihr Leben an die Erfüllung ihrer Pläne zu setzen. Aber sie werden Männer.

"Dieses Alles gefällt mir," unterbrach mich Balduin.

"Sie werden Männer, und die Ideale zerfließen ihnen unter den Händen. Zwar verschwindet ihre Philantropie nicht völlig, aber die Kosmopolitiker sind sich über ihre Schwäche klar geworden, und über die Stärke ihre Gegner. Sie beginnen einzusehen, daß sie gegen eine Welt kämpfen müßten im Streite für eine Welt. Was sollen sie also beginnen mit dem Schatz von Liebe, den sie im Herzen bergen. Können sie die Menschheit nicht glücklich machen, so wollen sie wenigstens ihr Scherflein beitragen zum allgemeinen Glück und das Land glücklich wissen, in dem sie geboren sind."

Balduin begann zu lachen. "Die Idealisten sind also egoistisch geworden aus Bescheidenheit—oder vielleicht gar bescheiden aus Egoismus. Sie lassen sich mit Ihrer ganzen Philantropie auf dem kleinen Fleck Erde nieder, den sie ihr Vaterland heißen. Und so sind wir wieder, von wo wir ausgegangen sind. O wie armselig ist doch, was wir unsere schönsten, erhabensten Gefühle nennen, wenn wir ihnen mit der Schärfe der Logik auf den Grund zu kommen suchen. Wenn der Patriotismus eine Tugend ist, so ist's der Egoismus auch,—eine Ansicht, zu der man sich übrigens allgemein zu bekehren scheint. Jeder sorgt für sich allein und es ist unfraglich leichter, dem Wahlspruch zu folgen: "Einer für Einen" als "Einer für Alle."

"Sehen Sie, Balduin, daß Sie mit einem Male dem Patriotismus das Wort sprechen! Denn der ist's, der da ruft: 'Einer für Alle!'"

"Nicht doch," erwiderte Balduin. Er sagt: "Einer, d.h. ich für die paar Leute, durch deren Wohlsein es selbstverständlich auch mir gut gehen muß, daß ich ein Glied des großen Körpers bin. Bemühen Sie sich also nicht, junger Freund, meine Weltanschauung auf andere Bahnen zu lenken, es wäre ein fruchtloses Bemühen. Auch ist es durchaus nicht verachtenswert, daß das Bewußtsein des Ich am stärksten ausgeprägt ist; da wir ja schließlich doch immer nur wir selber bleiben."

Arthur Schnitzler. "Über den Patriotismus". *(Der freie Landesbote,* München, 15 November 1880).

Appendix 4

Arthur Schnitzler's Response to Romain Rolland's
Collected Essays, *Au-dessus de la mêlée* , March 1916

Zu Rollands Gesammelten Aufsätzen "Au-dessus de la Mêlée".

Ich finde in ihnen den stärksten Beweis für meine Forderungen, daß zwischen denjenigen, die zu den Bedingungen und Möglichkeiten eines künftigen Weltfriedens das Wort ergreifen wollen, über die Vergangenheit, insbesondere über die Ursachen dieses Krieges nicht mehr gesprochen werden dürfe.

Nach dem Ruf, der diesen Aufsätzen voranging, erwartete ich in ihnen Gerechtigkeit und Objektivität zu finden, so weit siem [sic] Menschen überhaupt möglich ist.

Nicht etwa ein wirkliches Begreifen von Deutschlands Wesen (was ja dem Verfasser von "Jean Christoph" immerhin zuzutrauen gewesen wäre), nicht etwa den Versuch, sich mit den geographischen, politischen, historischen Problemen Deutschlands auseinanderzusetzen; aber doch wenigstens den Versuch, die Verteilung der Schuld an dem Krieg bei sämtlichen beteiligten Völkern und Regierungen gegeneinander abzuwägen.
Doch im ganzen Buch R.'s immer wieder Betonung der Schuld Deutschlands an diesem Krieg, der Verbrechen Deutschlands an diesem Krieg.—Kaum je eine Andeutung einer Schuld auf der Gegenseite.

Natürlich bemerkt er aus drücklich [sic], daß nur die deutsche Regierung, also nur tausend oder hundert Deutsche an dem Unglück

Schuld seien. Aber diese Regierung habe in Deutschland sogar die Intellektuellen so sehr belogen und so geknebelt, daß sie entweder die Wahrheit nicht erfahren oder sie nicht aussprechen dürften. Würde man versuchen, diese Verallgemeinerung auf ein den Tatsachen entsprechenden Maß zurückzuführen, so müßte man der Erwiderung gewärtig sein, daß man eben als Deutscher die Wahrheit nicht kennt, oder sie nicht aussprechen darf.

Sehen wir also hievon überhaupt ab. Die Frage ist nur, wieso sieht Rolland die Schuld auf der Ententeseite absolut nicht?

Im ganzen Buch ist von den Anteil, den die französischen Revanchschreier an dem Ausbruch dieses Krieges haben, von dem Verschwörertreiben in Serbien, von der Ermordung des Erzherzogs, von den Machinationen Englands, von den englischen Parlamentsreden gegen die deutschen Flotte, von der Mobilisation Rußlands in den letzten Julitagen mit keinem Wort die Rede. Der Name Poincaré, seine Reise zum Zaren, die Milliardenanleihe wird nicht erwähnt. Von Algeciras kein Wort, von der Einkreisungspolitik König Eduards ebensowenig. Immer nur der preußiche [sic] Militarismus, der deutsche Größenwahn und die deutsche Kriegslust. Von einem "orgueil français" der historisch etwa so beweisbar wäre wie der germanische, von der französischen Eroberungslust, die in Ludwig XIV, und in Napoleon Vertreter hat, die weit über das Maß aller preußischer Kriegshelden hinausgehen, ist nirgends die Rede. Von der Expansionslust Rußlands (Konstantinopel etc.) kein Wort.

Lieber keine Gegengründe gegen die Beurteilung des Deutschtums [sic] und Preußentums von Rollands Seite, sondern Anführung aller historischen und politischen Tatsachen, die er verschweigt, obwohl sie in den Zusammenhang gehören.

Was weiß er an Deutschland zu loben? Daß es einige wenige Intellektuelle gibt, die gegen das Gouvernement im Besonderen und gegen den Krieg im Allgemeinen ihre Stimme erhoben haben. Im Ganzen hätten sie versagt, wären Wortführer des preußischen Militarismus geworden. Er zitiert immer wieder den Artikel von Thomas Mann aus der N.R. "Gedanken im Kriege." Ich denke nicht daran, ihn zu rechtfertigen, aber er ist ein Feuilleton, für den keineswegs das intellektuelle Deutschland verantwortlich gemacht werden darf. Wieviele Artikel solcher Art sind wohl in dieser Zeit in Frankreich geschrieben worden, für den herrlichen Krieg zur Befreiung des geknechteten Elsaß-Lothringen—! Er zitiert ferner Ostwald, der in einem Artikel die preußiche [sic] Organisationskraft wohl etwas übertrieben feiert, ohne daß durch diesen Artikel die Behauptung gerechtfertigt erschiene, Ostwald verkündige für die Zukunft eine Hegemonie Deutschlands in Europa.

Rolland verurteilt die deutschen Intellektuellen, daß sie nicht gegen die Neutralitätsverletzung Belgiens, gegen die Zerstörung von Löwen, gegen die Beschießung der Reimser Kathedrale protestiert haben. Nehmen wir der Einfachheit halber an, in allen diesen Fällen wäre von deutscher Seite Unrecht geschehen,—hat je ein Deutscher von den französischen Intellektuellen verlangt, daß sie gegen Englands Völkerrechtsverletzungen, daß sie gegen den Treubruch Italiens, usw. Proteste erheben sollen? Rolland macht sich lustig über Hauptmanns Erwiderung, daß ihm das Leben eines deutschen Soldaten wichtiger sei als alle möglichen Kunstschätze Frankreichs und Belgiens. R. spricht wohl von der Zerstörung Löwens, aber kein Wort davon, daß die einziehenden deutschen Truppen von den Fenstern aus und aus Kellerlöchern zu Hunderten niedergemacht worden sind. Lauter Lügen der deutschen Regierung?

In dem Artikel "Pangermanismus oder Panslavismus" lehnt R. beide ab, findet aber doch den letzteren vorzuziehen. Seine Beweise? Daß Rußland einen Tolstoi und Dostojewski gehabt habe, Deutschland seit Wagner und Nietzsche niemanden, der jenen an die Seite zu setzen sei. Zugegeben.—Von der Musik sagt er, daß Deutschland nur Wagner-epigonen habe, des "virtuoses exaspérés comme Richard Strauss". Es stecke mehr Zukunft und wahre Originalität in einer Seite von Moussorgsky und Strawinsky als in allen Partituren von Mahler und Reger.

Rolland bringt den Brief eines Balten, der lieber und [sic] russischer als unter deutscher Herrschaft leben möchte.
Ohneweiteres zugegeben. Wo aber sind die Hunderte von—meinetwegen ungeschriebenen—Briefen von Juden, die lieber unter deutscher und österreichischer als unter russischer Herrschaft leben

190   Adrian Clive Roberts

möchten? Mit unbegreiflicher Zartheit geht Rolland über die Pogrome hinweg, die er gewiß ebenso verurteilt wie wir alle.

Er tritt für die kleinen Staaten ein, die von Österreich und Deutschland so sehr vergewaltigt werden. Er stellt die Forderung, daß die kleinen Staaten und die strittigen Provinzen über ihre Zugehörigkeit selbst zu entscheiden haben. So Schleswig-Holstein, Elsaß-Lothringen, die Juden. Ein Vorschlag von solcher Tragweite müßte in seiner politischen Durchführbarkeit zum mindesten angedeutet werden. Nehmen wir den Fall Elsaß-Lothringen. Eine Abstimmung würde etwa ergeben, sagen wir 60% für Frankreich, 40% für Deutschland. Sollen sich die 40% einfach fügen? Bedeutete es nicht die größte Ungerechtigkeit auf 40% zu Gunsten von 60% einen Zwang auszuüben?

Noch unlösbarer die Judenfrage. Es gibt keine jüdischen Provinzen. In Polen leben Russen, Ruthenen, Deutsche, deutsche Juden, russische Juden durcheinander. Ein Wahl, die getroffen würde, käme eigentlich nur dem Zwang zur Auswanderung gleich.

Rolland weiß nichts davon, daß im englischen Parlament, ebenso im italienischen die Vernichtung Deutschlands proklamiert worden ist. Er glaubt wirklich, denn an seiner Ehrlichkeit ist nicht zu zweifeln, nicht nur, daß Deutschland die Hauptschuld an diesem Kriege trägt, sondern daß es ihn gewollt hat aus Eroberungsgründen. Deutschland sollte tatsächlich gewünscht haben, zugleich gegen Frankreich, Rußland, England, Belgien Krieg zu führen?! Glaubt das ein vernünftiger Mensch? Welche Länder Deutschland eigentlich erobern wollte, ist niemals gesagt worden.

Gegen den Versuch Englands Deutschland auszuhungern, findet Rolland kein Wort.

Rollands Lob erhalten Wilhelm Herzog, der Herausgeber des Forum, René Schickele, der Herausgeber der Weißen Blätter, Annette Kolb, eine Deutsch-Französin und auch einige deutsche Dichter, die sich in ihren Feldpostbriefen gegen den Krieg im Allgemeinen aussprechen. Durch den Zusammenhang aber wird bei dem Leser der Anschein erweckt, als bedeute diese Stellungnahme gegen den Krieg als solchen auch eine Stellungsnahme gegen die deutsche Regierung, die diesen Krieg ja nach R.'s Meinung ausschließlich verursacht habe.

R. ist wegen einiger seiner Aufsätze in Frankreich angegriffen worden. Er hatte darin auszusprechen gewagt, daß es auch in Deutschland begabte, kluge und anständige Menschen gäbe. Man kann nicht gerade behaupten, daß dies eine Fanfare für Deutschland bedeutet, insbesondere da immer wieder die Schuld an dem Krieg so gut wie ausschließlich auf Deutschland, auf Preußen, auf die deutsche und preußische Regierung gewälzt wird. Der Herausgeber einer großen französischen Zeitung stellt ihm sein Blatt zur Erwiderung zur Verfügung. R. schreibt diese Erwiderung "a ceux qui m'accusent," und beansprucht für sich nichts weiter als das Recht, auch über Angehörige feindlicher Völker Gutes sagen zu dürfen, bekennt sich übrigens bei allem Weltbürgertum als Franzose, einer, der seiner Nation den Sieg wünscht und prophezeit. Auch diese bescheidene Erwiderung wurde niemals gedruckt. (Man bedenke, was doch immerhin zu gleicher Zeit in Deutschland erscheinen durfte.)

Trotzdem findet R. nicht ein Wort gegen den Chauvinismus seiner Landsleute und der Gedanke kommt ihm gar nicht, daß man auch das Vorgehen gegen ihn wohl zu den Versuchen rechnen dürfte, den Bölkern [sic] die Wahrheit zu verschweigen und sie mundtot zu machen.

Arthur Schnitzler. "Zu Rollands Gesammelten Aufsätzen "Audessus de la Mêlée." "Nachlaß." University of California, Los Angeles. Research Library, Special Collections. Microfilm Collection 511, Reel 23, File 230, pp. 34-38. (Unpublished portion of the folder entitled "Und einmal wird der Friede wiederkommen..."). The above is an exact rendition of the typewritten essay in Schnitzler's "Nachlaß." I have not attempted to correct any of the typographical errors which appear in the cited version but have designated them with the notation "[sic]."

Bibliography

Primary Works by Arthur Schnitzler:

Schnitzler, Arthur. *Aphorismen und Betrachtungen*. Gesammelte
    Werke. Ed. Robert O. Weiss. Frankfurt am Main: S. Fischer,
    1967.
——. *Arthur Schnitzler: Briefe 1875-1912*. Ed. Heinrich Schnitzler.
    Frankfurt am Main: S. Fischer, 1981.
——. *Arthur Schnitzler: Briefe 1913-1931*. Ed. Peter Michael
    Braunwarth, Richard Miklin, Susanne Pertlik and Heinrich
    Schnitzler. Frankfurt am Main: S. Fischer, 1984.
——. *Arthur Schnitzler: Tagebuch 1879-1892*. Ed. Werner Welzig.
    Wien: Verlag der Österreichischen Akademie der
    Wissenschaften, 1987.
——. *Arthur Schnitzler: Tagebuch 1909-1912*. Ed. Werner Welzig.
    Wien: Verlag der Österreichischen Akademie der
    Wissenschaften, 1981.
——. *Arthur Schnitzler: Tagebuch 1913-1916*. Ed. Werner Welzig.
    Wien: Verlag der Österreichischen Akademie der
    Wissenschaften, 1983.
——. *Arthur Schnitzler: Tagebuch 1917-1919*. Ed. Werner Welzig.
    Wien: Verlag der Österreichischen Akademie der
    Wissenschaften, 1985.
——. "Arthur Schnitzlers Protest." *Das Forum*, 1, 1914-1915, pp.
    489-491.
——. "Aufzeichnungen aus der Kriegszeit—Aus dem Nachlaß von
    Arthur Schnitzler." *Neue Rundschau*, 1, 1932, pp. 678-681.
——. "Ballade von den drei Brüdern." Ed. Reinhard Urbach. *Neues
    Forum*, 15, no. 178, 1968, p. 676.
——. "Briefe." Ed. Heinrich Schnitzler. *Neue Rundschau*, 68, no. 1,

1957, pp. 88-101.

——. "Briefe zur Politik." Ed. Reinhard Urbach. *Neues Forum*, 15, no. 178, 1968, pp. 677-680.

——. *Buch der Sprüche und Bedenken. Aphorismen und Fragmente.* Wien: Im Phaidon-Verlag, 1927.

——. *Das dramatische Werk.* 8 vols. Frankfurt am Main: S. Fischer, 1978.

——. *Entworfenes und Verworfenes—Aus dem Nachlaß.* Ed. Reinhard Urbach. Gesammelte Werke. Frankfurt am Main: S. Fischer, 1977.

——. *Das erzählerische Werk.* 7 vols. Frankfurt am Main: S. Fischer, 1982.

——. "Gedanken über Kunst. Aus dem Nachlaß von Arthur Schnitzler." *Neue Rundschau*, 1, 1932, pp. 37-39.

——. *Der Geist im Wort und der Geist in der Tat.* Berlin: S. Fischer, 1927.

——. *Jugend in Wien. Eine Autobiographie.* Ed. Therese Nickl and Heinrich Schnitzler. Wien: Verlag Fritz Molden, 1968.

——. "Kann uns zum Vaterland die Fremde werden? 2. Schularbeit." "Nachlaß." UCLA Research Library Special Collections. Microfilm collection 511, reel 2, File 4 - "School Essays." Undated.

——. "Kriegsgeschichte." Ed. Reinhard Urbach. *Literatur und Kritik*, 13, April 1967, pp. 133-134.

——. *Leutnant Gustl.* Mit einem Nachwort und Anmerkungen von Heinz Politzer. Hamburg: S. Fischer Verlag. Hanseatische Druckanstalt, 1965.

——. "Nachlaß." Microfilm Collection 511. University of California, Los Angeles. Research Library, Special Collections.

——. "Notizen über Politik. Aus dem Nachlaß." *Forum (Wien)*, 9, no. 101, May, 1962, p. 222.

——. *Ritterlichkeit. Fragment aus dem Nachlaß.* Ed. Rena R. Schlein. Bonn: Bouvier Verlag Herbert Grundmann, 1975.

——. *Some Day Peace Will Return: Notes on War and Peace.* Ed. and trans. Robert O. Weiss. New York: Frederick Ungar, 1972.

——. "Über den Patriotismus." *Der freie Landesbote*, München, 15 November 1880.

——. *Über Krieg und Frieden.* Ed. Heinrich Schnitzler. Stockholm: Bermann Fischer, 1939.

——. "Unveröffentlichte Tagebücher: 1893-1908 und 1920-1931." Wien: Österreichische Akademie der Wissenschaften. Diplomatische Abschriften.

——. *Das Wort. Tragikomödie in fünf Akten. Fragment aus dem Nachlaß*. Ed. Kurt Bergel. Frankfurt am Main: S. Fischer, 1966

——. *Zug der Schatten*. Ed. Francoise Derré. Frankfurt am Main: S. Fischer, 1970.

Secondary Works on Arthur Schnitzler:

Abels, Norbert. *Sicherheit ist nirgends. Judentum und Aufklärung bei Arthur Schnitzler*. Königstein/Ts: Athenäum, 1982.

Allen, Richard H. *An Annotated Arthur Schnitzler Bibliography*. Chapel Hill: University of North Carolina Press, 1966.

Allerdissen, Rolf. *Arthur Schnitzler: Impressionistisches Rollenspiel und skeptischer Moralismus in seinen Erzählungen*. Bonn: Bouvier Verlag Herbert Grundmann, 1985.

Althaus, Horst. *Zwischen Monarchie und Republik: Schnitzler, Kafka, Hofmannsthal, Musil*. München: Wilhelm Fink, 1976.

Apsler, Alfred. "A Sociological View of Arthur Schnitzler," *Germanic Review*, 18, no. 2, 1943, pp. 90-106.

Arens, Detlev. *Untersuchungen zu Arthur Schnitzlers Roman "Der Weg ins Freie."* Frankfurt am Main: Verlag Peter Lang, 1981.

Ayres, Gabriella Szekely. "The Theme of Transition in Arthur Schnitzler's Social and Historical Dramas." Dissertation. Tulane University, 1974.

Baumann, Gerhard. "Arthur Schnitzler. Die Tagebücher: Vergangene Gegenwart—Gegenwärtige Vergangenheit." *Modern Austrian Literature*, 10, no. 3/4, 1977, pp. 143-162.

——. *Arthur Schnitzler. Die Welt von Gestern eines Dichters von Morgen*. Frankfurt am Main: Athenäum, 1965.

Bergel, Kurt, ed. *Georg Brandes und Arthur Schnitzler: Ein Briefwechsel*. Bern: Francke, 1956.

Berlin, Jeffrey B. *An Annotated Arthur Schnitzler Bibliography 1965-1977*. München: Fink, 1978.

——. "Arthur Schnitzler Bibliography for 1977-1981." *Modern Austrian Literature*, 15, no. 1, 1982, pp. 61-83.

——. "Political Criticism in Arthur Schnitzler's 'Aphorismen und

Betrachtungen.'" *Neophilologus*, 57, no. 2, April 1973, pp. 173-178.

Berlin, Jeffrey B. and Hans Ulrich Lindken. "Theodor Reiks unveröffentlichte Briefe an Arthur Schnitzler, unter besonderer Berücksichtigung einiger Briefe Reiks an Richard Beer-Hofmann." *Literatur und Kritik*, 173/174, April/May, 1983, pp. 182-197.

Blume, Bernhard. *Das Weltbild Arthur Schnitzlers*. Stuttgart: Buchdruckerei Knöller, 1936.

Brandstätter, Christian and Reinhard Urbach, eds. *Arthur Schnitzler: Materialien zur Wiener Festwochen 1981*. Wien: Arthur Schnitzler Institut, 1981.

Daviau, Donald G. and Jorun B. Johns, eds. *The Correspondence of Arthur Schnitzler and Raoul Auernheimer*. Chapel Hill: University of North Carolina Press, 1972.

Davis, Evan B. "Moral Problems in the Works of Arthur Schnitzler." Dissertation, University of Pennsylvania, 1950.

Davis, Gustav. "Lieutenant Gustl." Feuilleton. *Die Reichswehr*, December 28, 1900, pp. 1-2.

Derré, Françoise. *L'Oeuvre d'Arthur Schnitzler. Imagerie viennoise et problémes humains*. Paris: Librairie Marcel Didier, 1966.

Dethlefsen, Dirk. "Überlebenswille: Zu Schnitzlers Monolognovelle *Leutnant Gustl* in ihrem literarischen Umkreis." *Seminar*, 17, no. i, February 1981, pp. 50-72.

Dickerson, Harold D. Jr. "Water and Vision as Mystical Elements in Schnitzler's 'Der Gang zum Weiher.'" *Modern Austrian Literature*, 4, no. 3, Fall, 1971, pp. 24-36.

Fritsche, Alfred. *Dekadenz im Werk Arthur Schnitzlers*. Frankfurt am Main: Verlag Peter Lang, 1974.

Goldsmith, Ulrich K., ed. "Der Briefwechsel Fritz von Unruhs mit Arthur Schnitzler." *Modern Austrian Literature*, 10, no. 3/4, 1977, pp. 69-127.

Heresch, Elisabeth. *Schnitzler und Rußland: Aufnahme, Wirkung, Kritik*. Wien: Wilhelm Braumüller, Universitäts—Verlagsbuchhandlung, 1982.

Janz, Rolf-Peter, and Klaus Laermann. *Arthur Schnitzler: Diagnose des Wiener Bürgertums im Fin de siècle*. Stuttgart: J. B. Metzlersche Verlagsbuchhandlung, 1977.

Kann, Robert A. "Die historische Situation und die entscheidenden

politischen Ereignisse zur Zeit und im Leben Arthur
Schnitzlers." *Literatur und Kritik*, 161/162, February/March
1982, pp. 19-25.

——. "Das Österreich Arthur Schnitzlers," *Forum. Österreichische
Monatsblätter für kulturelle Freiheit*, 6, no. 71, 1959, pp. 421-
423.

Kappstein, Theodor. *Artur [sic] Schnitzler und seine besten
Bühnenwerke.* Berlin: Franz Schneider, 1922.

Kaulen, Heinrich. "Antisemitismus und Aufklärung: Zum Verständnis
von Arthur Schnitzlers *Professor Bernhardi*." *Zeitschrift für
Deutsche Philologie*, 100, no. 2, 1981, pp. 177-198.

Körner, Josef. *Arthur Schnitzlers Gestalten und Probleme.* Zürich:
Amalthea, 1921.

——. "Arthur Schnitzlers Spätwerk," *Preußische Jahrbücher*, 208,
no. 1, 1927, pp. 53-83; 208, no. 2, 1927, pp. 153-163.

Krotkoff, Hertha, ed. "Briefwechsel Thomas Mann—Arthur
Schnitzler." *Modern Austrian Literature*, 7, no. 1/2, 1974, pp. 1-
33.

Lindken, Hans-Ulrich. *Arthur Schnitzler: Aspekte und Akzente.
Materialien zu Leben und Werk.* Frankfurt am Main: Peter Lang,
1984.

Liptzin, Solomon. *Arthur Schnitzler.* New York: Prentice-Hall, 1932.

Miklin, Richard. "Heimatliebe und Patriotismus: Arthur Schnitzlers
Einstellung zu Österreich-Ungarn im Ersten Weltkrieg."
Modern Austrian Literature, 19, no. 3/4, 1986, pp. 197-212.

Müller-Freienfels, Reinhart. "Das Lebensgefühl in Arthur Schnitzlers
Dramen." Diss. Frankfurt am Main, 1954.

Neumann, Gerhard and Jutta Müller. *Der Nachlaß Arthur Schnitzlers.*
München: Fink, 1969.

Nickl, Therese and Heinrich Schnitzler, eds. *Hofmannsthal-Schnitzler
Briefwechse*l. Frankfurt am Main: S. Fischer, 1964.

Offermanns, Ernst L. *Arthur Schnitzler: Das Komödienwerk als
Kritik des Impressionismus.* München: Fink, 1973.

——. "Arthur Schnitzlers Komödie 'Fink und Fliederbusch.'"
Modern Austrian Literature, 3, no. 2, 1970, pp. 5-24.

Perlmann, Michaela. *Arthur Schnitzler.* Realien zur Literatur. Band
239. Stuttgart: J.B. Metzler, 1987.

Reichert, Herbert W. and Herman Salinger, eds. *Studies in Arthur
Schnitzler.* Chapel Hill: University of North Carolina Press,
1963.

Reid, Maja D. "Die Hirtenflöte." *Modern Austrian Literature*, 4, no.

2, Summer, 1971, pp. 18-27.

Reik, Theodor. *Arthur Schnitzler als Psycholog.* Minden/Westf.: J. C. C. Bruns, 1913.

——. "Der Krieg bei Arthur Schnitzler." *Berliner Tageblatt*, Beiblatt "Zeitgeist", September 7, 1914.

Rey, William H. *Arthur Schnitzler. Die späte Prosa als Gipfel seines Schaffens.* Berlin: Erich Schmidt, 1968.

——. "Beiträge zur amerikanischen Schnitzlerforschung." *German Quarterly*, 37, no. 3, May, 1964, pp. 282-289.

——. "Judith—Aurelie—Seraphine. Zu Arthur Schnitzler's 'Komödie der Verführung.'" *Creative Encounter. Festschrift für Herman Salinger.* Ed. Leland R. Phelps. Chapel Hill: University of North Carolina Press, 1977/1978, pp. 133-144.

Roberts, Adrian Clive. "Arthur Schnitzler as a Pacifist Writer: The Critique of War and Militarism in Selected Works." In: *Germanistische Dissertationen in Kurzfassung. Jahrbuch für Internationale Germanistik.* Reihe B, Band 10, Liste XV. Bern: Peter Lang, 1987. pp. 162-169.

——. "On the Origins and Development of Arthur Schnitzler's Polemical Critique of Patriotism, Militarism, and War." *Modern Austrian Literature*, 19, no. 3/4, 1986, pp. 213-225.

Scheible, Hartmut, ed. *Arthur Schnitzler in neuer Sicht.* München: Wilhelm Fink, 1981.

Scheible, Hartmut. *Arthur Schnitzler in Selbstzeugnissen und Bilddokumenten.* Reinbek bei Hamburg: Rowohlt, 1976.

——. *Arthur Schnitzler und die Aufklärung.* München: Fink, 1977.

Schinnerer, Otto P. "Arthur Schnitzlers 'Nachlaß.'" *Germanic Review*, 8, 1933, pp. 114-123.

——. "The Early Works of Arthur Schnitzler." *Germanic Review*, 4, 1929, pp. 153-197.

——. "Schnitzler and the Military Censorship. Unpublished Correspondence." *Germanic Review*, 5, no. 3, July 1930, pp. 238-246.

——. "Schnitzler's 'Der Schleier der Beatrice.'" *Germanic Review*, 7, 1932, pp. 263-279.

——. "The Suppression of Schnitzler's 'Der grüne Kakadu' by the Burgtheater. Unpublished Correspondence." *Germanic Review*, 6, no. 2, April 1931, pp. 183-192.

Schlein, Rena R. "Das Duellmotiv in Schnitzlers Dramen 'Ritterlichkeit', 'Das weite Land' und 'Das Wort.'" *Modern Austrian Literature*, 8, no. 3/4, 1975, pp. 222-235.

———. "The Motif of Hypocrisy in the Works of Arthur Schnitzler."
    Modern Austrian Literature, 2, no. 2, 1969, pp. 28-38.

Schneider-Halvorson, Brigitte Lina. *The Late Dramatic Works of
    Arthur Schnitzler*. Bern: Peter Lang, 1983.

Schnitzler, Heinrich, ed. "Rainer Maria Rilke und Arthur Schnitzler.
    Ihr Briefwechsel." *Wort und Wahrheit*, 3, no. 4, 1958. pp. 283-
    298.

Schnitzler, Heinrich, Christian Brandstätter, and Reinhard Urbach, eds.
    Arthur Schnitzler: Sein Leben, Sein Werk, Seine Zeit. Frankfurt
    am Main: S. Fischer, 1981.

Schnitzler, Henry, ed. "Patriotismus und Schauspielkunst." Berlin:
    Selbstverlag der Gesellschaft für Theatergeschichte, 11, 1953,
    pp. 20-26. In: *Kleine Schriften der Gesellschaft für
    Theatergeschichte*.

Seidlin, Oskar, ed. *Der Briefwechsel Arthur Schnitzler Otto Brahm*.
    Tübingen: Niemeyer, 1975.

Selling, Gunter. *Die Einakter und Einakterzyklen Arthur Schnitzlers*.
    Amsterdam: Rodopi, 1975.

Swales, Martin. *Arthur Schnitzler: A Critical Study*. London: Oxford
    University Press, 1971.

Tarnowski-Seidel, Heide. *Arthur Schnitzler: Flucht in die Finsternis.
    Eine produktionsästhetische Untersuchung*. München: Wilhelm
    Fink, 1983.

Tax, Petrus H. and Richard H. Lawson. *Arthur Schnitzler and His
    Age. Intellectual and Artistic Currents*. Bonn: Bouvier Herbert
    Grundmann, 1984.

Urbach, Reinhard. *Arthur Schnitzler*. Dramatiker des Welttheaters.
    Velber bei Hannover: Deutscher Taschenbuch, Friedrich, 1972.

———. *Schnitzler-Kommentar zu den erzählenden Schriften und
    dramatischen Werken*. München: Winkler, 1974. Urban, Bernd,
    ed. in Verbindung mit Werner Volke. *Arthur Schnitzler. Hugo
    von Hofmannsthal. 'Charakteristik aus den Tagebüchern.'*
    Bamberg: Schadel und Wehle, 1975.

Vollhardt, Friedrich. "Wer etwas zu sagen hat, trete vor und schweige!
    Anmerkungen zu einer unbekannten Erklärung Dr. Arthur
    Schnitzlers (zum Fall Ernst Toller) aus dem Jahr 1919."
    Literatur und Kritik, 157/158, August/ September 1981, pp. 462-
    473.

Wagner, Renate. *Arthur Schnitzler: Eine Biographie*. Wien: Verlag
    Fritz Molden, 1981.

———. *Der Briefwechsel Arthur Schnitzlers mit Max Reinhardt und dessen Mitarbeitern.* Salzburg: Otto Müller, 1971.

Wagner, Renate and Brigitte Vacha. *Wiener Schnitzler-Aufführungen 1891-1970.* München: Prestel-Verlag, 1971.

Wassermann, Jakob. "Erinnerung an Arthur Schnitzler". *Neue Rundschau,* 1, 1931, pp. 5-13.

Weiss, Robert O. "The Human Element in Schnitzler's Social Criticism." *Modern Austrian Literature,* 5, no. 1/2, 1972, pp. 30-44.

Welzig, Werner. "Das Tagebuch Arthur Schnitzlers 1879-1931." *Internationales Archiv für Sozialgeschichte der deutschen Literatur,* 6, 1981, Tübingen: Max Niemeyer, 1981.

Werfel, Franz. "Arthur Schnitzler. Gedenkrede". *Neue Rundschau,* 1, 1931, pp. 1-4.

Zucker, A. E. "Im Spiel der Sommerlüfte." *Germanic Review,* 6, 1931, pp. 91-93.

Zweig, Stefan. "Arthur Schnitzler zu seinem sechzigsten Geburtstag." *Neue Rundschau,* 33, no. 5, 1922, pp. 498-513.

Secondary Works:

Aron, Raymond. *Clausewitz, Philosopher of War.* Trans. Christine Booker and Norman Stone. London: Routledge and Kegan Paul, 1976.

Aspetsberger, Friedrich, ed. *Staat und Gesellschaft in der österreichischen Literatur.* Wien: Österreichischer Bundesverlag, 1977.

Baldick, Robert. *The Duel. A History of Duelling.* London: Chapman and Hall, 1965.

Barbusse, Henri. *Le feu. (Journal d'une Escouade).* Paris: Flammarion, Editeur, 1917.

Barker, Christine R. *Erich Maria Remarque.* London: Oswald Wolff, 1979.

Baumer, Franz. *E.M. Remarque.* Berlin: Colloquium, 1976.

Berghahn, Volker. *Militarism 1861-1979.* Leamington Spa: Berg Publishers, 1981.

Bergquist, Gordon N. *The Pen and the Sword: War and Peace in the Prose and Plays of Bernard Shaw.* Salzburg: Institut für Englische Sprache und Literatur, Universität Salzburg, 1977.

Blackall, Eric. "Tobias Klenk." *Austriaca. Beiträge zur österreichi-*

200   Adrian Clive Roberts

schen Literatur. Festschrift für Heinz Politzer zum 65. Geburtstag. Ed. Richard Brinkmann, Winfried Kudszus and Hinrich C. Seeba. Tübingen: Max Niemeyer, 1975.

Boyer, John W. *Political Radicalism in Late Imperial Vienna: Origins of the Christian Social Movement 1848-1897.* Chicago and London: University of Chicago Press, 1981.

Brandes, Georg. *The World at War.* Trans. Catherine D. Groth. New York: Macmillan, 1917.

Brock, Peter. *Pacifism in Europe to 1914.* Princeton, New Jersey: Princeton University Press, 1972.

Chapple, Gerald and Hans H. Schulte, eds. *The Turn of the Century: German Literature and Art, 1890-1915.* The McMaster Colloquium on German Literature. Bonn: Bouvier Verlag Herbert Grundmann, 1981.

Chickering, Roger. *Imperial Germany and a World Without War: The Peace Movement and German Society, 1892-1914.* Princeton, New Jersey: Princeton University Press, 1975.

Eis, Egon. *Duell. Geschichte und Geschichten des Zweikampfs.* München: Verlag Kurt Desch, 1971.

Endler, Franz. *Österreich zwischen den Zeilen: Die Verwandlung von Land und Volk seit 1848 im Spiegel der "Presse."* Wien: Verlag Fritz Molden, 1973.

Field, Frank. *The Last Days of Mankind. Karl Kraus and His Vienna.* London: Macmillan Press, 1967.

Genno, Charles N. and Heinz Wetzel. *The First World War in German Narrative Prose.* Toronto: University of Toronto Press, 1980.

Germanistisches Institut der Humboldt-Universität Berlin, ed. *Frieden, Krieg, Militarismus im kritischen und sozialistischen Realismus.* Berlin: Rutten und Loening, 1961.

Goos, Roderich. *Das Wiener Kabinett und die Entstehung des Weltkrieges.* Wien: L. W. Seidel und Sohn, 1919.

Greve, Ludwig and Werner Volke, eds. *Jugend in Wien. Literatur um 1900.* Eine Ausstellung des Deutschen Literaturarchivs im Schiller-Nationalmuseum, Marbach am Neckar. München: In Kommission Kösel, 1974.

Hager, Philip E. and Desmond Taylor, eds. *The Novels of World War One. An Annotated Bibliography.* New York: Garland Publishing, 1981.

Hardach, Gerd. *The First World War: 1914-1918.* Berkeley:

University of California Press, 1977.

Helmreich, Ernst Christian. *The Diplomacy of the Balkan Wars: 1912-1913*. Cambridge: Harvard University Press, 1938.

Henriksson, Fritz. *The Nobel Prizes and Their Founder Alfred Nobel*. Stockholm: Alb. Bonniers Boktryckeri, 1938.

Hesse, Hermann. *Hermann Hesse and Romain Rolland. Correspondence, Diary Entries and Reflections, 1915 to 1940*. Tr. M. G. Hesse. London: Oswald Wolff, 1978.

Holl, Karl, ed. *Voices of German Pacifism*. Trans. Roger Chickering. New York: Garland Publishing, 1972.

Horwath, Peter. "The Literary Treatment of the French Revolution: A Mirror Reflecting the Changing Nature of Austrian Liberalism (1862-1899)." *Modern Austrian Literature*, 6, no. 1/2, 1973, pp. 26-40.

Houben, Heinrich Hubert. *Der ewige Zensor*. Kronberg/Ts: Athenäum, 1978.

———. *Hier Zensur—wer dort? Antworten von gestern auf Fragen von heute*. 1923; rpt. Hildesheim: Georg Olms, 1965.

———. *Verbotene Literatur von der klassischen Zeit bis zur Gegenwart*. 2 vols. 1924; rpt. Hildesheim: Georg Olms, 1965.

Huch, Ricarda Octavia. *Der große Krieg in Deutschland*. Gesammelte Werke, Vol. 3. Köln: Kiepenhauer und Witsch, 1967.

Iggers, Wilma Abeles. *Karl Kraus. A Viennese Critic of the Twentieth Century*. The Hague: Martinus Nijhoff, 1967.

Janik, Allan and Stephen Toulmin. *Wittgenstein's Vienna*. New York: Simon and Schuster, 1973.

Johnston, William M. *The Austrian Mind: An Intellectual and Social History, 1848-1938*. Berkeley: University of California Press, 1972.

Jünger, Ernst. *In Stahlgewittern*. 1920; rpt. Stuttgart: Ernst Klett, 1961.

Kann, Robert A. *The Multi-National Empire. Nationalism and National Reform in the Habsburg Monarchy*. Vol. 1: *Empire and Nationalities*. New York: Columbia University Press, 1950.

Kant, Immanuel. *Immanuel Kants Werke. Schriften von 1790-1796*. Vol. 6. Berlin: Verlegt bei Bruno Cassirer, 1923.

King, Jere Clemens. *The First World War*. New York: Walker and Company, 1972.

Klein, Holger, ed. *The First World War in Fiction. A Collection of*

Critical Essays. London: Macmillan Press, 1976.

Koszyk, Kurt. *Deutsche Pressepolitik im Ersten Weltkrieg*. Düsseldorf: Droste, 1968.

Kraus, Karl. *Die Fackel*, 20, no. 484-498, p. 127.

———. "In dieser großen Zeit." *Die Fackel*, 16, no. 404, December 1914, p. 2.

———. *The Last Days of Mankind. A Tragedy in Five Acts*. Edited and abridged by Frederick Ungar. Trans. Alexander Gode and Sue Ellen Wright. Critical analysis by Franz H. Mautner. New York: Frederick Ungar, 1974.

———. *Die letzten Tage der Menschheit*. 1922; rpt. München: Kösel, 1957.

———. *Karl Kraus. Werke*. Vol. 7. Ed. Heinrich Fischer. München: Kösel, 1967.

Latzko, Andreas. *Menschen im Krieg*. Zürich: Max Rascher und Cie., 1917.

Lindenberger, Herbert. *Historical Drama. The Relation of Literature and Reality*. Chicago: University of Chicago Press, 1975.

Luft, David. *Robert Musil and the Crisis of European Culture, 1880-1942*. Berkeley: University of California Press, 1980.

Majer, Friedrich. *Geschichte der Ordalien, insbesondere der gerichtlichen Zweikämpfe in Deutschland*. Jena: in der akademischen Buchhandlung, 1795.

McGrath, William J. *Dionysian Art and Populist Politics in Austria*. New Haven: Yale University Press, 1974.

Mendelssohn, Peter de. *S. Fischer und sein Verlag*. Frankfurt am Main: S. Fischer, 1970.

Mitchell, Allan. *The German Influence in France after 1870: The Formation of the French Republic*. Chapel Hill: University of North Carolina Press, 1979.

Nicolai, Georg Friedrich. *Die Biologie des Krieges. Betrachtungen eines Naturforschers den Deutschen zur Besinnung*. Zürich: Art. Institut Orell Füssli, 1919.

Nielsen, Erika, ed. *Focus on Vienna 1900*. München: Wilhelm Fink, 1982.

Prater, D. A. *European of Yesterday. A Biography of Stefan Zweig*. Oxford: At the Clarendon Press, 1972.

Prümm, Karl. *Die Literatur des soldatischen Nationalismus der 20er Jahre (1918-1933)*. Kronberg, Taunus: Scriptor, 1974.

Rasche, Friedrich, ed. *Fritz von Unruh. Rebell und Verkünder. Der Dichter und Sein Werk.* Hannover: Verlag für Literatur und Zeitgeschehen, 1960.

Reik, Theodor. "Zerstörung des ritterlichen Heldenbegriffes". *Pan*, 2, no. 1-45, 4 April 1912.

Remak, Joachim. *The First World War. Causes, Conduct, Consequences.* New York: John Wiley and Sons, 1971.

Remarque, Erich Maria. *Im Westen nichts Neues.* Berlin: Im Propylaen, 1929.

Renn, Ludwig. *Krieg.* Frankfurt am Main: Frankfurter Societäts-Druckerei, GmbH., 1929.

Richthofen, Manfred Albrecht Freiherr von. *Richthofen. Ein Heldenleben.* Berlin: Verlag Ullstein und Co., 1920.

Rolland, Romain. *Above the Battle.* Trans. C. K. Ogden. Chicago: The Open Court Publishing Co., 1916.

——. *Au-dessus de la mêlée.* Paris: Librairie Paul Ollendorff, 1915.

——. *I Will Not Rest.* Trans. K. S. Shelvankar. New York: Liveright Publishing, 1937.

——. *Je commence à devenir dangereux. Choix de lettres de Romain Rolland à sa mère 1914-1919.* Paris: Editions Albin Michel, 1971.

——. *Journal des années de guerre 1914-1919.* Paris: Editions Albin Michel, 1952.

Roth, Josef. *Radetzkymarsch. Roman.* Köln: Kiepenhauer und Witsch, 1963.

Rothenberg, Gunther E. *The Army of Francis Joseph.* West Lafayette, Indiana: Purdue University Press, 1976.

Russell, Bertrand. *Why Men Fight A Method of Abolishing the International Duel.* New York: Garland Publishing 1971.

Schorske, Carl E. *Fin-de-Siècle Vienna. Politics and Culture.* New York: Alfred E. Knopf, 1980.

Sked, Alan. *The Survival of the Habsburg Empire.* London: Longman Group, 1979.

Sonnenfeld, Marion, ed. *Stefan Zweig. The World of Yesterday's Humanist Today.* Albany: State University of New York Press, 1983.

Spencer, Herbert. *Essays: Scientific, Political and Speculative.* 3 vols. London: Williams and Norgate, 1891.

Stavrianos, L. S. *The Balkans 1815-1914.* New York: Holt, Rinehart and Winston, 1963.

Suttner, Bertha von. *Bertha von Suttner. Memoiren.* Lieselotte von Reinken, ed. Bremen: Carl Schünemann, 1965.

———. *Lay Down Your Arms. The Autobiography of Martha von Tilling.* Trans. T. Holmes. New York: Garland Publishing 1972.

———. *Die Waffen nieder.* 1889; rpt. Wien: H. Javorsky-Verlag, 1967 (?)

Taylor, Alan John Percivale. *The First World War. An Illustrated History.* London: Hamish Hamilton, 1963.

———. *The Habsburg Monarchy 1809-1918. A History of the Austrian Empire and Austria-Hungary.* 1948; rpt. London: Hamish Hamilton, 1964.

Unruh, Fritz von. *Ein Geschlecht. Tragödie.* Leipzig: Kurt Wolff, 1917.

———. *Opfergang.* Frankfurt am Main: Frankfurter Societäts-Druckerei, 1925.

———. *Der Sohn des Generals. Roman.* Nürnberg: Verlag Hans Carl, 1957.

———. *Vor der Entscheidung. Ein Gedicht.* Berlin: Erich Reiss, 1919.

Urbach, Reinhard. *Die Wiener Komödie und ihr Publikum.* Wien: Jugend und Volk, 1973.

Vagts, Alfred. *A History of Militarism, Civilian and Military.* New York: Collier-Macmillan, 1959.

Vidal, Annette. *Henri Barbusse. Soldat de la Paix.* Paris: Les Editeurs Français Réunis, 1953.

Wierschin, Martin. *Meister Johann Liechtenauers Kunst des Fechtens.* Münchener Texte und Untersuchungen zur deutschen Literatur des Mittelalters. Vol. 13. München: Verlag C. H. Beck, 1965.

Williams, Cedric Ellis. *The Broken Eagle: The Politics of Austrian Literature from Empire to Anschluß.* London: Paul Elek; New York:Barnes and Noble, 1974.

———. *Writers and Politics in Modern Germany (1918-1945).* London: Hodder and Stroughten, 1977.

Zweig, Arnold. *Der Streit um den Sergeanten Grischa. Roman.* Potsdam: Gustav Kiepenhauer, 1928.

Zweig, Stefan. *Meistererzählungen.* 1938; rpt. Frankfurt am Main:S. Fischer, 1980.

———. *Romain Rolland. The Man and His Work.* New York: Thomas Seltzer, 1921.

Name and Title Index